D1395291

JOHNNY

By the same author

The Successes and Sacrifices of the
British Army in 1914: Soldiers Marching, All to Die
(Edwin Mellen Press, Lewiston, NY, 2009)

JOHNNY

*The Legend and Tragedy of
General Sir Ian Hamilton*

John Philip Jones

Foreword by
General Sir Roger Wheeler GCB CBE,
Chief of the General Staff
1997–2000

Pen & Sword
MILITARY

First published in Great Britain in 2012
By Pen and Sword Military
an imprint of
Pen and Sword Books Ltd
47 Church Street
Barnsley
South Yorkshire S70 2AS

ISBN 978 1 84884 788 0

Printed and bound in England by
CPI Group (UK) Ltd, Croydon, CR0 4YY

Typeset in Times New Roman by
Chic Media Ltd

Pen & Sword Books Ltd incorporates the imprints of
Pen & Sword Aviation, Pen & Sword Family History, Pen & Sword Maritime,
Pen & Sword Military, Pen & Sword Discovery, Wharncliffe Local History,
Wharncliffe True Crime, Wharncliffe Transport, Pen & Sword Select,
Pen & Sword Military Classics, Leo Cooper, Remember When,
The Praetorian Press, Seaforth Publishing and Frontline Publishing

For a complete list of Pen and Sword titles please contact
Pen and Sword Books Limited
47 Church Street, Barnsley, South Yorkshire, S70 2AS, England
E-mail: enquiries@pen-and-sword.co.uk
Website: www.pen-and-sword.co.uk

Contents

Maps viii

Foreword xvii

Prologue xx

1. **Military Reputations** 1
   The Tragic Hero
   The Forbidding Peninsula

2. **Apprenticeship** 18
   'Gone for a Soldier'
   The *Gay Gordons*
   'The Land of Regrets'

3. **Beau Sabreur** 33
   The Military Pyramid
   Bobs Bahadur
   The 'Sharp End'

4. **'No End of a Lesson'** 48
   Army Reforms at Last
   Worthy Foes
   Disaster on the 'Hill of Doves'
   Fred Roberts Remembers

5. **Emerging from the Chrysalis** 65
   'The Refreshment of Adventure'
   The 'Roberts Ring'

6. **'The Last of the Gentlemen's Wars' and How it Degenerated** 86
    Two Encounters and Three Lessons
    'Fortified Towns are now Liable to Destruction'

7. **Learning from their own Mistakes**.......................................105
    Across the Veldt with the Mounted Infantry
    The Second Phase of the War: a Double Degeneration

8. **Observer of a Distant War** 129
    The First Large Twentieth Century War
    General Kuroki Carries the Honour of Japan
    General Oyama in Command
    The Russo-Japanese War as a Precursor
    What Hamilton Learned
    Forgotten Lessons from a Distant War

9. **An Abortive War of Words** 157
    Roberts versus Haldane
    The Ticking of the Clock

10. **'Corpses Lined up Like Rows of Broad Beans'**...................175
    Germany's Eyes turn South-East
    'The Attack on Turkey holds the Field'
    'You are to Have Command'
    Hamilton's Choice of the Least Bad Alternative
    Five Beaches and Fifteen Victoria Crosses
    Enemy Trenches Twenty Away
    The Last Roll of the Dice
    Three Questions Revisited

11. **Military Philosopher**..222
    The Crystal Ball
    Organisation, Discipline, Training
    Command
    The Legacy

12. **Index**..252

To the memory of the warriors
of all nations who lost their lives
at Gallipoli

Maps

Map 1 Majuba Hill, 26/27 February, 1881.

Map 2 The Gordon Relief Expedition up the Nile, 1884–85.

Map 3 South Africa during the Second Boer War, 1899–1902.

Map 4 Russo-Japanese War, Manchuria and Korea, 1904–05.

Map 5 The Dardanelles.

Map 6 The Gallipoli Peninsula.

Map 7 The Gallipoli Peninsula, 1915.

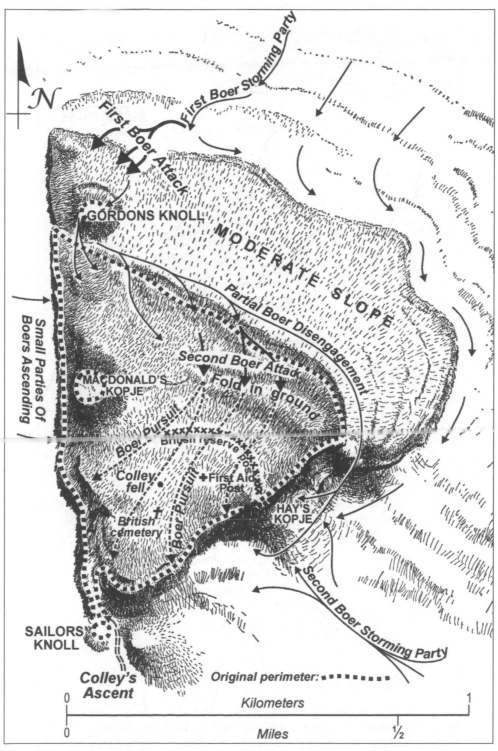

Map 1 Majuba Hill, 26/27 February 1881. The British force briefly occupied the summit before dawn on 27 February but were promptly ejected by the Boers.

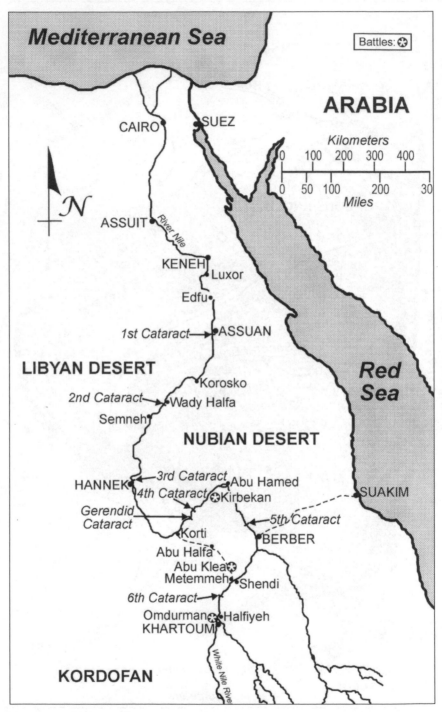

Map 2 The Gordon Relief Expedition up the Nile, 1884–85. The River Column made its difficult journey up the river, and the Desert Column embarked on its abortive *sortie* from Korti towards Khartoum. The British force retreated along the same routes after the death of Gordon.

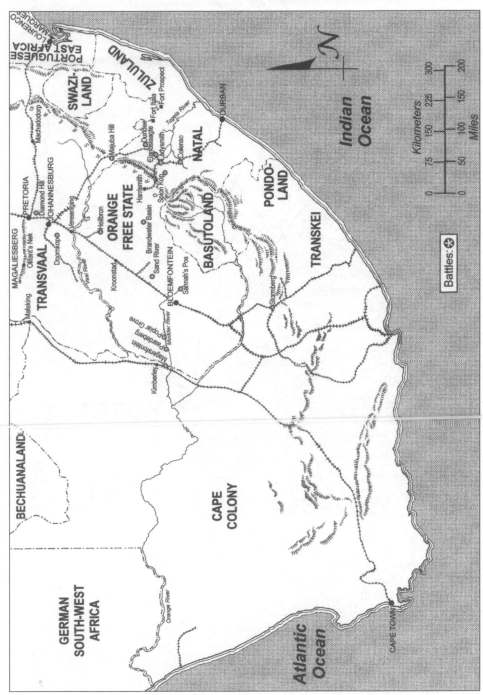

Map 3 South Africa during the Second Boer War, 1899–1902. Between October 1889 and February 1900, Hamilton fought in and around Ladysmith (Natal). From May to October 1900, he commanded the Mounted Infantry Division in its advance from Bloemfontein (Orange River Colony) to Johannesburg (Transvaal) and beyond.

Map 4 Russo-Japanese War, Manchuria and Korea, 1904–05. The Japanese Army, retaining the initiative throughout the War, deployed part of its force to besiege Port Arthur. The larger part of the Army pressed the Russian Army northeast along the Manchurian railroad, which was a branch of the Trans-Siberian Railway. Hamilton accompanied this larger Japanese force.

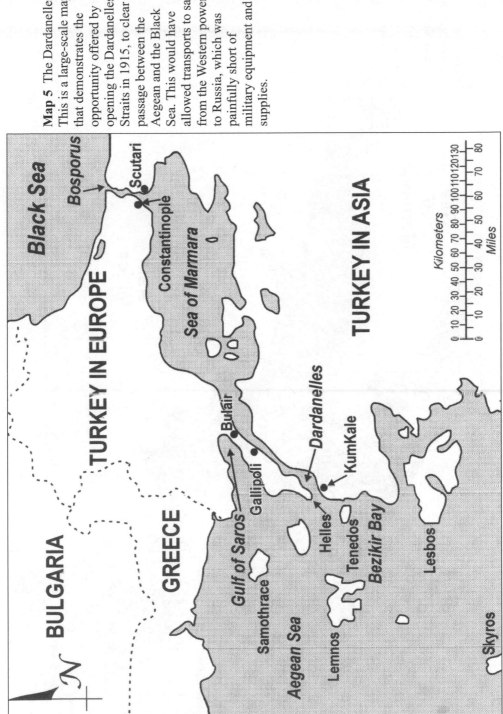

Map 5 The Dardanelles. This is a large-scale map that demonstrates the opportunity offered by opening the Dardanelles Straits in 1915, to clear a passage between the Aegean and the Black Sea. This would have allowed transports to sail from the Western powers to Russia, which was painfully short of military equipment and supplies.

BULGARIA

TURKEY IN EUROPE

GREECE

Black Sea

Bosporus

Scutari

Constantinople

Sea of Marmara

Bulair

Dardanelles

Gallipoli

KumKale

Gulf of Saros

Samothrace

Helles

Tenedos

Bezikir Bay

Aegean Sea

Lemnos

Lesbos

Skyros

TURKEY IN ASIA

Kilometers

0 10 20 30 40 50 60 70 80 90 100 110 120 130

0 10 20 30 40 50 60 70 80

Miles

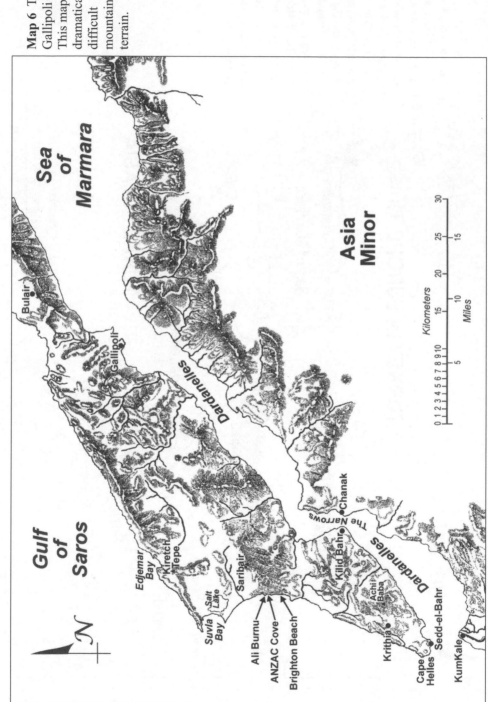

Map 6 The Gallipoli Peninsula. This map shows the dramatically difficult mountainous terrain.

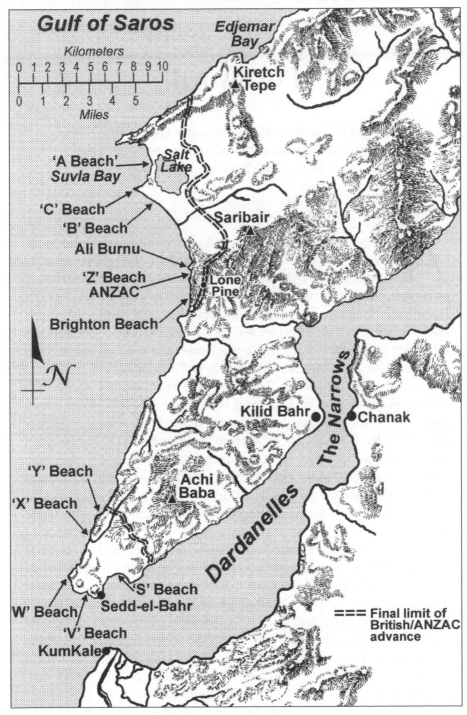

Map 7 The Gallipoli Peninsula, 1915. This map shows the British and ANZAC landing places, and the final limit of the advance. *Despite the most desperate heroism, the British and ANZAC troops did not manage to advance more than four miles from the coast.*

Foreword

by General Sir Roger Wheeler GCB CBE
Chief of the General Staff and professional head
of the British Army, 1997–2000

A s John Philip Jones remarks at the very beginning of this book, success in war results from leaders accepting onerous responsibilities and making the right decisions, from which they gain great admiration, particularly for displaying moral fibre and forceful leadership. This has been the case throughout the history of armed conflict, but there are many examples of those whose reputation has crumbled in the face of a greater challenge than their experience has prepared them for. This fascinating study of *The Legend and Tragedy of General Sir Ian Hamilton* is a fine example of a very senior General, with much experience of colonial wars in which he deservedly gained a high reputation as an operational commander in the field, being completely over-faced by the demands of modern warfare between sophisticated military powers for which he was ill-prepared. That said, it is especially interesting to read, in the final chapter, of General Hamilton's various publications after the First World War that show he had a remarkable understanding of the future development of warfare in the mid-twentieth century.

In this book John Philip Jones charts the experience of General Hamilton through various colonial campaigns, and indeed the General's propensity to learn from mistakes made in those campaigns. The most telling chapter ahead of the centerpiece of his chronicle of the failure of leadership at the strategic level at Gallipoli, is the account of General Hamilton's experience as an observer of the Russo-Japanese War at the beginning of the twentieth century. He also makes mention of General Hamilton's exposure to German military manoeuvres shortly after that. Whilst the General apparently appreciated the value of punctilious planning, good intelligence, admired the imperturbability of the Japanese

Generals, and was impressed by the toughness of the 'Japanese peasant soldiers' as well as the speed of their manoeuvre by fire and movement at the tactical level, he seems not to have appreciated the advantage gained by a defending force of the effect of modern weapons, particularly artillery and machine guns.

It is surprising therefore that, as John Philip Jones recounts, General Hamilton allowed himself to be bounced by Lord Kitchener and Winston Churchill into mounting the Gallipoli Expedition at great speed with insufficient intelligence of both the terrain and the forces opposing him. The 'peasant' army of the Turks was not dissimilar to the Japanese he had seen in Manchuria and furthermore they were led by a German General, Otto Liman von Sanders, with a very high reputation. There was no meticulous planning or gathering of intelligence and, most surprising of all after his experience observing the success of the Japanese against Russian defences in Manchuria, General Hamilton allowed his force to be launched onto a rugged peninsula without the superiority of forces and equipment that, after his experience in Manchuria, he should have appreciated that he needed.

The centrepiece of this study into High Command at the beginning of the First World War is the Gallipoli Campaign and General Hamilton's inability to think strategically, perhaps because his own experience was very much at the tactical level through command 'from the saddle' of mobile columns in the Second Boer War. As the author says, the Gallipoli Expedition was mounted a great speed, as a result of which insufficient attention was given to the terrain or the enemy. It was, as John Philip Jones describes, doomed to failure before the actual assault took place in spite of the unparalleled heroism which still lies deep in the national psyche of the ANZAC nations.

As John Philip Jones writes, the military leaders of many nations have failed in battle because they did not learn the lessons of previous conflicts, and often had not appreciated the changing nature of warfare through advances in technology. It is all the more remarkable, therefore, after the failure of the Gallipoli Campaign that General Hamilton should write with great clarity forecasting the end of trench warfare, that mechanization would replace horse cavalry, that aircraft would transform warfare, and that command of operations would become an all-arms affair. That he should show this perspicacity is reminiscent in today's military world of the way in which General Petraeus transformed the US Army's operational doctrine early in the twenty-first century and the British Army's appointment of a Director General of Force Development and Training to ensure that lessons of current campaigns are carried into the future.

The Legend and Tragedy of General Sir Ian Hamilton is a fascinating study of the fallibility of one British General at Gallipoli in the First World War, but the principles of High Command that John Philip Jones expresses in his book are every bit as relevant today.

Prologue

F ew if any events in history have generated such a prodigious and still-growing literature as the First World War. It was a long-maturing catastrophe of double importance. First, there were its colossal immediate effects: the bloodshed, which included the loss of a cohort of potential leaders in all countries whose absence would later be keenly felt; the cost in money to the majority (but not all) of the combatant nations; the dangerous rearrangement of political power between the leading nation states; and the war's immediate and permanent influence on the *mores* and attitudes and habits of all classes of society everywhere. If these things were not enough, the war had a second, delayed effect from the unfinished business that it left behind. With baleful inevitability, the First World War was followed after twenty years by the even greater horrors of the Second World War.

To British men who came of age between the late 1930s and late 1960s, the First World War etched a deep impression on their psyche. This was because the older men in the group volunteered or were conscripted to serve in the Second World War, and the younger ones were drafted to serve for a brief period in the armed services when they were of an impressionable age. I am a member of the latter category. And like so many of my contemporaries, in my early adulthood I developed a powerful, lifelong interest in the First World War. I spent hours talking to old warriors, now all dead; collecting and reading a large and eclectic range of books; and walking over most of the battlefields, map in hand. (I mention later the names of four of my friends who share my interest, and have made perceptive comments on earlier drafts of this book.)

For me, like most people who come from Britain, the First World War is associated primarily with the bloodshed and sacrifice – and also the heroism – in the mud and squalor of the trenches in France and Flanders. But in my early thirties, my eyes were opened to a lesser-known part of the conflict: a war of bloodshed, sacrifice and heroism, but waged in the torrid hills and gullies of the Gallipoli Peninsula. I became conscious of this different war from reading a long-forgotten book that impressed me by the elegance and sensitivity of its style. It was written by John North, and is called *Gallipoli, the Fading Vision.*

North draws the contrast between the Western Front and Gallipoli through two simple descriptions:

> There is no magic in the soil of France for the men who fought there; nor for an Englishman in that country is there anything quite as dead as the last war . . . the names of those tiny villages of France and Flanders that were once on the lips of the world already seem to belong to a past as remote as Ramillies and Malplaquet.[1]
>
> The ravines and the cliffs and the beaches of Gallipoli held for me an inward and spiritual meaning. I was ready to believe that the Peninsula had a personality; I persuaded myself that it could capture the imagination of the least imaginative of its visitors; I was almost prepared to argue that some spirit of doom still possessed its hills and gullies.[2]

North's central point about Gallipoli's greater hold on the imagination is persuasive, but it is incomplete. The missing ingredient is the evocative connection between Gallipoli and the world of Greek antiquity. This was not lost on the British Commander of the Gallipoli enterprise, Sir Ian Hamilton, whose diary, written when he was making his first reconnaissance of the Peninsula from a ship sailing around its coast, contains the following recollections of what he had long before learned about the classical world:

> There, Hero trimmed her little lamp; yonder the amorous breath of Leander changed to soft sea form. Far away to the eastwards, painted in dim and lovely hues, lies Mount Ida. Just so, on the far horizon line she lay fair and still, when Hector fell and smoke from burning Troy blackened the midday sun. Against this enchanted background to deeds done by immortals and mortals as they struggled for ten long years 5,000 years ago – stands forth formidably the Peninsula.[3]

Hamilton's words are arresting, not least because they open the door to his mind – not the mind of an historian, a classicist, a novelist or a poet – but of an infantry soldier, a rifle-and-boots man and a member of that most conventional, down-to-earth, unimaginative, 'brutal and licentious' fraternity. North's book, together with Hamilton's own *Gallipoli Diary*, convinced me that Hamilton was an individual worth studying. And in the decades since I first absorbed with pleasure these remarkable works, I have read and re-read the sixteen books that Hamilton wrote, and also the vastly greater number that describe his career and offer insights into his character. My fascination with Hamilton also took me to Gallipoli, up and down the Nile, to the battlefields of the First and Second Boer Wars, and many times to India, where Hamilton served for long periods until his late forties. In India I learned something about the unchanging slow pace of life, and the wide gaps between the races, castes and classes. In my reading about India I was also forcefully struck by Hamilton's military superior and patron, Sir Fred (later Lord) Roberts, who was small in stature, but a 'big' General. Roberts appears at various times in this book.

This all forms the genesis of my work, the most important part of which addresses the question of how such a successful and even brilliant man as Hamilton could have 'blown' his greatest professional opportunity. Many distinguished historians have attempted to answer this question, not least North:

> No commander has ever been more generously endowed with the gift of human sympathy and understanding; and just as he could never come to regard his troops as trussed creatures to be thrown into the battle, so also his immediate subordinates remained men rather than mere instruments of his will; and it is conceivable that a commander less sensitive to the common imperfections of humanity, and actuated only by a brutal determination to beat down opposition to his demands, might ultimately have succeeded where a compassionate and an exalted heart was to fail.[4]

Other analysts have provided different explanations. I disagree with them all. This book argues that Hamilton's problem was not caused by his inability or unwillingness to impose his will on subordinates. The problem was not sniping from political and military leaders in London and British Headquarters in France; nor was it due to breathtakingly bad luck. It stemmed in my view from the basic deficiency of Hamilton's strategic plan. This was partly driven by the inadequate size of his army – something for which Kitchener, the Secretary of State for War, had to take the blame – but Hamilton himself was content with what he was given.

War is a totally unforgiving activity. But there are differences in the penalties of tactical and strategic errors. The tactics of the initial British and ANZAC landings in Gallipoli succeeded as a result of the heroism, discipline and training of the assaulting troops. But the successful tactics were not transformed into strategic success. Such success depended on the soundness of the strategic plan, the resources available to the enemy, and – most importantly – the insight and energy of the enemy commander. Hamilton was faced by an unhurried and superbly professional opponent in the German General Liman von Sanders. He knew his job because of his experience and the fact that he had been baptised into the mysteries of high-level command at the formidable Prussian War Academy.

Hamilton, as the General Officer Commanding, was not responsible for the grand strategy of the campaign. But he controlled the pure (i.e. battlefield) strategy, and occupied a position that was the mirror-image of Liman von Sanders's. But Hamilton, isolated on the island of Imbros, forty miles from the battlefield, would by temperament have preferred being with his soldiers where the bullets were flying. He was less comfortable than his opponent in overall and distant command. In modern warfare, defence is less difficult to conduct than attack, and the Turks were of course defending their homeland. But the greater experience and training of Liman von Sanders had much to do with their defensive victory. This forced the British to withdraw from the Peninsula, leaving behind a legacy of wasted valour.

This book develops my argument, which is built from conclusions that emerge from various episodes during Hamilton's career. Any imperfections in the book are due to me and not my collaborators. I have in fact received generous help from family, friends and professional associates, to all of whom I am exceedingly grateful.

My first thanks as always go to my wife Wendy, who alone has the patience to work through the many drafts of my manuscript and produce at the end an immaculate version for the publisher. She is also my most unrelenting critic.

General Sir Roger Wheeler has contributed a most perceptive

Foreword, and I am greatly in his debt. He is a soldier of the highest distinction. He was GOC and Director of Military Operations for Northern Ireland, 1993–96; Joint Commander for British Forces on NATO operations in Bosnia in 1996–97; and Chief of the General Staff and professional head of the British Army, 1997–2000. One incisive point he makes in his Foreword is that the principles of High Command described in this book 'are every bit as relevant today'.

I am also extremely grateful to four friends who have combed through and commented on my early drafts of the whole work. They all have military experience from many years on the active list of the Territorial Army; and also have a greater than amateur knowledge of military history. Their names are James Colquhoun, Gordon Cumming, Charles Pettit, all of the Honourable Artillery Company (as am I); and Anthony Simpson of the 21st SAS Regiment (Artists). My warmest thanks also go to my son Philip, an experienced editor, who has gone through the entire manuscript and given me valuable comments on the content as well as cleaning up duplications and contradictions. My profound gratitude also goes to four friends and acquaintances who have seen specific chapters that relate to their own areas of expertise. They are Professor David Bennett (a prominent historian at Syracuse University); Major Gordon Corrigan (late of 2nd Gurkha Rifles); Colonel Tony Hare (late of 2nd Light Infantry); and Lord Montgomery (son of the Field Marshal). I have also benefited from extremely interesting insights into Turkey during the First World War from a Turk who lives in Britain, Ahmet Sapaz, who had learned about the War from his parents. His grandfather (whom he did not know) fought in the Ottoman Army and lost his life at the Battle of Kut al-Amara in 1916.

My wife and I have made four unforgettable visits to South Africa. Our hosts on all four occasions, and whom we can never thank enough for the warmth of their hospitality, were our friends Erik and Mariki du Plessis. They showed us all the major battlefields of the First and Second Boer Wars and the Zulu War. Not many people visit these spectacular sites which have remained largely unchanged, so that visitors receive a powerful impression of what they were like when they were the scenes of military action. At Magersfontein and Paardeberg in the Free State, I picked up a few artifacts from the ground: Mauser and Lee-Enfield bullet casings, shrapnel balls, and shards of thick glass from bottles carried by the combatants. They are sitting on my desk as I write these words.

My copy editor is Richard Doherty, to whom I am most grateful. He is knowledgeable, meticulous, energetic and constructive. He is in fact a well-recognized military historian, and his expertise shines through.

I must finally express my gratitude to my friend Ed Voytovich who has given my wife and me much advice on word-processing; and other expert collaborators in Syracuse: Scott Bunting, of Fresher Graphics, who designed the wonderfully clear maps; and Sharon Pickard and Collin Becker, of Industrial Color Labs, who handled the photographs with a high degree of skill.

Notes

1 John North, *Gallipoli, the Fading Vision* (London: Faber & Faber, 1936), p.15.
2 Ibid., p. 16
3 General Sir Ian Hamilton, *Gallipoli Diary* (Volume 1) (New York: George H. Doran, 1920), p.28.
4 North, *Gallipoli, the Fading Vision,* p.318.

CHAPTER 1

Military Reputations

If military leaders have a currency to spend, it is human lives. Their power over their own subordinates and their enemies is far greater than any weight loaded onto the shoulders of politicians in peace or war. And because success in war results from leaders accepting onerous responsibility and making the right decisions, soldiers and sailors who win battles are widely admired, both for their moral fibre and for the forceful masculine leadership that they display. This is what this book is about. It is devoted to the reputation of a number of prominent military figures, concentrating on one man in particular, General Sir Ian Hamilton, a beau idéal in colonial conflicts but a man who had to face greater challenges in the First World War.

Military reputations – the end product of public opinion – are usually only appreciated in a rough-and-ready way, because to do this properly requires specialist knowledge of what armies actually do and how they do it, which is knowledge not possessed by the population as a whole. Nevertheless, military leaders are widely and sometimes dramatically esteemed in their countries: in many cases more highly than top politicians, because successful soldiers and sailors catch the public imagination to a greater degree. And when successful generals themselves become political leaders – or are such leaders already – the majority tend to be remembered most dramatically for their battles. Shining through a period spanning more than two millennia are war winners who were also political leaders (although not always successful ones): Alexander the Great, Hannibal, Julius Caesar, Belisarius, Charlemagne, William the Conqueror, Edward I, Gustavus Adolphus, John Sobieski, Frederick the Great, Washington, Wellington, Grant, Kitchener and Eisenhower. The

1

most dramatic example of all is Napoleon Bonaparte, who left a permanent imprint on the law, geography, institutions and amour propre of France, yet in the porphyry marble surrounding his mighty sarcophagus in the Invalides, nothing is visible except the names of his battles (his successful ones at least).

Yet military reputations are illusory things, and it takes a number of years to determine whether or not a particular soldier's or sailor's reputation is fully justified. The reputation of military leaders crosses three distinct hurdles. The first and most immediate one condemns many, perhaps the majority, of the generals who hold the most important appointments when battle is joined; these lose their jobs after the enemy is encountered and they are caught wrong-footed. The Second Boer War (1899–1902), was the first colonial conflict in which the British fought against white opponents equipped with modern firearms, and was widely regarded as the first modern war fought by the British Army. Early losers in this who were sacked, frozen or sidetracked include Warren, Gatacre, White and Buller. The same fate awaited Smith-Dorrien, Hamilton, French and Jellicoe in the First World War; and Gort, Ironside, Dill, Percival, Wavell, Alan Cunningham, Auchinleck and Anderson in the Second. These leaders were not always forgotten, because British people tend to have nostalgic feelings towards ill-luck and even towards military defeat, although these commanders were no longer permitted to endanger the lives of their men.

The British Army is not unique in starting wars with incompetent generals. The two largest conflicts in American history were the Civil War and the Second World War. In the Civil War, President Lincoln had to suffer the agonizing experience of sacking a number of senior commanders until at last he decided to appoint Grant, who was someone with the right combination of talent and ruthlessness to defeat the Confederacy. And in the Second World War, Kimmel and Short lost their jobs after Pearl Harbor, as did Fredendall in Tunisia, Dawley at Salerno, and Lucas at Anzio.

Military leaders all too often rise in rank above their ceiling. This is not exclusively because their chiefs who promote them lack judgement. It is more often for lack of better alternatives. A successful leader in a major theatre of war needs to possess a formidable and varied menu of qualities: a wide range dictated by the fact that the highest military leadership is both an art and a science. I can number eleven qualities, some of which are related to one another:

(1) moral courage;

(2) raw intellectual horsepower;

(3) an understanding of battlefield tactics and the flexibility to adapt them to the nature of the ground and the dispositions of the enemy: the first step to military knowledge;

(4) the imaginative ability to think strategically with a broad vision: the second step to military knowledge;

(5) the ability to stand back in detachment to make his plans;

(6) mental clarity;

(7) the ability to pick good juniors;

(8) a rigid intolerance of incompetence accompanied by an occasional ruthlessness in sacking subordinates;

(9) obsessive determination;

(10) a feel for the psychology of the enemy;

(11) and – not least – a subtle understanding of the men he commands, which is the key to personal leadership.

All generals possess some of these qualities, otherwise they would not be appointed but it is very rare indeed for a man to possess them all. Some generals are so strong in individual qualities that other qualities become overwhelmed, e.g. determination to follow a specific course defeats the ability to think of imaginative alternatives. Ian Hamilton published his own views about generalship: views that were obviously relevant to how he executed his command. His clear but limited vision is discussed in Chapter 11. In Chapter 9, I attempt myself to evaluate how Hamilton measured against my eleven criteria. He had great strengths but some weaknesses, at least two of which I judge to be very serious.

The second hurdle in the path of military reputations is erected at the end of a war, when victory signals the start of revisionism, as the successful military leaders begin to be sniped at. Haig and Foch in the First World War; and Eisenhower, Montgomery, Alexander, Mountbatten and Harris in the Second, were commanders whose achievements have been questioned and in some cases demolished: not only by journalists with a sensational story to tell, but even by well-informed inside observers.[1] These leaders' reputations come increasingly under fire for a variety of reasons: because of their mistakes, the opportunities they had missed, and the failings of their personalities, not to speak of general disenchantment with war itself. From the names in the list above, only Montgomery has come through relatively unscathed: he was the only major British battlefield commander in the two world wars who came close to combining the eleven qualities listed in the last paragraph. This is partly because he managed to bridge the personal command exercised by successful generals during the nineteenth century, and the large-scale pyramidal control demanded by twentieth-century industrial warfare. In contrast, Haig was highly polarized. He had six qualities in great strength: moral courage, knowledge of his profession, the ability to stand back in detachment to make his plans, mental clarity, rigid intolerance of incompetence, and – most important of all – obsessive determination. However, Haig was weaker in other respects, as has been discussed in the many books that have been written about him. Most remarkably, he was not very brainy.

Negative appraisals of the successful generals of the First World War began to be published a few years after the end of that war. In 1928 the writer who was later to become Britain's leading military analyst, Basil Liddell Hart (a man with superb insight who had been invalided out of the Army at the rank of captain), gave a degree of respectability to this revisionism with the publication of his book *Reputations*. In this he examined ten leading generals of the war: four French, two British, two American and two German. This book is not a 'hatchet job', as many later ones were, but the analysis was searching, as can be seen by the following extract from what the author had to say about Marshal Foch, the generalissimo who was widely thought to have won the war, and who was a proponent from first to last of the relentless offensive.

> His theories were so ingrained in his mind – and soul – that during four years he had persevered in carrying them into practice without heed to the reality of conditions which make them hopeless. And, because the balance of battle so often turns on the moral element, his 'will to conquer' prevailed in certain defensive

crises through the very intensity of his belief in the illusion that he was attacking. This faith remained, but hard experience awakened him to the value, if not to the obstacle, of material factors.[2]

What Liddell Hart was implying, albeit gracefully, is the terrible truth that Foch was responsible, because of his blind beliefs, for a hideous loss of life during his earlier years of command.

It is perhaps well that we should begin to doubt the wisdom of successful generals, because of the real danger that their strategies and tactics might become embodied in the military doctrines of the armies they formerly commanded. Paradoxically, this is practically a guarantee of failure in future wars, because wars do not follow the paths of previous ones. Hence the truth of the cliché that generals spend most of their time planning for the last war rather than the next one. The missing ingredient is always flexibility: in particular the ability to cope with the unexpected, and this is something that all wars bring in their wake.

We finally get to the third and last hurdle, when all secrets have been revealed and a reasonable consensus emerges about those who will enter the pantheon of great captains. It is not easy to think of many First World War generals who are fit to join this select group: perhaps the Germans Ludendorff, Liman von Sanders, and von Lettow-Vorbeck; the Frenchman Galliéni; the Turk Mustafa Kemal; the Russian Brusiloff; the Australian Monash; and the British Rawlinson, Allenby, and Lawrence, although there is no unanimity about these ten figures, especially since three of them made their names in minor campaigns. But, in contrast to the First World War, the Second provided opportunities for military artistry because it was a war of movement; and there is also the important point that the best Second World War generals learned harsh and direct lessons from their experiences as junior officers between 1914 and 1918. As a result there is a bumper crop of great figures, with widespread informed support for the following: the Germans von Manstein, Guderian, Kesselring, Rommel and Dönitz; the Japanese Yamamoto; the Russians Zhukov and Chuikov; the Americans Marshall, King, Nimitz, MacArthur and Patton; and the British Brooke, Andrew Cunningham, Dowding, Montgomery and Slim. Note the presence of three figures, Marshall, King and Brooke, who were concerned mainly with grand strategy, a matter of key importance in a war of such scale. These names embrace a great richness of talent; but the total number of eighteen names is as nothing compared with the vast numbers of men and women under arms in the Second World War.

The Tragic Hero

Ian Hamilton, the tragic hero of this book, typifies the pattern of early hope overtaken by failure: the leitmotif that runs through this biography. Hamilton's career before 1914 had been unusually successful, and his energetic and widely recognized exploits in command of a mounted infantry division in the Second Boer War had put him ahead of most of his contemporaries. Moreover, the powerful men who appointed him to the big job of commanding the expedition to force the Dardanelles in 1915 had believed unhesitatingly that he would succeed, otherwise he would not have been appointed. Success in this expedition would have propelled Hamilton into my third group of successful generals, the great captains. Yet when he did reach the highest level of command, he failed. This book will argue that the key reason for this failure was his weakness in the fourth of the eleven qualities needed for a general of the first rank: he lacked *strategic* understanding. And his strength in the third attribute, his practical feel for battlefield *tactics*, was not enough to compensate.

Although Hamilton had weaknesses – failings as serious as nearly all the other British military leaders of the First World War – he was nevertheless a fascinating person: a complex man, and one who was far more attractive and interesting than his military contemporaries, whose preoccupations were strongly influenced by the deeply-entrenched military traditions of the armies in which they served. These traditions, despite their merits, never encourage flexibility and open-mindedness. Hamilton put tradition in its place and was more interested in the future than the past. Although, like most of his contemporaries, he had a long and varied military career and was endowed with great moral and physical courage, unlike them he also had a sharply-honed imagination. Endowed with a variety of interests as well as a deep involvement in his profession, he was observant and pro-active, and had a natural glint of humour: qualities that made him long remembered with affection by people who knew him, and even by the public who knew him only by reputation or from his writings.

A remarkable and very rare quality that Ian Hamilton possessed was his ability to write. One only has to work one's way through the memoirs of important figures in public life to realize quite how good Hamilton's writing was by contrast. He was prolific and wrote engagingly on a wide range of topics. And, more importantly, he combined a rare felicity in the use of words with a searching power of observation and an imaginative spark that lightened every page he wrote. Hamilton had spent his early years of schooling in carefully supervised grammatical writing, but his magical touch came from a combination of his inborn Celtic sensibility and his absorption of the poetry of the Greeks and Romans: 'a touchstone sunk darkly into my subconscious whereby the rhythm of a line of poetry let me savour a drop or two of that ecstasy which is surely the elixir of life.'[3] It is difficult to imagine any other soldier who could have written a piece of enchanting prose like the following description of his first encounter with military hierarchy:

> I was seated, so I have often been told as good as gold between Grandpapa Gort and HRH the Duke of Cambridge, C-in-C of the Army, when, after the blessing, the Duke picked me up, stroked my curls, and said he had taken me for a pretty little girl; whereupon, so the family legend runs, I, prompted I suppose by the devil, grabbed hold of one of the royal whiskers and gave it a good hard tug. If a military career could begin worse you must tell me.[4]

A feature – perhaps the secret – of Hamilton's style is that it is slightly elliptical. He does not have to strain the reader's patience by spelling out what author and reader already know and this common knowledge acts as a link between them. Because Hamilton's readers are well-informed, he did not need to say much about Hannibal's qualities as a general when recounting this single moment of high drama at the Battle of Lake Trasimene:

> It was in training that the best armies of the Carthaginians excelled. The troops were unmercifully drilled. Swiftness in execution and cohesion of shock were the ideas . . . . The Consul Flaminius lay in Foesulae in his camp. Hannibal trailed his coat close by and drew him out of his covert in hot pursuit. The road along which Hannibal seemed

to fly ran between rocky hills on the one hand and the waters of the lake on the other. As the head of the Roman pursuing force was about to debouch into the open it was held up by a detachment. At that moment the main body was charged in flank by the bulk of the Punic Army. That Army had not passed through the defile, but had lain in ambush on the heights whence they had watched the legionaries march in column of route across their front . . . The Roman Army was wiped out of existence.[5]

Hamilton published far more than any other leading military figure before or since; a total of eighteen books carry his name. The most important are his two volumes of scrap-books – more properly seen as a detailed commentary – on the Russo-Japanese War of 1904–05 (when he was an official Indian Army observer); and his two-part diaries of his command of the Gallipoli expedition. Both are substantial works and should be seen as primary sources relating to those campaigns. A further book deals with Hamilton's experiences in the Second Boer War, a period when he was in the field, commanding substantial bodies of troops in mobile warfare. There are two volumes of delightful personal memoirs, and also two smaller-scale reminiscences: a tribute to his wife (shortly after her death), and – long before this – his first published work, the story of a voyage in a small boat around the coast of India. He also published a novel and two collections of poetry. The remaining six books are concerned with the author's thoughts and speculations about the leadership, recruitment, organization and future of military forces. Everything he wrote is worth reading, and much is very broad in its scope and provides insights into the calibre of Hamilton's mind. I shall be referring to most of these works in the following chapters: chapters all based on first-hand sources, i.e. the witness of people who were actually present at the events portrayed.

One point that he made in his scrap-book of the Russo-Japanese War is vivid and far-seeing enough to make here. This is his comment on the tenacity and fighting power of Japanese soldiers.[6] In 1905 and 1907, when Hamilton published these unexpected ideas, they were an unwelcome surprise to the military establishment in western European countries. During the years before the First World War European empires straddled the world and their Imperial warriors were considered to be vastly superior to oriental and other 'natives'. However, Hamilton's perceptions were emphatically confirmed during the years of bitter fighting between 1941 and 1945, when Japanese soldiers – for a number of reasons, not least their adaptability to different types of terrain – were astonishingly successful in the attack. And in defence, they were prepared to sacrifice their lives in the unwavering expectation of religious and patriotic glory.

The Forbidding Peninsula
Hamilton, despite his shining qualities of intellect and spirit, had an underlying impetuosity that influenced his conduct of the Gallipoli campaign. Impetuosity is a theme that will recur throughout this book. It can be a good quality in a junior officer, but it can be dangerous in a senior one who is responsible for the lives of many men. Hamilton also had the great misfortune to be a general who, like so many others, was given a big job at the beginning of a major war full of the more-than-usual unknowns: and crashed in failure.

The story of the Gallipoli expedition will be told in detail in Chapter 10. In 1914, Hamilton was a senior general in the British Army and had just completed his command of the British Army in the Mediterranean. At the age of sixty-one, he was unlikely to receive any further appointment in peacetime, but the coming of war meant that Hamilton was back in line for an important job somewhere. Sir John French had already been nominated to lead the British Expeditionary Force (BEF), the Army sent to support the French. Hamilton would have been qualified for that plum job, but it was not therefore open to him. Instead he was given a large but non-active command in Britain, the three armies in training called the Central Force, responsible for resisting any invasion. The grand strategy for a British assault on the Dardanelles to clear a passage for the Royal Navy to attack Constantinople, and force its way into the Black Sea to bring support to Russia, came from the strategic imagination of two big figures: Lord Kitchener, political head of the Army, and Winston Churchill, political head of the Navy. Both Kitchener and Churchill knew Hamilton well from the Second Boer War, and picked him to command the Dardanelles expedition, although one or two other generals also had enough experience. The enterprise was soon shown to be a task for the Army and not the Navy, since at an early stage it was obvious that there had to be an assault on the Gallipoli Peninsula, the narrow land mass to the north of the Dardanelles Straits. This is where the problems really began.

In 1914 Hamilton and indeed all senior officers in the British Army were experienced leaders in colonial wars, and he was accustomed to commanding 'from the saddle'. This meant that a general lived with the soldiers and imposed his personality on them, and conducted a war of movement based on improvisation and fast reaction, with very little reliance on what is today called logistics (and sometimes referred to impolitely as plumbing). This aspect of how armies operate – something that became enormously important during the course of the First World War – covers the multitude of different supplies that an army needs: the transport of troops and such supplies; reinforcements; bases; support services; treatment and evacuation of casualties; prisoners; soldiers' welfare; and many other things. In British Army doctrines in 1914, movement was thought of in terms of horses and marching men, and supplies meant ports and railheads and then what could be carried on horse-drawn wagons and a limited number of motor vehicles. The reliance on horse transport meant specific and well-defined problems, notably maintaining animal health and supplying huge quantities of fodder. But the number of men on the ground in colonial wars could not be compared with the numbers in the wars of the twentieth century. This meant that logistics now had to become a major preoccupation for modern commanders as well as for staff officers in the Quartermaster branch.

As the twentieth century progressed, a war between European nations became likely. This meant a conflict between rich industrial powers, with unprecedented numbers of soldiers and huge and increasing problems with logistics. The new style of generalship that was demanded was a novelty to British military leaders. Sir John French, first commander of the British Expeditionary Force in France and Flanders, soon became perplexed and almost paralyzed by it all, although his Army was much smaller than the BEF in 1916, 1917 and 1918, when all the problems multiplied. In 1915, French's command suffered horrendous problems due to a shortage of artillery ammunition, something for which the British Government should be blamed, since it had been unable to anticipate and gear itself up to conduct the new type of warfare. Soldiers were not therefore the only people at fault. As the war developed, the increasingly insistent mantra became *planning*, which called for a large increase in the number of staff officers and a growth in military bureaucracy. Unfortunately in this change the most important role of the general – to make the most of his personal qualities of mind and spirit in order to impose his will both on his own troops and on the enemy – was pushed into second place. This is why the First World War produced so few great captains.

In view of all these developments it is no surprise that the Gallipoli expedition encountered immediate difficulties. Because of the geography of the place that the Army was to attack, Hamilton was forced to be distant from it, with his headquarters isolated on an island forty miles away. He was therefore unable, at least at first, to live among his troops and make the personal contribution that he was accustomed to do. His problems were compounded by the fact that, since everything was mounted at such short notice, planning for the expedition was of necessity an improvised affair. The numbers of assaulting troops were shown in retrospect to have been inadequate. The strategic plan was later shown to have had serious flaws, partly the result of Hamilton's zeal to get to grips with the enemy. And when battle was joined, a disastrous and unanticipated problem soon made itself felt, as it had already done in France and Flanders: the strength of modern defences.

After the German army had crushingly defeated the Russians at the Battle of Tannenberg in August 1914, the Western Front in France and Flanders became the cockpit of the war and the scene of continuous conflict during its whole course. The unanticipated tactical problem that Hamilton faced, and the same terrible drag on his plans, was also the one that confronted French, British and German commanders on the Western Front, and one that should have been foreseen but was not. This problem, which was soon shown to be virtually insoluble, was the technical advance in defensive firepower from troops in dug-in positions: torrents of lead from small arms, especially medium machine guns, and from artillery of all calibres. It is a remarkable and surprising fact that Hamilton had observed and written about the dominance of entrenchments and defensive firepower during the Russo–Japanese war of 1904–05.

In the notes that he made at the time, Hamilton discussed on many occasions the importance of entrenchments. As he correctly observed, defenders of fixed positions, in good trenches and deploying plentiful small-arms and machine-gun fire, were able to make their positions impregnable. In short, these were the conditions that ruled during the First World War. Hamilton had devoted much of his career to improving army musketry, so that what he saw of effective firepower in the Russo–Japanese war could not have come as a surprise to him. It therefore raises serious questions about Hamilton's judgement that he visualized a successful assault on the hostile Gallipoli shore when the enemy was well aware that an attack was impending, and he also knew that the Commander-in-Chief of the Turkish Army opposing him was a seasoned German professional, Liman von Sanders. The superb quality of the German Army was well known in most European countries, and Hamilton had learned at first hand something of this professionalism when he had spent a few months in Germany before going to Sandhurst, and when he had also returned on a number of later occasions. It was obvious that the importance of defensive firepower had still not really sunk into Hamilton's psyche.

But in contrast, he was optimistic about the value of rapid-fire small arms in the attack, and he had also seen an example of this in the Russo–Japanese war:

> the first practical exemplification of a theory I have several times had the temerity to put forward publicly. It is to the effect that the power of the magazine rifle is now so great against anything fairly exposed to its action, that if even half a dozen men can penetrate and enfilade the line held by an army, they may cause such local loss and confusion as to enable a frontal assault to be delivered. This view has been considered fanciful.[7]

This was the precursor of the infiltration tactics developed by the German Army and used by the intensively-trained 'storm troops' against the British trench lines in 1918, a series of assaults that achieved astonishing early success. Nevertheless, for most of the war, rapid fire from magazine rifles and machine guns was the main weapon that made defensive positions impregnable. The evidence for this was already becoming evident from British experience in 1914, at the Aisne in September and during the First Battle of Ypres in October and November. Hamilton had obvious faith in rapid fire from small arms in the attack while he paid little attention to its greater importance in defence, and this is something that goes to the heart of the disaster suffered by the British Army on the Gallipoli Peninsula.

The difficulty of assaulting modern defences was compounded by a special circumstance in Gallipoli, which was different from an equally serious difficulty in France and Flanders. In Gallipoli, the terrain – the high ground dominated by the enemy that Hamilton required his Army to attack – soon produced a situation that became virtually suicidal for assaulting troops. (Note the phrase *Hamilton required his Army to attack,* which again raises the question of his judgement.) The British and the Australian and New Zealand Army Corps (ANZAC) assaults had to be made uphill, in plain view of the enemy. This was much less true of France and Flanders, even in the notorious Ypres salient, where the surrounding hills are modest bumps.

But there was a different complication in France and Flanders: the vast size of the armies relative to the limited area of the territory in which they operated made manoeuvre virtually impossible. As at Gallipoli, the result was a bloody deadlock. The deadlock at Gallipoli was the inevitable outcome of the Turkish defences, the small size of Hamilton's force, and his decision to assault the peninsula in the most tactically difficult (and most obvious) place. The reason for this decision was his lack of strategic subtlety, his unawareness of what Liddell Hart called 'the strategy of indirect approach'.

The Gallipoli catastrophe cost Hamilton his career. He was to receive no further military preferment, no glow of victorious celebrity, no peerage or cash grant to support it (a reward given to a substantial handful of British generals in 1919). After the war he received a consolation prize when King George V gave him another splendid decoration to wear on his uniform, the Grand Cross of the Royal Victorian Order (GCVO). And the sympathy that all sorts of people felt toward him helped to cushion the blow of his dismissal. This made the books he published after the war popular and talked-about, at least among the narrow but influential audience to which they were directed. It also ensured that Hamilton was always warmly received whenever he appeared at public ceremonies, and his obituaries in the leading British newspapers after he died in 1947 at the age of ninety-four, were well-informed and positive about his achievements, and truthful about his failings and ill-luck.[8]

During the early part of the First World War, after the expenditure of rivers of blood, all the leading operational commanders on the Western Front lost their jobs. The German commander, the younger von Moltke, was the first to go, only months after the beginning of the war. The British commander, French, was dismissed at the end of 1915. And both the French commander, Joffre, and the German, von Falkenhayn, were also relieved in late 1916. Hamilton's failure was therefore a part of a broader pattern. And since the failure at Gallipoli was recognized earlier than the increasingly unsuccessful British offensives on the Western Front, Hamilton was the first British Commander-in-Chief to be sacked.[9] And the downward fizzle of his comet was the most dramatic of all, and was not equalled until much later in the war, when three high-level commanders were dramatically dismissed: the Frenchman Nivelle and the Italian Cadorna in 1917, and in 1918 General Gough, a member of an old Irish fighting family, who commanded the British Fifth Army.

These three generals' failures were even greater than Hamilton's in terms of the numbers of casualties for which they were considered responsible. There was also the matter of territory: ground lost in the cases of Cadorna and Gough, and not gained despite big promises in the case of Nivelle. With all three generals, the disasters brought the Western Allies noticeably closer to losing the war. This was never the case with Gallipoli, but what made the failure there so exceptionally tragic was the lost opportunity. Success at Gallipoli could have led the way for the Allies rapidly to win the war by keeping the Russians supplied and the Eastern Front alive and active.

The Gallipoli disaster raises three questions that, in retrospect, go to the heart of the whole enterprise. These will be discussed further in Chapter 10:

• First, given the state of military technology in 1915, was the assault on the Gallipoli Peninsula a viable operation of war?

• Second, if time and resources had been available, would greater force and more effective army-navy co-operation have been successful, given no change in the basic strategic plan? Hamilton deployed four divisions which had only recently been put together, and there had been no time for each division to train as a formation or for the divisions to work in partnership with one another. In addition, although the Navy provided enormous supporting firepower, the actual methods of landing troops had to be improvised: during the crucial initial landings there were no specialist landing craft such as those developed during the Second World War. It is instructive to compare Hamilton's acceptance of the need to 'get the show on the road' with Montgomery's iron resolution before the battle of El Alamein. Despite the most insistent pressure from London and from the Prime Minister personally for the British Army to attack, Montgomery refused to move until he was satisfied that he had all the manpower he required, that they were properly trained in desert conditions, and that his Army had an overwhelming superiority in quantities of artillery, tanks and aircraft.

• Third – and most importantly – could the Gallipoli assault have succeeded with a different strategic plan?

There is no evidence that these questions were considered either by the War Office in London or by Hamilton and his small hastily assembled staff. (Chapter 10 discusses and quotes from the unpublished correspondence between Hamilton and the War Office.) He addressed the expedition with his usual enthusiasm, and he was naturally aware of its importance to him personally, since in all circumstances of success or failure, the Commander-in-Chief alone accepts the responsibility. This is a point that Hamilton made in his own words:

> great and sometimes terrible as these responsibilities are, the commander who is unwilling or unable to accept them has no right to accept the command.[10]

Hamilton made enormous personal contributions in providing charismatic leadership, confidence, energy and resolution, although his impulsiveness was a problem. He was invariably caught up with the day-to-day pressures of his command, a legacy perhaps of his experience of leadership 'from the saddle'. What was needed, especially during the initial phase of planning, was for the Commander-in-Chief to shut himself off and *think*, as Montgomery always contrived to do. Although many plausible excuses can be provided for the failure at Gallipoli, there is no doubt at all that the fault was substantially Hamilton's, and was due particularly to his emphasis on the tactical rather than the strategic. He always wanted to get to the enemy, but he seemed not to have had the time to consider the best way to do it. Kitchener, who appointed Hamilton, must bear the main responsibility for the inadequate size of the Gallipoli force, but there is no evidence that Hamilton himself made a case for more men (although he had good reason to fear that Kitchener would have said no).

The overarching question that must be faced is this: why did a successful career turn sour when Hamilton faced his greatest challenge? His life has been well described in two biographies, published in 1966 and 2000. The first of these, written by his nephew, is a very personal work based to a large extent on Hamilton's personal papers.[11] There are, in addition, Hamilton's own two volumes of autobiography, published in 1939 and 1944,[12] plus his own diary of the Gallipoli campaign.[13] The field has therefore been thoroughly tilled. The focus of my book is, however, rather different, because I am attempting to analyze the events of Hamilton's career with the aim of uncovering clues to explain his positive – and negative – contribution to the Gallipoli campaign. My basic structure is to concentrate on individual episodes in Hamilton's military life, and these are covered in Chapters 3 to 10 inclusive, the last of which and also the longest being devoted to all aspects of the Gallipoli expedition. Chapter 11 discusses Hamilton's frequently arresting contributions to the theory and practice of war, as these are revealed by the books he wrote on these subjects. The contents of these works give a good idea of his warm and attractive personality, although they also provide clues to why the Gallipoli campaign went wrong.

Notes

1 Critical comments on famous military figures are extremely common in the professional literature. Typical examples can be found in the following works: on Haig and Foch, see B. H. Liddell Hart, *Reputations* (London: John Murray, 1928); on Eisenhower, Alexander, Mountbatten and Harris, see Field Marshal Lord Alanbrooke, *War Diaries 1939–1945* (Alex Danchev and Daniel Todman, eds.) (London: Weidenfeld & Nicolson, 2001); on Montgomery, see Omar N. Bradley and Andy Clay Blair, *A General's Life* (New York: Simon & Schuster, 1983).

2 Liddell Hart, *Reputations*, p.178.
3 General Sir Ian Hamilton, *When I Was a Boy* (London: Faber & Faber, 1939), p.106.
4 Ibid., p.43.
5 General Sir Ian Hamilton, *The Soul and Body of an Army* (London: Edward Arnold, 1921), pp.169–70.
6 Lieutenant General Sir Ian Hamilton, *A Staff Officer's Scrap-Book* (London: Edward Arnold, Volume 1, 1905; Volume 2, 1907), especially Volume 2, pp.198, 280.
7 Ibid., Volume 1, pp.175–6, 242, 249, 312, 355.
8 Obituaries of Sir Ian Hamilton were published by all leading British newspapers. A good example is the one published in the *Manchester Guardian*, 13 October 1947, pp.4, 6.
9 The facts are available in any good history of the First World War, e.g. John Keegan, *The First World War* (London: Hutchinson, 1998).
10 General Sir Ian Hamilton, *The Commander* (Major Anthony Farrar-Hockley, ed.) (London: Hollis & Carter, 1957), p.12.
11 Ian Hamilton (nephew), *The Happy Warrior. A Life of General Sir Ian Hamilton* (London: Cassell, 1966); and John Lee, *A Soldier's Life. General Sir Ian Hamilton, 1853-1947* (London: Macmillan, 2000).
12 Hamilton, *When I Was a Boy*; and General Sir Ian Hamilton, *Listening for the Drums* (London: Faber & Faber, 1944).
13 General Sir Ian Hamilton, *Gallipoli Diary,* Volumes 1 and 2 (New York: George H. Doran, 1920).

CHAPTER 2

Apprenticeship

Hamilton was a quintessential Scotsman. His family was from the upper layer of Scottish society and known as the Hamiltons of Westport; they had lived nowhere except in the barren but beautiful northern kingdom of Scotland, and their ancestry was well documented over hundreds of years. He was a believing Presbyterian, the established Church of Scotland. And he carried out his regimental soldiering in a distinguished Scottish regiment, the Gordon Highlanders, in which his father had also served. Scottish society is tribal, with its clans, like extended families, providing strong cohesion. In the nineteenth century, when families were rarely uprooted, the lairds and their many servants had clan connections, which meant remote family kinship. This led to a stronger relationship between them than was the case in England, where employers and servants were rigidly divided along the lines of social class.[1] This clannishness goes some way to explain the special esprit de corps of Scottish regiments and even that of larger Scottish army formations, such as the legendary 51st (Highland) Division that made such a mark in the two world wars of the twentieth century.

Ian Hamilton was his father's elder son and it was inevitable that he should follow a military career and serve in his father's regiment, the Gordons, which Hamilton père commanded when his elder son was in his late teens. Officers in the nineteenth century British army virtually all came from the top five per cent of British society.[2] (This simple number is clearer than the descriptions 'upper class' and 'upper middle class', particularly because those are confusing to readers outside Britain.) The sine qua non for an army officer was an expensive private education provided by a family that could also give him some continuing financial support, since a junior officer's pay was very low and was absorbed by his basic living expenses in the officers' mess. Marriage was actively discouraged during an officer's early years of service.

When Ian Standish Monteith Hamilton was born, on 16 January 1853, on the Mediterranean island of Corfu where his father was serving at the time, the top five per cent of British society accounted in round terms for 350,000 families (out of a total population of approximately 35,000,000 people and 7,000,000 families). Officers in the army and navy came from five main sources: the landed aristocracy (a very small group); the rather larger numbers of gentry who had enough private money to live on, generally from the estates they owned; sons of serving and retired service officers; offspring of members of the learned professions, the Church, law and medicine; and (to a limited degree), those from prosperous industrial and commercial families. Ian Hamilton came from both the second and third of these classes, the gentry and the officers. His mother died young, and during his childhood his father was serving in India. He and his younger brother Vereker (who later became a well-known artist) therefore spent their early years among their extended family headed by their paternal grandfather. They all lived on a beautiful rambling Scottish estate overlooking the Holy Loch in Argyllshire, a home inhabited by numbers of kinsfolk and even larger numbers of outdoor and indoor servants; Hamilton's earliest friends were the children of estate workers. During Hamilton's early years, his life was under the control of his Swiss nurse, with whom he spoke French. He therefore had the unusual advantage of being brought up comfortable in two languages.[3]

In the customary way for boys of his class, Hamilton was despatched early to a boarding school. He went at the age of ten, while most boys went away when they were eight. From the ages of ten to thirteen he received an excellent education at Cheam, a prominent private school for young boys in the south of England, where he had to lay aside the kilt he had worn every day in Scotland, and don English schoolboys' trousers and breeches. Private education in Britain is described in its own language. Cheam is known as a preparatory school (a different terminology from that used in the United States). Between the ages of thirteen and seventeen he went on to Wellington College, an institution with strong military associations, also in the south of England. This was an English public school, which means (in British English) a fee-paying private school.

British boarding schools did not believe in soft treatment for the boys (and there were of course no girls). They were a reflection of a British society which was much more abrasive than in the twenty-first century, and was divided by many lines of demarcation, the most important being social class. Such schools provided a good formal education, based on divinity and the Greek and Latin classics. However, for the pupils there was physical discomfort, there were long hours of study, and vigorous and often rough sports. There were all sorts of artificial divisions between groups of boys, particularly between the seniors and juniors, and these led to conflict, bullying, flogging, and widespread rumors of homosexuality (with some justification). By today's standards, British boarding schools were deplorable places, but the boys in such schools, despite their mutual antipathies, developed a strong corporate spirit because they were all victims in adversity. And since the older boys played a large part in the day-to-day running of public schools, this was something of obvious value for the career of an army officer. In addition, the austere living conditions in these schools prepared young officers to withstand the rigours of active service. Today, the system might be called tough love, although such schools are now pale shadows of what they once were. The majority today are populated by both boys and girls, and such schools still offer a very good education but one based on a far broader curriculum than that under which Hamilton suffered as a boy. Cheam was a strongly disciplined school, and during his three years there Hamilton had a great deal of knowledge pumped into him, and he learned how to write clear, vivid, grammatical English. Wellington was a disappointment; the boys had much more freedom and as a result Hamilton did not apply himself to his studies. This caused a problem when, at the age of seventeen, he wanted to realize his long-held ambition to become an officer in the Gordon Highlanders.

'Gone for a Soldier'

This phrase, in eighteenth century English, was always used in the context of disapproval. At that time, soldiers in the ranks were widely regarded as 'the scum of the earth, enlisted for drink' (to use the words of the Duke of Wellington). Officers were seen as not much better: improvident, debauched, and reactionary in their political and social views. These attitudes had softened by the mid-nineteenth century, but they still remained below the surface, as Kipling demonstrated disapprovingly at the end of the century. Nevertheless to Ian Hamilton, who was a Highlander from an idealistic military family, soldiering was never anything but a noble calling.

The 1870s, when Hamilton was embarking on his military career, saw the beginning of a series of major changes in the organization of the British Army.[4] These were proposed and steered through Parliament by Edward Cardwell, the Secretary of State for War. One change that affected Hamilton directly was the abolition of purchase. This ancient system meant that most officers bought their first commissions, then sold them when they moved up in rank, when they had to pay an increased amount of money for their next commissions. This method of appointing and promoting officers was supposed to offer two advantages: first, it ensured that officers were motivated by ideals of service rather than financial gain; and second, it provided a pot of money for retired officers to keep them in their old age. (There were no army pensions at that time.) These arguments did not stand up too well to Cardwell's common sense and his ambition to attack the Army's profound conservatism. Purchase came to an end.

Until the abolition of the purchase system, some candidates could not afford to buy their first commission. Instead, these men could spend a year at the fee-paying Royal Military College, Sandhurst, if they were intended for the infantry or cavalry. If they wanted to enter the artillery, engineers and other specialist arms that required technical knowledge (in which commissions were not available for purchase), they spent eighteen months at the Royal Military Academy, Woolwich. Non-purchase officers did not have good promotion prospects, since those who could buy their next steps in rank had preference.

As part of the transition away from purchase, all candidates for commissions now had to sit a two-day examination comprising formal written papers and interviews, and the best candidates were selected. In Hamilton's batch, fewer than 500 succeeded out of a total of 1,000 who sat the examination. But before getting to the examination, Hamilton and his family realized that, after he had left Wellington, he was totally unprepared for this difficult process that was decisive for his future career. Action was urgently needed, and he managed to acquire enough (mostly superficial) knowledge to handle the examination papers. He did this by spending two months under the hard regime of a 'crammer', an ex-army officer with considerable knowledge of military examinations and who could make inspired guesses about the questions that were going to be asked in future ones. In the event, Hamilton did unexpectedly well and took seventy-sixth place in the order of merit; his knowledge of French was particularly useful when he was tested in a viva voce interview. He was not yet eighteen years of age. His family was surprised and delighted at this triumph but, during this transition period in the British army, Hamilton was still going to purchase his commission, as his father had done before him.

But there was one more complication. The top one hundred candidates in the examination were offered the chance of one year at Sandhurst instead of being directly commissioned, and the advantage of this was that they did not need to pass any promotion examinations until they reached the rank of major (as was necessary for those officers directly commissioned). Hamilton decided to accept the offer, and this meant that he spent a year, 1871, at Sandhurst. But before going there, he had time on his hands, and he decided to study for six months in Germany. He lived with the family of a retired general in Dresden and quickly learned to speak the language. The General himself acted as a tutor to improve what he saw as Hamilton's inadequate education and, most importantly, taught him a good deal about the German Army. This was the time of the Franco-Prussian war, and the victorious German military machine was regarded all over the world as the most formidable one that had ever been raised and trained. Hamilton's time in Germany was well spent, and he was so independent and accustomed to looking after himself that he found it an enjoyable adventure.

Sandhurst was a less inspiring experience. Living conditions were uncomfortable, the food was inadequate, and the instruction was unimpressive. Hamilton thought that he was wasting his year at the College and did not work very hard. The most successful graduates had the dates of their commissions advanced by two years, and those in the second rank were advanced by one year. But Hamilton did not manage to get into either group, which meant that many of his Sandhurst contemporaries, together with candidates who had taken their commissions directly without going there, were all now senior to him. This was a matter of some importance at a later stage in his career, when promotion largely depended on an officer's place in the pecking order. During his time at Sandhurst, Hamilton bought a horse – a hunter with considerable staying power – and he devoted most of his time to improving his ability to ride hard: a useful attribute for an army officer during the 1870s, even one intended for the infantry. Before his time at Sandhurst came to an end, Hamilton became at last an officer in the British army. He was not yet twenty. He had grown tall, thin and wiry and, in accordance with army regulations, he did not shave his upper lip and was sprouting rather an untidy moustache. Like most of his contemporaries he was active and kept himself very fit.

As seemed inevitable after the glitches in Hamilton's progress to date, a further problem had now developed. There was no vacancy in the Gordon Highlanders, and one was not likely to be opened for a year. Hamilton was helped out of his difficulty by his father, who arranged for him to be accepted by the 12th (Suffolk) Regiment, and also agreed to pay the considerable expense of the 12th Regiment's uniforms. This regiment was relatively senior, indicated by its number, and had a fine fighting record. The 12th was to be Hamilton's home for a busy and instructive year. Its Commanding Officer was Colonel Meade Hamilton, who came from a different branch of the family, the two branches having been separated two centuries earlier. The Colonel was known as 'Tiger' Hamilton, a reflection of his ferocious appearance and manners. The young Hamilton who wished to join the Suffolk Regiment for a year was introduced to 'Tiger' Hamilton over lunch, and he was riveted by the Colonel's moustache which was long even for a Victorian Army officer, as well as by his brusque conversation during the vetting process. The 'Tiger' was the father of two soldiers who subsequently became Generals and also of Lady Colley, the wife of the General who commanded the British force on Majuba Hill, where the young Hamilton greatly distinguished himself.

Hamilton (carrying the rank of Sub Lieutenant, the title then used for the lowest commissioned rank) spent a happy year in Ireland, where the Suffolks were stationed. Since the terrifying 'Tiger' Hamilton was being transferred to another job and was for most of the time off the scene, the atmosphere of the officers' mess was tranquil, and Hamilton found his comrades, officers and other ranks alike, to be the most pleasant companions with whom to spend soldiering days. He learned a good deal about the routine of peacetime regimental activity and he had plenty of time for riding and fishing. He even had a day of military action, helping to quell a riot, a job 'in aid of the civil power' that the Regular Army had to carry out occasionally. The whole Battalion was called out, and because Hamilton's immediate superior was away from the garrison, the young man stepped in to command a company of about 100 men. The rioters were unable to stand up to the long lines of well-disciplined Suffolks, and peace was restored.

At last, after twenty years of interrupted progress that had seen some successes but more failures, Hamilton was ready to move on. He was high spirited and optimistic; he had learned a modest amount about regimental soldiering; he could write English well, a legacy of the excellent basic education in English and the Classics that he had received, in particular during his three years at Cheam; he could speak two foreign languages; and he had a good seat on a horse. Now, just before his twenty-first birthday, he embarked for India, accompanied by trunks containing the equivalent of a wardrobe full of expensive sealed-pattern uniforms, with kilts and trews cut from the distinctive Gordon tartan, again all paid for by his father who also passed on his own sword. He was going to join the regiment – the military family – of which he had long planned to become a member.

The *Gay Gordons*

The *Gay Gordons* is a phrase coined well before any suspicion of a double-entendre and meaning simply the *light-hearted Gordons*. It is the name of one of the most energetic and elegant Scottish reels, formal dances performed by men and women of all ages and classes. The *Gay Gordons*, and the song *A Gordon for Me*, not to speak of ever-popular martial music like *Heilan' Laddie* and *Scotland the Brave,* are small pieces of evidence of the important place of Scotland's regiments in the culture of that self-contained and once remote kingdom.

In Ian Hamilton's day, Scotland raised twelve regiments for the Regular Army: the Royal Scots Greys, an ancient cavalry regiment; the Scots Guards, a part of the Royal Household; four infantry regiments from the Lowlands; and six from the Highlands, of which the Gordons were one. During the twentieth century and later, changes in the size and shape of the British Army led to many regiments being amalgamated and some disbanded, so that the overall organization is quite different today.

Since the British Army has always been based on individual self-contained regiments recruited from separate parts of the country, there had inevitably been differences between them, and these had grown over time and been constantly fostered by each regiment's officers and other ranks. Each regiment had a culture embracing idiosyncrasies in uniform, customs and even in the language of the barracks. The regiment's precedence (signalled by its number) was jealously guarded, and it is not surprising that there had always been an unstated but widely understood social ranking.[5] This was based on the regiment's attraction for the commissioned ranks, with regiments with the highest cachet attracting the wealthiest officers and those from the oldest families, especially if the family had a connection with the regiment. The Scottish regiments have always held a high position in this social hierarchy, much more so than the general run of those from England, Wales and Ireland. Soldiers from the Highlands had (and perhaps still have) a stronger natural pride even than those from the Lowlands. A sharp reminder of this is provided by an event that took place during the Second World War. During the campaign in the Western Desert of North Africa, a battalion of the Seaforth Highlanders had lost many junior officers through enemy action. A number of reinforcements were sent forward from rear headquarters, all excellent platoon commanders from Lowland Scottish regiments. Yet the Commanding Officer of the Seaforth refused to accept the newcomers because they had not been commissioned into his own regiment.[6] Many soldiers as well as members of the public would regard this attitude as deplorable, but to the Scots it was neither capricious nor vain but a right and proper reaction, and one that helps explain the strength of the morale of the regiments recruited in the Highlands. Warfare alongside their comrades was the Highlanders' raison d'être. It has always been common for those reaching the end of their full-time service to volunteer to extend it if the regiment was warned for active service. But they would only do this so long as they kept their own places in the ranks and were not transferred to any other regiment.

In Hamilton's day, there were more than a hundred infantry regiments in the British Army, all carrying their original numbers representing the chronological order. The Gordons were the 92nd Regiment, having been formed in 1794. Although they were not quite as ancient as many others, this did not reduce the esteem in which the Gordons were held, because it was based on their heroic and bloody fighting record. The soldiers in infantry regiments were at that time recruited for a long period of voluntary service, although later in the nineteenth century this was shortened to seven years with the Colours and five years in the Reserve (an innovation that Hamilton thought was a very bad idea[7]). Recruitment to the ranks of the army was always difficult and depended on the level of unemployment among industrial and agricultural laborers, but Highland regiments were always up to strength because of the lack of better jobs in northern Scotland. (Large numbers of men in the ranks were generally good for a regiment's *morale.*) A regiment – the basic tactical unit in the infantry – contained rather fewer than 1,000 men, about three per cent of the total being officers. The commanding officer was a lieutenant colonel, and each regiment was composed of a headquarters and eight rifle companies, each commanded by a captain.

'The Land of Regrets'
The Land of Regrets is the name of a once-popular poem written in 1885 by Sir Alfred Lyall, a prominent member of the Indian Civil Service. At the time when Lyall served in India, British expatriates only returned to Britain on leave at infrequent intervals: every five years in the case of army officers. The poem acknowledges without sentimentality that long service in the sub-continent by men and women born in Britain was accompanied by the continuous pang of homesickness. Ian Hamilton served for twenty-five years continuously in India and its periphery (with two relatively brief intervals on active service in Africa) but, despite the success he made of the increasingly responsible jobs he undertook, he expressed great relief when his quarter-century serving the Raj eventually came to an end.

When Hamilton arrived in India, he joined almost 190,000 soldiers in that country. Two-thirds of these were members of the Indian Army. In the Indian Army, most subaltern officers and all the lower ranks were Indians, with regiments recruited from men of individual races; but all senior officers, nearly all those with the rank of captain and above, were British. The remaining one-third of the total force in India were units of the British army, of which the Gordon Highlanders were one.[8] A force of 190,000 soldiers, the majority being infantry but also including cavalry, artillery and engineers, was a small body considering that the population of the country was not far short of 300 million. The army units were spread over the country in garrisons, known as cantonments. Besides being ready to fight small wars on the frontiers, their job was essentially to be prepared for immediate action if an insurrection were to take place in any part of the country. Only sixteen years before Hamilton arrived in India, the Mutiny, a bloody uprising that had infected large numbers of native soldiers, had been suppressed with great brutality, *pour encourager les autres*.

Hamilton spent five years of peacetime soldiering with the Gordons before he embarked on his first active campaign, in Afghanistan in early 1879. During those five years he was stationed at Mooltan, a barren, hot, unattractive cantonment, and later at Dera Ishmael Khan, an equally unattractive fort. These are both in the north-west, the Muslim region of India that is now Pakistan. Since the role of the army was to be in situ and ready for trouble, it did not demand day-and-night activity. Daily parades were brief, and much of the soldiers' time was spent on sports. During Hamilton's time in the Regiment, he spent his time on five main activities: first, the routine of regular garrison duty, working closely with his brother officers and the men in the ranks, which led to his early acceptance into the military fraternity of the Regiment. Second, there was sport; third, the infantry specialties of musketry and marching; fourth, he learned to speak Hindustani, the lingua franca of British India; and fifth – a pursuit that occupied very little time indeed – tactical training in the field.

Sport mostly meant riding, polo and shooting: rough shooting, using shotguns to pepper a variety of birds in and around camp and on the line of march; and more seriously, what was then called *shikar*, stalking larger animals with the rifle in the foothills of the Himalayas. Officers had plenty of local leave, and Hamilton devoted two long spells to shikar. The second of these lasted two months, and he embarked on a major expedition, accompanied by two Indian guides and a number of bearers to carry supplies and camping equipment. He returned with a number of trophies of a record size: spectacular horns from elusive mountain goats and sheep.

Shooting game had a natural relevance to the military skill of musketry, and this became Hamilton's overriding passion. When he was on leave in Britain, he had attended the course at the School of Musketry at Hythe (where he became Commandant much later in his career). He had passed the course with top honours, and this led to his appointment as the Gordons' Musketry Instructor. This was to be for him a very important stepping stone as well as the most interesting part of his early career.

> I sweated; I lectured; I begged; I made bad jokes; I even filled the pouches of the men with ball cartridge for private practice out of my own slender purse. As my propaganda began to take effect, the Adjutant and the Sergeant-Major became first uneasy, then furious, to see so much time lost to the barrack-square for the sake of the rifle range; the field officers, however, were astonished, and not altogether displeased.[9]

Hamilton's enthusiasm and effort paid off. The Gordons crept up the ranking to become the best shooting regiment in India; and he himself became a man who might in the future climb the ladder.

There was, however, little else in Hamilton's life that was directly valuable in improving his military skills. Most of his time was spent in barracks, and he tackled with enthusiasm the only-too-infrequent marches that the Regiment undertook, when they covered twenty miles in a day. On one of these marches he described a delightful picture of his soldiers crossing a deep ford, to the wild tribal music of the bagpipes. The men hung around their necks the sporrans they normally wore in front of their kilts, and lifted the skirts of their kilts under their arms as they splashed across the water. (In Highland regiments, no underclothes are worn under a kilt.) Hamilton also worked hard to master the Hindustani language and achieved a certificate of competency which earned him the job of Interpreter, with a modest increase in pay. This was not entirely a wasted effort, although knowledge of the native language would have been far more useful if he had been serving in an Indian rather than a British regiment.

An astonishing deficiency in the British army's training during the nineteenth century was the lack of attention to practical training in field tactics. In defence, soldiers formed infantry squares; and in attack they moved forward in close order. In both cases they concentrated on volley fire, in which accuracy was not particularly important since the volleys were a preparation for the soldiers to use their bayonets. Things changed during the twentieth century, and from the time of the Second World War tactical exercises have been carried out in conditions that, for the participants, bear some resemblance to active service in lack of sleep, exhaustion and other hardships, if not in actual danger. But in Hamilton's day things were totally different; at that time, on field days, which were often supervised by a general, regiments would carry out rigid and formal exercises better fitted for the eighteenth century than for a period that had seen a great increase in firepower and had witnessed in the Crimea and the American Civil War a very different type of conflict. Hamilton describes a typical and wonderfully unrealistic field day:

> First the march past – all the officers of the Garrison to be present in uniform – the order said nothing about the ladies, but they were all there and all in full kit; next, the rapid formation of squares two deep and four deep to resist cavalry; next, a practice performance to show the new-fangled 'attack' . . . . The enemy was supposed to be entrenched under a clump of palm trees about 600 yards distant. At our Colonel's command the Regiment deployed at the double from Quarter Column into line, lay down and opened fire. Next came an order for the Regiment to advance by Companies, beginning from the left, with short sharp rushes of fifty paces. Having made its rush each Company had to fling itself on the ground, fire three rounds rapid 'independent' – make another rush and so *da capo* until we got within 100 yards of the enemy when we would fix bayonets and charge.[10]

But on this particular occasion things did not go quite right. Two hundred yards short of the objective, Hamilton spotted a strong brick wall and ordered his men to fall out behind it and shoot over the top. As he was doing this, he realized that he was committing a mortal sin because his orders did not brook any variation in how they should be interpreted. He was, however, saved by the general who was supervising the exercise, who unexpectedly gave him a strong commendation for his initiative. There were not many signs of hope for the British Army during the 1870s, but this was perhaps one.

Field tactics are – or should be – the main preoccupation of all infantry soldiers. The main elements are first, the use of the battleground itself – the shape of the topography – in order for infantry to use it effectively in the four phases of war, advance to contact, attack, defence, and withdrawal. This means moving troops quickly without bunching, and making the best use of dead ground. The second element is tight control of the infantry sub-units; every officer and non-commissioned officer should all the time strive to control his own small part of the battlefield. The third principle is the use of fire and movement, based on the infantry's own small arms; and during the twentieth and twenty-first centuries a battalion's own support weapons, plus the artillery, armoured and air support provided by attached units. Fire and movement has become very complex, which means that effective tactics demand continuous practice and unrelenting attention. This is simply and persuasively explained by Brigadier Peter Young, a Second World War Commando and a highly successful battalion commander:

> I believe that a good infantry unit is one that is fit and hard, is superlatively good with its weapons, and widely trained in tactics. The Commanding Officer may sleep when he has taught all his followers all that he knows himself and is confident that they will act as he would wish when he is not there and hasn't been for six months.[11]

The British Army during the nineteenth century paid no attention to these principles, although generals proclaimed vague and self-serving generalizations such as that fox-hunting improved an officer's eye for the shape of ground. It is therefore no surprise that, when the British Army met an enemy quite different from the ill-armed native levies against whom they had fought during the last four decades of the nineteenth century, disaster followed disaster. The British Army did not lack bravery but, rather seriously, it lacked skills. Their new enemy was the irregular bands of farmers who had become guerrilla soldiers and were Britain's opponents during the two Boer Wars. These men lived on scanty rations, which meant that they subsisted on dried meat, tough bread and coffee. They were all hardy and moved fast on their scrawny ponies. They had the important military quality of an excellent 'feel' for ground. And they were practised shots; in the Second Boer War they were equipped with modern German rifles. In fighting the Boers, the British had to learn about field tactics the hard way. But this was all in the future.

Young officers of the Victorian army were always enthusiastic about volunteering for active service in any campaign that seemed likely to be on the cards. These were invariably small affairs fought at the periphery of the British Empire and were usually forecast to be brief and triumphant. To young officers, active service offered a break from the tedious routine of garrison duty and an opportunity for glory and promotion (but also of course for wounds and death for the unfortunate). Hamilton had made an attempt to volunteer during his early days with the Gordons, but he was considered then to be too young and inexperienced. But his opportunity came in 1879. As an unconscious precursor of an event that was to take place in the twenty-first century, a campaign was planned to invade Afghanistan. By that time the hero of this book had spent five years in India and he was just twenty-six years of age.

Notes

1 General Sir Ian Hamilton, *When I Was a Boy* (London: Faber & Faber, 1939), p.27. Much of what I write about Hamilton's early life is based on this book.
2 John Philip Jones, *Keynes's Vision. Why the Great Depression Did Not Return* (London and New York: Routledge, 2008), pp.135–7.
3 Hamilton, *When I Was a Boy*, pp.29–30.
4 Jock Haswell, *The British Army* (London: Thames & Hudson, 1975), pp.100–06.
5 John Philip Jones, *The Successes and Sacrifices of the British Army in 1914. Soldiers Marching, All to Die* (Lewiston/Queenston/Lampeter: Edwin Mellen, 2009), pp.22–4; also David French, *Military Identities: The Regimental System, the British Army, and the British People, 1870-2000* (Oxford: Oxford University Press, 2005), pp.164–5.
6 Neil McCallum, *Journey with a Pistol. A Diary of War* (London: Victor Gollancz, 1959), pp.48–9.

7 General Sir Ian Hamilton, *Listening for the Drums* (London: Faber & Faber, 1944), p.141. As with the listing in Note 1, this book is an excellent primary source.
8 Philip Mason, *A Matter of Honour. An Account of the Indian Army, Its Officers and Men* (Harmondsworth, Middlesex, UK: Penguin Books, 1974), p.319.
9 Hamilton, *Listening for the Drums*, p.120.
10 Ibid., pp.69–70.
11 Alison Michelli, *Commando to Captain-Generall. The Life of Brigadier Peter Young* (Barnsley, South Yorkshire, UK: Pen & Sword, 2007), p.40.

CHAPTER 3

Beau Sabreur

The half-century between the late 1850s and 1914 – the year that pointed like a signpost to a changed world – brought Britain continuous peace punctuated by colonial wars. If nothing else, these taught British soldiers something about their profession, and some unpalatable lessons were certainly learned from the Second Boer War of 1899–1902. It was during the early years of the twentieth century that Ian Hamilton reached high rank. The reasons why he rose above the pack were real enough, but some clues to his success are easier to detect than others. One clue has been described already: Hamilton's passionate interest in musketry and the resulting measurable improvement in the soldiers' performance in his Regiment. During the late nineteenth century, this became something of much greater importance than a means of advancing a unit's performance in a competitive league table. The adoption of rapid-fire magazine rifles and smokeless powder had the immediate effect of making fast and accurate small-arms fire a decisive factor in infantry combat. These developments came too late for the American Civil War, but the Second Boer War demonstrated the power of modern musketry quite clearly, and this relatively small conflict pointed the way to an even more important role for individual marksmanship – accurate and rapid small-arms fire – during the much larger war that broke out in 1914.

Two further clues will be revealed in this chapter. The first is the reputation that Hamilton earned for himself as a *beau sabreur* – a thrusting young officer – and he began to make his mark during his first exposure to enemy fire, in Afghanistan. The second clue, and a matter of decisive importance, is the influence of Frederick Roberts, a rapidly rising general who took Hamilton under his wing.

The Military Pyramid

I shall try to avoid the mistake, all too common in military biographies, of describing Hamilton's rise as an automatic progression from subaltern to full general, as if such a movement were smooth, uninterrupted and inevitable, like a teenager's progress each year to the top form at his school. In contrast, the structure of an army means that the higher the rank, the fewer the number of jobs. For every brigadier or higher grade, there are at least a hundred officers in more junior ranks, and of course the limited number of higher appointments determines the opportunities for promotion. The military pyramid is an accurate metaphor, although it does not communicate the painful fact that, at every step, large numbers of careers come to an end to make way for the men who succeed. The interesting point is *why* a soldier came to be selected at each upward step in a competitive race, and what qualities he possessed that his contemporaries did not. This is a subject very rarely addressed.

Promotion to lieutenant colonel is where the real difficulties begin, and they grow greater at each further upward move beyond that. This is anyway true of peacetime. In major wars, vast numbers of conscripts in the ranks call for increases in the number of officers of all grades to command them. But at the end of the war, most of the surviving Regular lieutenant colonels and higher ranks are obliged to step down at least one grade and often stick there for the rest of their careers. During the nineteenth century, Regular officers were promoted as a result of four factors. (This is less true today, when the second factor – ability – is a more important determinant.) The first was seniority, which was determined by the date of an officer's commission in each rank he obtained. This system has always applied in a general sense, but there were ways in which an officer could leapfrog. The best known was the system of brevet ranks (known disparagingly as 'promotion on the cheap'). As a reward for outstanding service, an officer could receive a higher, or brevet, rank which did not mean any extra pay but did count towards seniority. There were also rare individual examples of leapfrogging to a more dramatic degree as a result of most exceptional direct nomination.[1]

The second factor influencing promotion was, quite rightly, an officer's demonstrable competence: his power of leadership, administrative ability, knowledge, dedication, and – rather importantly – his courage and the example he set to his juniors when on active service. Towards the end of the nineteenth century, passing the Staff College course (carrying the prestigious initials *psc* after an officer's name in the seniority list) became an important rite of passage to the senior ranks. Military tradition lays down that an officer receives an annual report based on a formal although subjective evaluation of his performance by his direct superior, one or more grades higher. However, in the Victorian army, a greater part was played by the third determining factor, what is best described as patronage: whether an officer was recognized and selected for interesting jobs by a general who knew him or his family personally and/or was particularly impressed by his abilities. The fourth factor – influencing all the others – was quite simply luck, which meant being in the right place at the right time, as well as beating the odds and surviving his encounters with the enemy.

The first two points – seniority and ability – were necessary conditions for promotion; many officers had both. However, they were not sufficient in themselves. Nor were a variety of personal strengths – presence, charm, personal persuasiveness, and the ability to write engagingly – strengths that were distributed randomly over the whole officer corps.

It was the two additional factors that were both necessary and decisive: patronage and luck. It is an interesting exercise to review the historical records and count the number of senior officers whose various promotions were governed by the combination of these two ingredients. Two of the most striking examples are Haig, the controversial British Commander-in-Chief during the second half of the First World War, [2] and Montgomery in the Second World War.[3] Ian Hamilton is another, despite his lack of the *psc* initials after his name. Taking a long view, Montgomery was an outstanding success while Haig and Hamilton were not, which means that further factors kick in if a soldier in the exalted ranks is to leave a positive mark on history, or even if he is to keep his job. These additional factors will be discussed in Chapter 10, where Hamilton's performance at Gallipoli is described. However, his ascent in rank before the First World War was driven by his seniority, ability, patronage and luck. In particular, it is impossible to understand his rise without examining his relations with Lord Roberts, the most important British soldier during the second half of the nineteenth century. Roberts first noticed Hamilton's performance under fire during the Afghan fighting in 1879. Before too long he became one of Roberts's favourites and was welcomed into the General's military family. Not surprisingly, Roberts himself had received the benefit of the same factors of patronage and luck as would influence Hamilton's preferment. But to be fair, both Roberts and Hamilton had demonstrable ability, and patronage and luck were extra (albeit decisive) ingredients. Because of the similarity in the factors that influenced the upward progression of both Roberts and Hamilton, it will illuminate Hamilton's career to look first at Roberts and how he built his formidable reputation.

Bobs Bahadur

Frederick Roberts, later Sir Frederick and eventually Lord Roberts, was the most distinguished of Queen Victoria's generals, rivalled only by Lord Wolseley. But Roberts's decisive contribution to the Second Boer War gave him the winning advantage in their rivalry. Roberts was always popular with his soldiers, both because he won battles and because he looked conscientiously after his troops. British soldiers called him *Bobs*; and Indian soldiers gave him the name of respect and affection *Bobs Bahadur* (enshrined in the writings of Rudyard Kipling).

Roberts was Irish and was born in 1832.[4] His father was a well-known soldier who served in India and ended his career as a major general. The younger Roberts had little conventional schooling although he benefited from an unusually intensive specialist education for a Victorian army officer: one year at Eton, two years at the Royal Military College, Sandhurst, and a further two years at the East India Company School at Addiscombe. Roberts was intended for the artillery, and graduated from Addiscombe at the age of nineteen and received his commission in the artillery of the East India Company. He was intelligent and enthusiastic, and was technically well-qualified. He was a strikingly short man, although this did not inhibit his natural air of authority.

Before the bloody Indian Mutiny of 1857–59, the British possessions in the Indian sub-continent were ruled by an organization that had originally been a totally commercial enterprise, the Honourable East India Company, which had received in 1600 a Royal Charter giving it a monopoly to carry out all types of trade in India. However, over the years the Company had led the way in conquering provinces and then ruling them on behalf of the British Crown. It also arranged treaties with the Indian Princely states which, as a result of bribery and intimidation, mostly accepted overall British direction in important matters. In this curious way, Britain exercised control over the vast and variegated territory of India. In order to do its job properly, the Company recruited military and naval forces, and the structure of its army set the pattern for the Indian Army that came directly under British government rule after the Mutiny had been quelled.

The individual units were recruited from different Indian races, each regiment coming from a single race, with its own religion, customs and eating habits. As described in Chapter 2, half the officers – the more junior ranks – were appointed by promotions from the rank and file. The remaining officers were British, and were recruited in the same way as Roberts. They usually made their entire career in India: a system that remained in place until the end of the Raj in 1947. In addition to the regiments recruited in India, there was an old-established custom of units of the British Army spending long periods of time there, just as the Gordon Highlanders were doing when Ian Hamilton was a junior officer. (The number of British regiments in India was greatly increased after the Mutiny.) The fact that the British and Indian regiments served alongside one another led to close and continuous comradeship, which flowered wonderfully during the Second World War and contributed powerfully to the reconquest of Burma from the Japanese in 1944–45. General Sir William Slim, the commander of the victorious Fourteenth Army, was an Indian Army officer.

Roberts served for forty-one years in India. He carried out very little normal regimental duty because, soon after his arrival in 1851, he was given a job on the staff. This was because he was recognized as a result of his father's reputation, and was anyway thought to be a promising young officer. But the Mutiny, which erupted suddenly in 1857, shook to its foundation the slumberous routine that characterized peacetime soldiering in India, and gave Roberts a series of opportunities for active service, opportunities he seized enthusiastically. He carried out many special jobs for his military superiors, which involved him in many hot engagements. He did extremely well, showing no sympathy at all for the mutineers and their reasons for taking up arms against their British officers. He was tough, ruthless and aggressive, as can be seen in his description of the execution of two mutineers, which he witnessed:

> A parade was at once ordered. The troops were drawn up so as to form three sides of a square; on the fourth side were two guns, to which the mutineers were bound. The word of command was given; the guns went off simultaneously, and the two mutineers were launched into eternity. It was a terrible sight, and one likely to haunt the beholder for many a long day; but that was what was intended. I carefully watched the sepoys' faces to see how it affected them. They were evidently startled at the swift retribution which had overtaken their guilty comrades, but looked more crest-fallen than shocked or horrified.

(This account comes from Roberts's engaging and vivid memoirs, which he wrote without any help from professional writers or editors after the end of his service in India.[5])

Roberts's highly visible junior leadership earned him the Victoria Cross, a decoration recently introduced to take precedence over all other awards granted by the British Government. It was and is open to all ranks and granted solely for the highest valour in the face of the enemy, witnessed by a superior officer. Its unique eminence has never faded. Roberts's service during the Mutiny gave his career a strong surge, and he was given the rank of brevet major: good progress for an officer of twenty-six. He now returned to the routine of staff work. By this time, the old Army of the East India Company had been transformed into the Indian Army, under the direct control of the British Government of India.

During Roberts's remaining thirty-four years in India, he spent a lengthy period as a staff officer, during which time he took part in three minor expeditions on active service. But he was at last given a major command in the field, in the second Afghan War which began in 1878. After this conflict, which established his reputation, his career progressed upward and he was the Commander-in-Chief during his last eight years in India.

The first Afghan War that lasted from 1839 to1842 was a disaster for British arms. Roberts's important opportunity came with the second, and surprisingly successful, Afghan War that was fought in two phases, in 1878 to1879 and 1879 to1880. At the beginning, Roberts was a major general, relatively newly promoted. At the end of the second phase of the war, he was a hero, known throughout the British Empire. The wars in Afghanistan fought during the nineteenth century (like those before and during the first decade of the twenty-first century) were not the outcome of a direct quarrel with the indigenous population. The local population was targeted because it was thought to harbour dangerous outsiders. During the 1870s, these outsiders were the Russians who were regarded in Britain and India during the nineteenth century as aggressive interlopers with designs on Britain's possessions. In 1878, the Russians signed a treaty with the Afghans' tribal leader: something immediately seen by the British as a serious warning that called for action.

It is difficult to imagine a country worse than north-eastern Afghanistan in which to fight a war. It is a mountainous and arid desert, with deep valleys that channel the paths of invading troops, and with inadequate roads and poor lateral communications (at least before the days of radio and helicopters). Worst of all, the Afghan defenders, both regular and irregular, were hardy, brave and wily; and they did not obey the conventions of 'civilized' war. They had an instinctive grasp of field tactics and were able to conceal themselves easily when firing at their enemies with their antique firearms; not all were antique because there was an active trade in stealing modern rifles from Indian Army encampments.[6] The Afghans fought in natural defensive positions which they occupied skilfully until the time came for the defenders to melt away.

The only way in which a general could command a mobile column in such an unpromising environment was by leading 'from the saddle': living among the troops surrounded by a very small staff, and personally exhorting and cajoling the men in the ranks. He also needed subordinate commanders – lieutenant colonels in their battalions and captains in their companies – to operate in the same way. By and large this is how the army in Afghanistan worked.

The British invaded with three columns of troops, acting independently but following a broad overall plan. The strength of these columns was 16,000, 13,000, and 6,300 men respectively. Roberts commanded the smallest, which had a strength somewhere between a division and a brigade in size, composed mainly of native troops reinforced by eighteen guns. The troops wore native headdresses or cork sun-helmets, with the infantry dressed in scarlet tunics; and like armies of the eighteenth century they carried their regimental colours into battle. Roberts marched at the end of November 1878. It was his good fortune to fight and win the decisive battle of this phase of the war within days of entering the country. This was at Peiwar Kotal, where Roberts defeated an Afghan army six times as large as his own, and which was occupying dominant hillside positions. He carried out this feat by deception: by making visible preparations for a frontal attack and then secretly encircling the enemy position by a long and hazardous flanking march over inadequate mountainous tracks. He led this himself, as Stonewall Jackson had done at Chancellorsville. It was a master stroke, and Queen Victoria sent her personal congratulations. She was a conscientious ruler and was always knowledgeable about her men in uniform and was intensely interested in their victories and defeats. Parliament also voted its thanks and Roberts received a knighthood.

With the war apparently concluded, Sir Louis Cavagnari, a fascinating politician-cum-soldier from a mixed English, Irish and French family, was despatched in July 1879 as a permanent political agent to the Afghan capital, Kabul, to keep an eye on the continued neutrality of the government there. He was promptly murdered: a disaster consistent with the violence and treachery endemic to that country (a condition that has not changed much with the passage of time). As a consequence, Roberts had to carry out a number of small but brisk battles to bring some sort of finality to the conflict. Because further trouble had been anticipated, substantial reinforcements had arrived, including the Gordon Highlanders, with whom the twenty-six-year-old Ian Hamilton was to hear his first shots fired in anger. When Roberts finally reached Kabul, he ordered the murderers of the British envoy to be hanged publicly on a row of gibbets. This was intended to be a severe example to others, but the gesture did not succeed in bringing peace.

Roberts garrisoned Kabul and built a strong fortress there to guard against the still antagonistic local population. But insurrections continued in various parts of the country, and these led to the second phase of the war. The most dramatic action in this was the relief of the British garrison in Kandahar, where British troops were under siege and badly demoralized. The relief was highly dramatic and, until that time, the most notable feat of arms of Roberts's career. He led a march of 313 miles over inadequate roads from Kabul to Kandahar. His strength was 10,000 men and large numbers of camp followers, and he drove them forward to reach their goal in twenty-two days in the ferocious heat of August 1880. The feat caught the imagination of the British public, and Roberts received a shower of rewards, including promotion to lieutenant general. The British now felt sufficiently comfortable to leave the country, but little had been achieved by the two phases of the war. A lesson was learned that is still relevant in the twenty-first century: Afghanistan is a country that can be subdued at least temporarily, but it can never be occupied or even pacified by an outside power. During the period of the Raj, the British continued to garrison the North-West Frontier of India and were involved in a number of small campaigns to quell insurrections on the Afghan side of the frontier. But there was no question of a full invasion of Afghanistan until the twenty-first century, when they entered the country as the junior partner of the United States in a major invasion with ill-defined objectives: an enterprise that seems to have no end despite the optimism of many politicians. This is a military adventure in which the lessons of the past have been forgotten, as is so often the case.

Roberts spent his remaining thirteen years in India doing what he did best: commanding troops. He was initially chief of Southern India based in Madras, one of the three big commands into which the country was divided; and then from 1885 he was commander-in-chief. This appointment was by no means a certainty, since the natural candidate was Wolseley, the senior soldier in Britain and who had fought his battles in Africa. (As mentioned earlier, Roberts had a formidable fighting reputation, but he only demonstrated his lead over Wolseley much later, during the Second Boer War.) Roberts got the job as Commander-in-Chief in India as a result of an extraordinary stroke of luck.

Some time before a new commander-in-chief was due to be appointed, Lord Randolph Churchill (Winston Churchill's father) visited India. He was a leading politician who was not in office at the time since his party was in opposition. He met Roberts and they went to a camp and inspected an Indian Army brigade that was scheduled to join the Nile expedition to rescue General Gordon in Khartoum. This brigade was not under Roberts's command. The men looked smart and capable, and Lord Randolph – an intelligent and observant amateur – was very impressed by their appearance. But Roberts – an experienced professional – did not think much of them since he judged that the battalions had been softened by too much peacetime soldiering. Lord Randolph was incredulous, but Roberts was correct. The brigade performed inadequately in the field, and Churchill never forgot his conversation with Roberts. When the time came to appoint a new commander-in-chief of the Indian army, Lord Randolph's party had formed a government and he was personally responsible for the India Office, which controlled all high-level appointments. This was the way in which Roberts was selected in 1885, and Winston Churchill wrote subsequently that nothing gave his father more pleasure than to have given Roberts his greatest professional opportunity.[7]

During his eight years in the job, Roberts proved himself the best commander-in-chief who ever ran the affairs of the Indian Army. He was a diligent trainer of men, emphasizing the importance of infantry, since he questioned the future value of cavalry as shock troops and planned to use them as mounted infantry, whose best contribution would be to operate as trained foot-soldiers with greatly increased mobility. He co-operated in the annexation of Burma and occupied that country relatively smoothly. He paid great attention to the North-West Frontier of India, by both reinforcing the local defences and maintaining good relations with the Afghan tribes, who were as dangerous as ever. Most important of all, he improved the barren living conditions of the British troops who were far from home in an uncomfortable climate and did not have enough work and other activities to occupy their time. He did not attempt to ban liquor, but he did much to encourage soldiers to drink less, in well-appointed recreation rooms. Because of the measures he took to make the life of the troops less onerous, he justified his nickname *Bobs*. His departure in 1893 was regretted by everybody, although he left India at last as Lord Roberts and a field marshal.

He did not have a tranquil retirement. The tocsin summoned him to arms in 1900, to help the British army in South Africa recover from their disheartening series of defeats during the first months of the Second Boer

War. His successes there deserve to be examined in detail, in the context of the role that Ian Hamilton played as a staff officer and column commander. This is the topic of Chapters 6 and 7. Even after Roberts's labours in South Africa had been crowned with great (although not complete) success, he decided to devote his remaining years to promoting an unpopular but sensible political cause – universal military service – although it was a cause that could never be accepted by British politicians, who were petrified about what it would cost, both in money and in the disapproval of the electorate. Universal military service for the whole nation meant, for Roberts, conscription for only a few months, to be spent absorbing rudimentary military discipline and learning how to shoot. This system would have provided an invaluable reserve in the case of a big war. The campaign for universal military service that Roberts spearheaded brought him into conflict with Ian Hamilton, as will be described in Chapter 9.

Finally, after all his incomparable contributions to his country, the ancient Field Marshal greeted with military determination the outbreak of the First World War. In December 1914, he visited France and Flanders and inspected many troops, in particular soldiers of the Indian Army, who hated the northern European climate; and, as if marking a poetic closure, he died of pneumonia while he was among them.

The 'Sharp End'
The Gordon Highlanders were, as mentioned, summoned to action in 1879, and crossed the frontier into Afghanistan. Lieutenant Hamilton, much to his annoyance, was not with the main party and did not participate in the small but dramatic actions in which the Regiment was soon engaged. He was stricken with fever, an all-too-common occurrence in India, and this put him out of commission although his determination to play his part drove him to follow the Regiment independently.

The Gordons fought four limited but very sharp engagements, and their successes burnished the Regiment's already high reputation.[8] Two Victoria Crosses were awarded, one of which went to Major George White, the temporary Commanding Officer. He will reappear in Chapter 6, which describes the 1899 siege of Ladysmith in Natal. White commanded the garrison there, and one of his senior subordinates was

43

Ian Hamilton, by then a colonel who fought his own battles during the siege. The first of the four skirmishes in Afghanistan fought by the Gordons, witnessed an especially striking example of junior leadership. A Colour Sergeant in one of the rifle companies, Hector Macdonald, son of a Highland crofter, distinguished himself by his bravery and natural power of command. His men immediately responded to him, with one man's cry echoing through the ranks: 'We'll make ye an officer for this day's work, Sergeant!' and another soldier shouting: 'Aye, and a General too!'[9] Macdonald did receive from Roberts the rare honour of a battlefield commission. His career prospered. As a colonel, he commanded a brigade in the Battle of Omdurman in the Sudan in 1898. And he fought with courage and skill during the Second Boer War, where he was wounded and was promoted major general and then knighted. But no one was to forecast his tragic end. In 1903 he shot himself in a hotel room in Paris, in the face of charges of homosexuality, a criminal matter that at the time was not treated lightly.[10]

While the Gordons were being sharply engaged with the Afghans, Hamilton (by now known in his regiment as 'Johnny') was in a groggy state and was riding his pony alongside another junior officer, who was nicknamed 'Polly' Forbes. They reached Peiwar Kotal, the site of the successful battle that Roberts had fought in November 1878, and the two young men saw that the battlefield was still littered with debris.[11] But, more arrestingly, they were shocked to see a party of soldiers, without their rifles, rushing helter-skelter down a hill. Hamilton and Forbes immediately investigated, drew their revolvers, and accompanied 'at a discreet interval' by a lone soldier who still had his rifle, the three of them mounted the hill. The soldier who went with them was lucky enough to avoid a court martial, but this was the fate of those who had run away. These were inexperienced soldiers, the first batch recruited for what was then called 'short service', or seven years with the colours. Hamilton bitterly opposed short service because it deprived the army of fully experienced men: a view that was to cause (as already mentioned) a public disagreement with Lord Roberts over conscription during the years before the First World War.

Hamilton and Forbes had sent for help, and at the top of the hill they found a defence post unoccupied and in perfect peace: and, of course, containing the rifles that had been left behind by the scattered soldiers. Appropriately for someone who was so enthusiastic about musketry, Hamilton, joined by his companion, armed themselves with rifles from this collection, loaded them and stood guard. Before too long they were relieved by a British infantry company. The two young men, with dramatic impulsiveness now went alone down the other side of the hill to search for the Afghans who had caused the trouble. These turned out to be a raiding party who, outnumbering the two young officers, still had much fight in them. There followed a pantomime of inaccurate pistol and musketry fire. Hamilton let off six shots from his revolver, but due to his weak physical state he hit nobody. In turn he was enfiladed by three tribesmen, one of whom fired at him with an ancient blunderbuss. He fortunately missed, and he was soon himself shot.

It was a highly charged encounter, and one that led to a meeting that was to have a decisive influence on Hamilton's career:

> Lord Roberts, or Sir Fred Roberts as he then was, sent for me to his tent and made me tell it to him. He then gave me a glass of sherry and said he would write home and tell my father what had happened and so he did – longhand and at length. The indirect sequel was Sir Fred's offer to me two and a half years later to come on his Staff and the sherry and the letter give a useful glimpse of the secret of his popularity.[12]

An immediate reward also came Hamilton's way. Still not fully fit, he was appointed an aide-de-camp (ADC) to General Redan Massy, who commanded the Cavalry Brigade in Roberts's army. With this Brigade, Hamilton savoured the danger and the acute thrill of an old-fashioned cavalry charge. This was an unusual experience for an infantry officer:

> The dust clouds of the Chardeh Valley – the 5th Punjab Cavalry – red puggarees – blue swords flashing; the galloping line, and I also galloping with that sensation of speed which the swiftest motor car can never impart; my little grey arab snorting and shaking his head, galloping obliquely towards them again . . . . Nearer, nearer, every stride nearer! These dust clouds of the Chardeh Valley, flecked here and there with the flicker of moving colours; the foot-hills speckled with puffs of white smoke . . . Afghans in little knots, or else lying

on their backs whirling their big knives to cut off the legs of our horses, a hell of a scrimmage in fact.[13]

After this adventure Hamilton was granted some sick leave, but he returned to Afghanistan and rejoined the Gordons on the last day of the final battle of the war.

During his brief but intense baptism of fire, Hamilton became more than ever enthusiastic about his calling. With even greater eagerness he continued *Listening for the Drums* (the title of his second volume of memoirs). His attitude was more emotional than intellectual, and he rationalized it in words he wrote when he was an old man:

> War to us British is a process of running into danger voluntarily for the sake of others. Looked at in that light it is quite another process from that of working for selfish reasons whether as a cat-burglar or a company promoter. War then is an ordeal and the man who has been through it adds to his self-esteem.[14]

The most important single event of Hamilton's adventures in Afghanistan was that his enterprising gallantry had brought him to Roberts's attention. This was a stroke of luck comparable with Roberts's own meeting with Lord Randolph Churchill which had secured him his appointment as Commander-in-Chief of the Indian Army. Hamilton was to take part in two further expeditions against colonial enemies, in South Africa and North Africa, before he began his many years of service as a member of Roberts's military staff. His bold participation in Afghanistan and in the two campaigns in Africa won him his spurs.

Notes

1 The most egregious example of leapfrogging comes from America. In 1942 General Marshall, the United States Army Chief of Staff, selected Brigadier General Eisenhower, who had shown that he was an outstandingly able staff officer in Washington, DC, to command Operation TORCH, the invasion of north-west Africa. Eisenhower, who had been only a major in 1935, was appointed in 1942 over the heads of a large number of officers who were senior to him. Marshall took a great risk, but his judgement was sound. Within ten years, Eisenhower had advanced from major to five-star general, an upward move of seven ranks, certainly a world record. In the Royal Air Force, also in 1942, Air Vice Marshal Bennett, a flier with formidable

technical abilities, was appointed to create the elite Pathfinder Force. Although he was not a Regular officer, he was moved up before his thirty-second birthday from the rank of wing commander, and very quickly jumped three grades. (This was the equivalent of rising from lieutenant colonel to major general in the army.) Again, his success justified his promotion.

2 Haig benefited from Royal patronage. His career was followed favourably by King George V, because Haig's wife was a lady-in-waiting. Haig's major stroke of good fortune was that Grierson, his fellow corps commander and a better qualified officer, died in France in 1914 before the British Army engaged the enemy. It is likely that Grierson rather than Haig would have succeeded to the Supreme Command within a year, after Sir John French had been sacked.

3 Montgomery's patron was Brooke, the powerful Chief of the Imperial General Staff. The extraordinary stroke of luck that determined Montgomery's future career was the death in action of Gott, the lieutenant general who had been appointed by Churchill to command the Eighth Army in North Africa. Montgomery stepped into his shoes.

4 Details of Roberts's life come from David James, *Lord Roberts* (London: Hollis & Carter, 1954).

5 Field Marshal Lord Roberts of Kandahar, *Forty-One Years in India, from Subaltern to Commander-in-Chief* (London: Richard Bentley, 1897), pp.124–5.

6 Frank Richards, *Old Soldier Sahib* (London: Faber & Faber, 1936), pp.92–107.

7 James, *Lord Roberts*, pp.194–6.

8 Patrick Mileham, *The Scottish Regiments, 1633–1996* (Staplehurst, Kent, UK: Spellmount, 1988), p.248.

9 Byron Farwell, *Queen Victoria's Little Wars* (New York: Norton, 1972), p.207.

10 John Montgomery, *Toll for the Brave: The Tragedy of Hector Macdonald* (London: Max Parrish, 1963), pp.144–6.

11. Hamilton's own reminiscences of the war in Afghanistan appear in his memoirs: General Sir Ian Hamilton, *Listening for the Drums* (London: Faber & Faber, 1944), pp.125–7.

12. Ibid., p.125.

13. Ibid., p.126.

14. Ibid., p.123.

CHAPTER 4

'No End of a Lesson'[1]

After Afghanistan Ian Hamilton, still a junior officer, was only too anxious for the further opportunities for glory and advancement offered by active service. These opportunities came from two further campaigns, both in Africa: the First Boer War of 1880–81, and the 1884–85 Gordon Relief Expedition, which sailed up the Nile towards the Sudan, to rescue General Gordon who was surrounded in Khartoum by followers of the Mahdi, the charismatic Muslim leader. Both expeditions were serious failures, although the British army learned some limited lessons from them. When these conflicts were resumed, eighteen years later against the Boers and thirteen years later against the Sudanese, the British army finally triumphed, despite the fact that in the Second Boer War it took the British almost three arduous years to bring the fighting to a successful conclusion. Both examples illustrate the familiar bon mot that in its many wars, the British Army is defeated in all battles – except the last one.

In early 1881, when Hamilton was nearing twenty-eight years of age, his Battalion at last left India to return to Britain. They were diverted to South Africa and duly arrived in Durban, the capital of Natal, when they were summoned to join the expedition to invade the neighbouring colony of the Transvaal, which had reverted to being an independent Boer republic after a short and unhappy period of British rule. Four subalterns of the Gordons were now persuaded by Hamilton to add their names to a cable that he signed, paid for, and sent to Sir Evelyn Wood, Second-in-Command of the British Army in Natal. It said that the Gordon Highlanders were ready and more than willing to join the campaign.[2] The cable was sent, but its outcome is only speculation although Wood, who did not yet know Hamilton personally, was the sort of man who appreciated initiative and would have been influenced by it.

Army Reforms at Last

At this time a change took place in the British Army that directly affected the Gordon Highlanders. This was the final stage of the reforms initiated by Edward Cardwell, the Secretary of State for War from 1868 to1874, in the administration of the Liberal Prime Minister William Ewart Gladstone.[3] These reforms all carried Cardwell's name, but the last and most important of them was only implemented by his successor Hugh Childers in 1881, the date when the Gordons, like a number of other regiments, were expanded and reshaped.

The reforms were all intended to overcome some of the deadly conservatism in the British Army, an endemic condition that had been reinforced by the long years of rarely-interrupted peace since the defeat of Napoleon Bonaparte in 1815. By the late 1860s, the more knowledgeable and alert politicians (and even some soldiers!) were realizing that after the experience of the Crimean War, the Indian Mutiny, and the American Civil War, the nature of warfare was changing radically and rapidly. And at about this time, the Prussian Army, which had in short order defeated the Danes, the Austrians and the French, was setting the pace of military innovation, technically and organizationally. One immensely important improvement was the introduction of breech-loaded rifles, which were soon adopted by the British Army, as they had been by both the Prussians and the French. The first ones were single-shot, but later models had magazines from which the rounds were fed into the firing chamber by bolt action.

Cardwell's original reforms began with the reorganization and strengthening of the War Office in London, a department of state answerable to Parliament. The Army Commander-in-Chief, the holder of an archaic appointment, was at last firmly subordinated to the War Office, although the Commander-in-Chief's job was not finally abolished until the twentieth century when Lord Roberts was to be the last soldier to hold the post.

In order to reduce costs, the overseas garrisons in Australia, New

Zealand, and Canada were reduced in size. A more radical reform was the introduction of short-service enlistment, by which soldiers served for six (later seven) years with the Colours. This was intended to reduce the average age of the soldiers in the ranks, although (as mentioned in Chapter 3) Hamilton thought that the scheme had serious drawbacks, because it deprived the infantry of men with many years of experience who had acquired hard-bitten physical resilience. The purchase of commissions was also abolished, something that had taken place when Hamilton first joined the Army, but this did not change greatly the social composition of the officer corps and was yet another example of inbred military conservatism.

The most important of all the reforms applied to the infantry alone, and was introduced regiment by regiment in 1881 and subsequent years. This was the imaginative and eminently serviceable system of linked battalions. The basic infantry unit in the British Army had for a long time been the regiment, numbering about a thousand men. The Cardwell reforms retained units of this size, but they were renamed battalions. Regiments were reconfigured as combinations of two Regular battalions (in exceptional cases more than two) and various Militia and Volunteer battalions for home service were affiliated to the Regulars. The regiment became essentially an entity to organize recruitment and to be the centre of regimental pride. In each, one of the Regular battalions (in some cases the 1st and in other cases the 2nd) served overseas while the other served in Britain, with the job of receiving and training recruits and feeding the overseas battalion with reinforcements. This met the eternal problem of there being too few soldiers on the ground in overseas stations, although the home battalions still remained generally under-strength. From now on the basic tactical unit of the British infantry was to be the battalion and not the regiment. Battalions were in the future going to fight in brigades and divisions composed of battalions of different regiments. It was only during the vast expansion of the British Army during the First and Second World Wars that battalions of the same regiment were occasionally brigaded together.

The creation of multi-battalion regiments meant that there were many shotgun marriages. The 92nd Gordon Highlanders, in which Hamilton served, became in 1881 the 2nd Battalion of the Gordon Highlanders. The

1st Battalion was the new title of the old 75th Stirlingshire Regiment, and its ranking as the 1st Gordons was the result of its earlier number in the regimental hierarchy (i.e. its greater seniority).[4] Hamilton was to join the 1st Battalion temporarily during the Gordon Relief Expedition, but in India he returned to the 92nd, his home battalion, from which he was detached when later he became a staff officer.

Worthy Foes

The Boers were by far the most formidable opponents the British Army ever faced in any of its colonial wars. And because the Boers fought with such skill and endurance against the British Army in both the 1880–81 war and the much larger one in 1899–1902, it is appropriate to compare them with the British and later the Germans against whom the Boers took up arms during the two world wars. In bravery, individual initiative and fighting skills, the Boers were the equals of both the British and the Germans. The Germans outperformed the British during the First World War, according to the macabre measure of 'net body count' – a monthly calculation of British casualties minus German ones – an analysis that favoured the Germans across the whole course of that war.[5] Yet in all wars the British eventually get their act together and win the last and decisive battle: a generalization that holds for both the Second Boer War and the First World War. How do the Boers compare with that most formidable antagonist the Japanese (against whom very few South Africans fought in the Second World War)? The Boers had great endurance, as did the Japanese, but they lacked the Japanese soldiers' frightening power of self-immolation.

'Boer' is the Dutch word for farmer. The Boer people, who came mainly from the Netherlands but also included numbers of French Huguenots and German Protestants, arrived in South Africa over the seventeenth, eighteenth and nineteenth centuries. They brought with them their Dutch language which evolved over time into Afrikaans. After the Cape became a British colony during the Napoleonic War (joined by Natal in 1843), the Boers remained the largest national group among the white colonists, and became increasingly uncomfortable with British rule. One point of difference was that the Boers were strict Sabbatarian Calvinists, with each Church ruled by its Elders, while the British were only intermittently observant Anglicans. An even worse difficulty stemmed from the fact that the black population, both indigenous and the descendants of immigrant slaves, was ten times the size of the white nationalities (a proportion which today is tilted even further toward the indigenous). Before and during the nineteenth century, the blacks who lived alongside the whites became farm labourers and servants, receiving barely adequate board and lodging plus wages that did not provide for luxuries. The Boers kept their black workers firmly in their place. Intermarriage was discouraged, although it did happen and the offspring became known as Coloureds. The British had a far more relaxed relationship with the native population and were inclined to live and let live.

The tensions between the British and the Boers, especially after the British ordered slaves to be emancipated in 1834, caused large numbers of Boers from the Eastern Cape Province to pack up their belongings and move away. In 1835–37, they began a legendary journey that became known as the Great Trek, when 14,000 Boers plus black servants, with all their possessions loaded onto ox-drawn wagons, moved north. Many were killed fighting African tribes, and others formed a republic in uncharted territory beyond the Orange River, 500 miles north-east of Cape Town, which became the Orange Free State. The remaining 5,000 – including many who were the most extreme Calvinists, the most virulent anti-Britishers, and those who were most uncompromising about the superiority of the white race – crossed the Vaal River, 800 miles from Cape Town, and founded the independent republic of the Transvaal. In both republics, the whites were substantially outnumbered by the blacks who were originally there, in a proportion of roughly twenty to one. This meant that the newly-settled farmers lived with the threat of insurrection and had to be prepared to defend their homesteads. Over the years they fought a series of small-scale wars against the original black population, who obviously resented the newcomers. During this fighting, the Boers acquired tactical skills, especially a good 'feel' for the shape of ground, and their brown homespun clothing made for excellent camouflage.

The Boers, being courageous pioneers, were supremely self-reliant. They were hardy because they were accustomed to living rough and continuously surrounded by active and potential enemies. They rode strong and agile ponies, which made them mounted infantry, something that gave them a tactical advantage over the conventional armies that they were to meet in the future, which were composed of marching infantry and anachronistic cavalry armed with lances, swords and carbines. Most importantly, the Boers could shoot. They were accustomed to filling their pot from wild game, mainly small buck, which made them able to live off the country. Boers of all ages became crack shots, and the majority could hit a buck at 400 yards range. They owned relatively modern British rifles, single-shot and, later, repeat-action. During the Second Boer War the majority had modern German repeat-action Mausers, early versions of the rifles used by the German Army in the First World War.

However, the Boers suffered the severe disadvantage that, since they were so robustly independent, they were largely incapable of working together and running their own political affairs with any efficiency. Both republics were constantly teetering on the brink of bankruptcy. They did not welcome outsiders, whom they called *uitlanders* and considered interlopers. In 1877 they reluctantly accepted British rule as a means of providing some degree of sound administration, although three years later they renounced their association with the British. This was the cause of the First Boer War.

An important point about Boer military organization is that it was based on mounted fighting units of different sizes, set up to defend themselves against the natives. This system continued during the First Boer War and even more widely during the Second. These Commandos, which were rough-and-ready groups of varying strength, were run by elected officers, some of whom demonstrated high talent despite their lack of any training in conventional military organization and operations. (The Afrikaan word *komando* is derived from the verb *komandeer*, which means that service was compulsory.) The Boers' discipline was self-imposed, and occasionally men floated into and out of the ranks. They also had a streak of laziness and the discipline of the Commandos could not correct this. The Boer military system worked well, especially during the later stages of the Second Boer War, although it was quite different from how the British organized their Army, which was a system based on an inflexible organization cemented by rigid regulations and orders, with severe punishment for disobedience. During the Second Boer War the

British system proved eventually to be the more efficient, and the British Army, after learning many harsh lessons, became unstoppable.

Disaster on the 'Hill of Doves'
The sonorous word Majuba is a translation of the African phrase 'Hill of Doves', with its alluring reminder of the tranquillity of a native dovecote which the hill resembles in shape. During the battle fought on 26–27 February 1881, nothing at all could be described as tranquil on that dreadful hill.

Major General Sir George Colley was forty-five years of age when he headed the British Army in Natal and was in local command of the operations against the Boers. He was expecting to be reinforced by 5,000 men under Sir Evelyn Wood, who was Colley's senior although he had agreed to play second fiddle during the forthcoming conflict. The First Boer War proved to be a rich example of British military incompetence. Colley had very little idea of the strength and fighting power of his adversaries. His own Army was initially weak in numbers and many British troops were widely scattered in garrisons all over the Transvaal, where they were besieged by the Boers and soon became *hors de combat.* The British field tactics of fighting in close order were dangerously unsuitable, not least because the infantry wore scarlet and were therefore inviting targets against the brown South African veldt. It was the last war during which Regimental Colours were carried into battle, a historical practice that provided even more 'high value' targets for enemy marksmanship. Worst of all, Colley was a staff officer with high intellectual achievements but was an inexperienced commander; and although personally brave he was temperamentally ill-attuned to the grittiness of battle. Despite his friendly disposition that made soldiers warm to him, Colley had a streak of stubbornness. After a series of small yet bitter British defeats, both the government in London and the leaders of the Boers were willing to patch up their differences and make peace, but Colley was not.[6] The War Office was anxious for Sir Fred Roberts to be given command, but since he was far away in India his appointment was not a practical possibility, especially in view of Colley's unreasoned determination to continue pressing the Boers with no delay until he was victorious.[7] If Roberts had been appointed, there would have been a very good chance that the Battle of Majuba Hill would have turned out less disastrously than it did for the British. However, it is unlikely that the eventual outcome of the War – the continued independence of the two Boer republics – would have been any different.

The road from Durban, on the Natal coast, to Pretoria, the capital of the Transvaal, runs north-west for almost 400 miles as the crow flies, although it is a greater distance to travel because the road winds north before returning north-west. The magnificent Drakensberg mountain chain that runs south-west to north-east divides Natal from the Boer republics: the Orange Free State on the Drakensberg itself and then inland to the Transvaal beyond the Vaal River. Leaving Newcastle, the last town on the Natal side of the mountains, the road passes through a broad cleft in the mountain range. This was to be the cockpit of the war.

The main pass through which the road runs is called Laing's Nek, a saddle 500 feet above the plain. This was firmly entrenched by the Boers, who obviously appreciated its importance since it effectively blocked the British advance into Boer territory. As mentioned, Colley had already suffered some reverses. The most significant of these had been at Laing's Nek itself. On 28 January, Colley leading 480 men made a leisurely left-flanking attack which was bloodily repulsed and cost the British 150 casualties. The Boers' losses totalled only forty-one.[8] This defeat was followed by another, at Ingogo, before Colley got around to planning his next assault, which was aimed at Majuba to use it as a springboard for a major attack on Laing's Nek.

Majuba Hill is better described as a mountain, 2,000 feet higher than Laing's Nek and 6,000 feet above sea level. It is a striking feature like a sliced-off pyramid. The slopes leading to the top make for a stiff climb, and the summit forms an uneven ten-acre plateau, triangular in shape. (See **Map 1**.) Majuba sits two miles south-west of Laing's Nek, which it dominates.

By this time Colley's force comprised three infantry battalions, including the newly-arrived 92nd Gordon Highlanders. Colley spent a long time studying the hill carefully and made a plan to seize it. The point missed by Colley – a very serious deficiency and the first of five major blunders he made during the battle – was that from the north-east, the

Boer side, the ascent was much easier than from the south, the route of the British approach.

On Saturday, 26 February, Colley took the calculated risk that the hill would be unoccupied and decided to ascend the southern point of the triangle with part of his small force: 365 men, a similar number to the Boers at Laing's Nek, although the Boers were rapidly reinforced. Colley had originally detailed 600 men: two companies from each of the three battalions, plus sixty-four sailors to provide artillery support, although the guns could not in the event be manhandled up Majuba. A third of the men were left behind in a makeshift camp at the bottom of the hill. Colley's second error was to rely on such a small force. This would have been inadequate for any further assault on Laing's Nek; and, as soon became obvious, 365 men was too small a body to defend the plateau at the top of the hill. The 365 men of the assault force were anyway made up of small groups from four different units. A complete battalion would have provided much greater cohesion and control. Not deploying a battalion was Colley's third major mistake.

The climb in the darkness of the evening of 26 February was very difficult because the path was steep and so narrow that the men had to follow one another in Indian file. What made for a particularly exhausting climb was that the men were carrying waterproof sheets, blankets, greatcoats, picks and shovels, enough food for three days, and seventy rounds of ammunition per man (which proved inadequate for many of them during the fight on 27 February). But everyone finished the climb as dawn was breaking, and they were all thrilled and surprised to find the plateau at the top of the hill unoccupied. They looked down on Laing's Nek and heard the Boers there praying and singing hymns. It was now Sunday, and the Boers later criticized the British for desecrating the Sabbath. At about this time the British soldiers in South Africa acquired a name that they were to keep for decades. They wore tunics with high collars, and their cork sun-helmets were dome-shaped, with brims not wide enough to shade the face and neck. To the Boers these soldiers inevitably became *rooineks* – rednecks – a name that seemed to symbolize insensitivity and stubbornness.

The British troops were by now more elated than exhausted, and they took it easy and wandered around the hilltop. Colley's fourth error, and a matter of decisive importance, was that there was no attempt to build defensive positions, with the single exception of the sailors, who built a small redoubt. Many officers on the spot asked for orders to dig or to build stone sangars – crude defensive positions – but Colley made no response. Naturally the junior officers commanding the 'penny packets' did not have the authority to order strong defences to be improvised. This was the most important reason why the British were defeated at Majuba, in the opinion of Ian Hamilton, from what he saw on the ground.[9] It says something about the rigid, hierarchical, top-down way in which the British Army of those days carried out its business that such a decision had to be made by the general in command. Colley appeared to everybody to be too distracted to think about the next stage of the action. It is no surprise that he gave no instructions to his subordinates about further phases of the operation – which was his fifth mistake – since his mind did not seem to grasp how he was going to exploit his considerable and unexpected success. Some people believe that he was waiting for Sir Evelyn Wood's reinforcements. But the key point about Colley was his astonishing lack of that quality so important for any commander, 'grip.' Before the battle opened on the top of the hill, the men were directionless; and after the bullets began to fly, all the men could do was to fight for their lives.

Among the small party who reached the top of Majuba Hill was Lieutenant Ian Hamilton, one of five officers of the Gordons; Hector MacDonald was another. Hamilton was quite certain that his own men were as excited as he was and would have had plenty of energy to prepare strong defensive positions. But General Colley remained mute despite Hamilton's pleas. Colley was behaving like a staff officer rather than as an experienced and energetic leader of men. Hamilton believed that a fighting commander – or even any private of the Gordons – would have reacted instinctively to a successful seizure of enemy territory by consolidating the position and reorganizing the men on the ground.[10]

The Boers were much faster to react to what the British had achieved. Covered by accurate rifle fire from the base of the hill, parties of Boers moved up at about 0600 hours. They advanced steadily as if executing a well-thought out plan, although actually a piece of improvisation. They naturally advanced by the comparatively easy approach from the north-east, making the best use of dead ground:

What military genius possessed these burghers! What instinctive aptitude they had for war! Here were a few hundred men prepared to assault a position which any professional soldier of the time would have insisted was impregnable. Yet everything was planned by the Boer commander Smit that morning with Napoleonic facility and speed; it was then carried out with an exact precision scarcely equalled in the annals of warfare.[11]

The triangular perimeter on the plateau crowning Majuba is roughly one mile in circumference and has the following features:

 • The longest of the three sides runs north to south. From the north and south ends – corners of the triangle – the other two sides of it angle east until they meet.
 • Along the north-south side of the triangle there are three small rises in the ground: in the north corner, Gordons' Knoll; half way down, Macdonald's Kopje (named after Lieutenant Hector Macdonald); and at the southern corner, Sailors' Knoll, where the naval party had erected their small redoubt. The path from which the British climbed the hill is at the southern corner.
 • The north-south side of the triangle is the safest from attack because the ground rises steeply from the plain below. To the north-east there is a much less precipitous approach that makes it much easier to get to the top of the hill. Three storming parties of Boers moved up from the lower ground to get to the British from three different directions: north-west, north-east, and south-east. The Gordons, under Major Hay, were strung along the north-east of the triangle: the most vulnerable sector. Hamilton's men were spread out at intervals of twelve paces.
 • With a total British strength of 365 troops, the perimeter was only too obviously thinly occupied, especially with a third of the men in a central reserve and who were barely committed until the battle was virtually over.

When the Boers first appeared below the hill, the British soldiers were told to stop firing. This was because their senior officers, being obsessed by the normal top-down system of giving and accepting orders, did not know whether the General wanted them to engage. By 1100 hours, the storming parties of Boers had approached the plateau from north, north-east and south, and some hundreds were forming up under the plateau in fairly well concealed places, ready to rush the British positions. By this time everyone was firing energetically – the British demonstrating more energy than accuracy – and some Boers got to Gordons' Knoll from where they could enfilade the Highlanders' line. A Boer marksman, firing from the astonishing distance of half-a-mile, shot and mortally wounded the commander of the naval detachment who was also Colley's second-in-command. Colley, who had been unthinkingly optimistic for most of the morning, was soon overcome by extreme pessimism.

Hamilton, controlling and encouraging his men, was by now increasingly anxious about his own sector, which was the one under the greatest potential threat, with the Boers infiltrating around the Gordons' right. He forcefully made his presence felt, not only to his own soldiers but also to his General. He kept rushing back through the storm of small arms fire to reach Colley to report the numbers of Boers who were approaching the plateau: 100, then 200, then 350, then 400. Some were firing buckshot, which gave out a menacing whizzing noise. But Colley paid little attention even when Hamilton, whose own men had been pushed back, came up with a bold, perhaps desperate plan to counter-attack the Boers with bayonets. Major Hay did not think it would have worked, but others considered that Hamilton's impulsiveness might have saved the day. Hamilton was anyway confident enough to write afterwards, when he was recovering from his wounds:

> It is my firm belief that had a charge been ordered at this moment we should have cleared the hill. The men, near me at any rate, were furious at having run back from the first position, and had a few encouraging words been spoken to them, and the pipes told to play up, I feel confident they would have followed their officers anywhere.[12]

By this time, most of the British soldiers were in disarray, and the plateau was thick with acrid smoke from the rifle fire. Since the time the Boers began to move up the hill – a period of heated action – Hamilton demonstrated energy, leadership and fearlessness, and his impetuosity was certainly excusable in view of the flaccid leadership at the top. Hamilton was lucky to avoid being hit, but the odds were shortening that a Boer round would soon have his name on it. Colley was standing some distance from the southern point of the plateau: a curious-looking figure in white cork helmet, scarlet tunic and light shoes, like those worn by tennis players; he was strolling up and down with his pistol in his hand. There were soon troops all around him moving back rapidly, and Colley was calling out to them – not too successfully – to assemble behind a defensive position he had selected. Hamilton was himself busily although temporarily occupied with a private war. He had picked up a rifle and was taking careful aim at a single Boer when his antagonist got his shot in first. Hamilton's left wrist was shattered and a spent round or piece of rock hit the back of his head and knocked him out cold. When he awoke, he saw two fourteen-year-old Boers picking over the equipment he was carrying. He was worried most about his sword, which had been his father's and was now taken from him. After the Second Boer War he eventually traced it, but it was immediately lost in a flood and never recovered.

General Colley had been despatched by a Boer bullet about the time that Hamilton had been hit, and the wounded Hamilton was taken to where the General was lying, to help the Boers identify the body. Colley was reported to have been on the point of surrendering and was tying a white handkerchief to the point of his sword. There were now about 1,200 Boers on the top of the hill, and many British soldiers were lying about wounded, while a number had got away by rushing helter-skelter down the hill: not an edifying sight, but Hamilton later said that they could not be blamed too greatly because there was nothing they could have done on the hilltop. Hamilton, weak and in pain, with the help of a Boer managed to improvise a splint for his arm out of a bully beef can, and for a bandage to tie it, his helper gave him a large red bandana neck scarf.[13] He spent as much time as he could bringing brackish water to the wounded before he himself managed to slip away because the Boers were too preoccupied to notice. Before too long he had lost consciousness, but at about 1100 hours on 28 February he was located by his pet dog and brought into the British lines. Hamilton's behaviour from first to last had been exemplary, and his actions that day were duly noted by his superiors.

Majuba cost the British force 226 casualties in killed and wounded: sixty-two per cent of the men who had climbed on that Saturday evening to discover to their delight that the hill was unoccupied. In incredible contrast, the Boer losses were only six men.[14] One half of the British troops had been recruited by the new short-service system, and Hamilton was not surprised that they did not perform as well as the long-service Regulars of the old school. Majuba was a very small engagement when judged by the butcher's bill. But it taught the Boers and British no end of a lesson.

The Boers immediately understood that they had nothing to fear from the British *rednecks*, and their confidence was to lead eventually to the Second Boer War which broke out in 1899. The Boers' fighting skills carried them through the early months of the Second War, months that were disastrous for the British. But the invaders eventually pulled themselves together and formulated and carried out plans that over two years were to bring some sort of victory. Hamilton said that Majuba led to the loss of 20,000 men: the total count of losses from enemy action and sickness suffered by the British Army between 1899 and 1902.[15]

The immediate lesson the British learned from Majuba was that there was no future in prolonging their fight with the Boers although, shortly after Majuba, Sir Evelyn Wood arrived among the demoralized British troops and demonstrated such an obvious grip that the morale of the men visibly improved. He was very keen to muster all his forces and end the war victoriously. However, although Queen Victoria did not like the idea of peace, the British government was happy to patch up an end to hostilities that acknowledged the independence of the Boer republics, although the restrictions imposed were fairly quickly evaded by the Boers. Within the British Army, Colley, although a popular and clever man, had obviously been promoted above his ceiling. He was a protégé of Garnet Wolseley, the most important general serving in Britain, while Fred Roberts was the leading general in India. Wolseley, whose supporters were given the name of the 'Wolseley Ring', was the main proponent of short service, while Roberts (and the 'Roberts Ring') favoured the old long-service system. Unfortunately Colley's failure did not end or even seriously erode the patronage system associated with Wolseley, and the numbers of failed generals provide plentiful evidence of the promotion of much second-class talent. And it is not necessary to emphasize what I have said already about the depth of military conservatism in the British Army.

For Hamilton personally, Majuba made him well-known for an officer of his rank. It also reinforced his obsession with musketry. However, the musketry worth remembering from Majuba was emphatically that of the Boers. They made little use of volley firing, although their few volleys were effective because they were accurately directed. More importantly, their excellent musketry was based on accurate individual sharpshooting. Both the British and the Boers used single-shot breech-loading rifles, and there was not much to choose between their weapons. They both fired enormous bullets, with a bore of .450 inches, compared with the .303 inch bore of the British Lee-Metfords and long Lee-Enfields used during the Second Boer War (and the similarly small bore of the Boer Mausers). However, many British .450 bullets had weak casings, which caused misfires.[16] One astonishing reason for the generally poor quality of the British musketry was that in the close-quarter fighting, many of the British rifles had their sights set at 400 yards. It should be no surprise that the Boers managed to maintain their superiority during the Second Boer War, although by that time the British troops were taking a much greater interest in their shooting, partly through Hamilton's efforts. During that conflict, both sides were using excellent magazine rifles which enabled the rounds to be loaded by bolt action, a system that obviously increased greatly the rate of fire.

Fred Roberts Remembers
Hamilton had a very rough and incomplete recovery from his wound.[17] In the military hospital to which he had been brought, he was thought to be dying. But he revived in time to greet Sir Evelyn Wood, who visited him with the news that his name was going to be published, with a favourable commendation, in the official British Army Despatch on the War. Wood actually submitted Hamilton's name for the Victoria Cross, although he did not in the event receive this dazzling decoration. As a general rule, the Victoria Cross, which is granted rarely enough when the recipient had fought in a successful action, was awarded even more rarely when the recipient was on the losing side.

The medical officers in South Africa thought that Hamilton's arm would have to be amputated, but his own doctor in the Gordons detected a sign of life, and the arm was saved. A number of surgical operations followed, both in South Africa and London. In London, Lord Lister, who was the leading surgeon of his day, re-broke Hamilton's wrist without anaesthetic, which must have been an indescribable experience, and then broke it yet again but with anaesthetic this time. But although his left arm remained intact, Hamilton had a stiff and useless wrist and hand for the rest of his long life.

In England, the young officer was entertained by society hostesses; and most unexpectedly he was invited to dine with the Royal Household and had the heady experience of a long talk with Queen Victoria herself. But all this time Hamilton remembered his profession. He realized that with his record as a fighting soldier, further promotion was possible, but to improve his chances he needed to enter the Staff College, which had difficult entry requirements. In thinking of the Staff College, Hamilton was striking out on his own:

> it was the proud boast of the Gordons that none of their officers had ever entered the Staff College. To permit oneself even to breathe the name of such a place was held to be excessively bad 'form'.[18]

Hamilton had earlier demonstrated that he was able to absorb enough knowledge to pass examinations. He therefore rented a room over a public house and returned to the same retired officer who had crammed him with enough facts to get him into Sandhurst. He worked assiduously until a few days before the examination. Then, quite out of the blue, he was summoned to London and given the news that General Roberts had requested his services as ADC. The General had obviously recollected their meeting in Afghanistan, the young man's story of his encounter with the enemy, the glass of sherry, and the letter Roberts had written to Hamilton's father. There was very little delay before Hamilton made up his mind, and he actually burned the books he had been using with his crammer. He then informed his father in a letter dated 24 January 1882, and after a delayed departure eventually sailed for India. He was twenty-nine years of age and it was a year or so since Majuba: a disaster for British arms, but by no means a disaster for Ian Hamilton. He had accepted Roberts's offer impetuously and with much enthusiasm. The decision he made was to devote his future to the up-and-coming and talented general who had obviously spotted him as a young man of promise, but he had thereby closed himself off from what was becoming a normal route to military preferment, staff jobs alternating with regimental duty.

Notes

1 This is Rudyard Kipling's comment on the Second Boer War. It is equally applicable to the First.
2 General Sir Ian Hamilton, *Listening for the Drums* (London: Faber & Faber, 1944), p.31.
3 Edward Spiers, 'The Late Victorian Army, 1868-1914', in *The Oxford Illustrated History of the British Army* (David Chandler, ed.) (Oxford: Oxford University Press, 1994), pp.189–93.
4 Patrick Mileham, *The Scottish Regiments, 1633–1996* (Staplehurst, Kent, UK: Spellmount, 1996), pp.244–9.
5 Niall Ferguson, *The Pity of War* (London: Allen Lane, the Penguin Press, 1998), p.301.
6 Oliver Ransford, *The Battle of Majuba Hill. The First Boer War* (New York: Thomas J. Crowell, 1968), pp.62–3. Much of my description of the First Boer War comes from this source.
7 Colonel W. H. H. Waters, *The German Official Account of the War in South Africa* (London: John Murray, 1904), p.16.
8 Ransford, *The Battle of Majuba Hill*, pp.42–51.
9 Hamilton, *Listening for the Drums*, p.138.
10 Ibid., p.133.
11 Ransford, *The Battle of Majuba Hill*, p.90.
12 Hamilton, *Listening for the Drums*, pp.136–7.
13 After the war, Hamilton by coincidence found the Boer who had helped to put the splint on his arm. He gave him an elegant memento of the original bandana neck cloth: a small silver box containing a new bandana. Ibid., p.143.
14 Byron Farwell, *Queen Victoria's Little Wars* (New York: W.W. Norton, 1972), p.250.
15 Hamilton, *Listening for the Drums*, p.130.
16 Information supplied by the War Museum of the Boer Republic, Bloemfontein, South Africa.
17 Hamilton, *Listening for the Drums*, pp.145–9.
18 General Sir Ian Hamilton, *The Commander* (Major Anthony Farrar-Hockley, ed.) (London: Hollis & Carter, 1957), p.50.

CHAPTER 5

Emerging from the Chrysalis

etween 1881 and 1885, Sir Frederick Roberts commanded the
Army in Southern India, based in Madras. The majority of the
troops came from native Indian regiments, but a third came from
the Regular British Army. A single British battalion served alongside three
Indian ones to form a composite brigade. There were also units of British
cavalry, artillery, engineers and supporting troops. This was a successful
arrangement that continued with very little change during the long and
eventful period until the Raj came to an end in 1947, with the grant of
independence to India and Pakistan by the British Labour Government
then in power. It certainly relieved Britain of the burden of garrisoning
and policing a country that was struggling hard for independence.

After his delayed departure from England, Ian Hamilton arrived in
June 1882 to join Roberts's personal staff. Although the General had a
number of senior staff officers running headquarters departments covering
his large Command, his personal staff comprised only three officers. The
most senior was Colonel Pretyman, the Military Secretary, whose job was
to provide his chief with informed advice about all officers' appointments
in the command. There were also two ADCs: Lieutenant Neville
Chamberlain (the inventor of snooker and later Inspector General of the
Royal Irish Constabulary but no relation to the politician of the same
name who was the British Prime Minister at the beginning of the Second
World War) and the newly-promoted Captain Ian Hamilton. The job of
the ADCs was to accompany their chief the whole time and act as

'gallopers' and general helpers, which meant that they carried out a multitude of tasks both military and social. They lived *en famille* with the General.

At 0530 hours on the day of his arrival, Hamilton's train steamed into the railway station of Bangalore, one of the largest military cantonments in the Madras Army, and there he was greeted by Sir Fred Roberts himself. This thoughtful gesture gave Hamilton an immediate insight into the secret of Roberts's popularity with his troops: that they had number one priority, and therefore deserved untiring attention. By 1130 hours that same morning, Hamilton had begun his duties. In an immaculate uniform and mounted on an obstreperous charger, he followed Roberts along the long line of soldiers in a grand parade of the whole garrison.[1]

All the time that Hamilton was ADC, he was confronted at first hand with the effective and sometimes subtle ways in which the General exercised his command. Roberts's tenure at Madras was tranquil in that his Army was not engaged in any active operations.[2] He could therefore apply himself to what he saw as the urgent matter of army reform: something that became even more important to him when he became Commander-in-Chief of the Indian Army in 1885. One specific concern to Roberts was the controversial matter of short versus long service for British troops. In the 1880s, what was then known as short service had been introduced for the rank and file. This meant seven years with the Colours followed by five years in the reserve after the soldiers had returned to civil life. Roberts was convinced that was an unsatisfactory compromise between genuinely short and truly long service: in particular it deprived the army of fully experienced long-service men. He favoured and lobbied for two alternative types of enlistment. The first was a three-year term followed by reserve service: something that would be offered to young recruits who wanted to join the army on a trial basis. This would have the advantage of providing quickly a substantial force of reserves in Britain. The second type of enlistment would be for an active service period of twelve years, or longer for men who wanted to make the army a progressive career. Despite the merits of his case, Roberts made no progress in persuading the authorities in London, notably the ancient and reactionary Commander-in-Chief the Duke of Cambridge, and the War Office which was headed by politicians and staffed by bureaucrats. The

Duke and the War Office moved at the pace of a glacier (if they moved at all) and, in frustration, Roberts publicized his views in the London press, a not unusual step for generals to take at that time. But his efforts were to no avail and Roberts never won his battle for long service. After he had retired from the army, he would still be fighting it, and add the important and revolutionary idea of brief compulsory service to provide a massive reserve of trained manpower. This dispute will be taken up in Chapter 9, when Hamilton will be seen on the opposite side. Roberts's disciple and former ADC still favoured long enlistment, and he was against the supplementary idea of compulsory service.

Roberts nevertheless did much to improve the well-being of the young British soldiers in India. He was genuinely concerned with the troops' welfare, but in parallel he was anxious to maintain the numbers of men in the ranks. This meant attracting new recruits, so that good conditions of service were important for that reason also. He engineered greater leniency for those convicted of military crimes and misdemeanours, and he lifted some of the petty restrictions in barrack life. The soldiers were far from home and living in an uncomfortable climate, and were receiving low pay and had little to occupy their time, although they suffered long hours of sleepless guard duty. Roberts eventually improved food, clothing, education, barracks and canteens; and it was with the younger soldiers in mind that he developed his plan to open up military careers with prospect of promotion for the most able and ambitious, although he was not able to implement it.

At Madras, Roberts also embarked on his long-term programme to improve the musketry of the infantry. British infantry soldiers were at this time armed with breech-loading rifles that fired single shots and used smokeless ammunition; they were soon to receive repeat-action weapons. These would revolutionize the defensive power of infantry because of their rapid rate of fire. By 1914, the British infantry had achieved worldwide pre-eminence in the speed and accuracy of their rapid fire – 'fifteen aimed shots a minute' – something that was widely mistaken by the Germans in 1914 for the dangerous clatter of machine guns. At that time, each British battalion had only two machine guns, but the majority of the men in the ranks were either marksmen or first-class shots.

Roberts spent his time during the long months of moderate heat (India is never cool except in the foothills of the Himalayas), inspecting the many and variegated units of the Madras Command. This was repetitive activity, but it never lost its appeal to Roberts. It was something supremely important because it was his contact with the men in the ranks. He cherished his soldiers without any self-consciousness, and this was the real secret of his success as a fighting general:

> If, after an exhausting march Lord Roberts reached camp with a sharp go of fever on him – do you suppose he would go to his tent and lie down? Not much! There he would sit, half-dead, his Staff simply writhing in their saddles with fatigue, while he watched the long column march in for four long hours and exchanged kindly greetings with any of the extra exhausted.[3]

Roberts, with his constant focus on the men he commanded, was invariably thoughtful in saving them time and trouble by always issuing simple written instructions: 'It only takes one minute, my dear Johnny, and it is so much more satisfactory.'[4]

During the months of extremely hot weather, Roberts and his staff moved to the pleasant hill station of Ootacamund (Ooty), which is 7,000 feet above sea level. Here, Hamilton's duties were primarily social: greeting guests, arranging receptions and dinner parties, amateur theatricals, and – not least – arranging shooting competitions for the team from Roberts's own headquarters. It did not take long for Hamilton's personal charm to win over the clique of professional and personal friends who surrounded General 'Bobs'. Hamilton made many lifelong friends here, and this is where he was to meet his wife.

After Majuba, a totally unexpected urge had come over Hamilton – the urge to write – and it was to hold him captive for the rest of his long life. His first work was a slim booklet entitled *The Fighting of the Future*, devoted to his belief in the importance of good rifle shooting.[5] Written in June 1884, it was the end-product of his years as Musketry Instructor with the Gordons; his ideas were developed on a broader scale in India, where he was soon moving in step with Sir Fred Roberts to improve the Army's ability to shoot fast and accurately. The booklet was published and received some attention. Meanwhile, Hamilton had another and quite different type of work in mind and was being planned. This was a book of 269 pages that he published anonymously, entitled *A Jaunt in a Junk*.

A Ten Days' Cruise in Indian Seas.[6] The good writing cannot conceal the thinness of the story, and the book was not well received on its publication in 1884: something that did not shake Hamilton's natural resilience.

During the summers at Ootacamund, Hamilton's writing took a more light-hearted form. Two ladies in the garrison, the daughters of an army officer there, had founded a literary club that held regular writing competitions. After some unsuccessful efforts, Hamilton won a prize for his translation of the familiar Goethe poem *Der Erlkönig*, something made possible by the knowledge of German that he had acquired before he went to Sandhurst. As a result of this small prize, he was invited to be an occasional correspondent for the newspaper *The Madras Mail*. This led him to write some journalism, all long disappeared.

In 1886 came a novel called *Icarus*, a convoluted story set in Britain about a man-about-town who had a number of unusual adventures.[7] It was reviewed, not entirely favourably, and a typical comment was that it was 'a book which is distinctly entertaining, although the situations are here and there far more risqué than is necessary or desirable, while the author indulges in a certain blunt and somewhat coarse fashion of calling a spade by its ordinary name'.[8] There then followed a slim volume entitled *The Ballad of Hádji and Other Poems*, published in 1887.[9] The poetry is well constructed, but to the critical eye Hamilton uses too many adjectives, and the thoughts occasionally verge on the banal. In 1926, he published his second volume of poetry, *Now and Then*.[10] It is a more mature work although it reprints a few of the poems in the earlier collection. The ideas are generally not arresting enough to be remembered. Hamilton's considerable writing talents lay in a different direction.

Although *The Fighting of the Future* revealed, or at least hinted at, a vision that was eventually to be realized, Hamilton's early works for the most part were the fruits of his apprenticeship as an author. One quality that comes through is his capacity to write clear and rhythmic prose, in a way that is appealing to the reader. Hamilton's work was to gain much greater substance in later years when he had vivid personal experiences to describe. His really important books started after the Second Boer War. In the first of these books, Hamilton was joint author of a reminiscence describing episodes in the fighting on the veldt.[11] A few years later, he revealed extraordinarily sharp insights into the Japanese Army during the

Russo-Japanese War of 1904-1905.[12] And his diary of the Gallipoli Campaign of 1915 was to be a work of historical importance.[13] Finally, after the First World War, he was to write thought-provoking books that spelt out his convictions of a lifetime: convictions about armies and the officers and men who formed their fabric. The First World War had seen greater technological changes in warfare than at any time since the invention of firearms, and Hamilton now directed his focus on the command of armies in this radically different environment.[14] These books are discussed in Chapter 11.

Hamilton took ship from India in October 1884 on six months' leave to visit Britain. Although he had not commanded troops since the disaster at Majuba in February 1881, and had spent two years and four months in the relatively placid surroundings of an Indian headquarters, Hamilton was now emerging from his chrysalis. Before his arrival in India, he had been a young officer who had done well; he was now clearly a man with a future. There were four reasons for this. First, he had gained a powerful patron, who was obviously going to ease his further steps up the ladder. Second, although he had already made his mark in the field of musketry training, what he had done already was much less than what he was certainly going to achieve with the active support of General Roberts. Third, he had profoundly absorbed the secret of Roberts's popularity with his men – something that explained his almost unique talent as a field commander – his unrelenting attention to the welfare and morale of the troops he led. This lesson was going to yield a dividend when Hamilton later found himself commanding large bodies of men in South Africa. Finally, he had been powerfully struck by the urge to write. He had so far found little to write about that demonstrated originality, and what he had written (with the possible exception of *The Fighting of the Future*) has left no permanent mark. But his lucid style showed potential, and his early writing helped him towards his later success as a staff officer. A feature of clear writing is that it illuminates the author's mind in the sense that it opens a window into his thought processes. Hamilton's ability to think straight and grasp essentials was to prove extremely important when, surprisingly soon, he began to rise in the hierarchy of the Indian Army staff.

'The Refreshment of Adventure'
These words were written by Winston Churchill. They describe the lift
that Churchill experienced when he moved away from garrison life as a
junior officer in a cavalry regiment and began to pursue danger and
excitement as a freelance soldier and war correspondent in a number of
small wars. Churchill described these wars in a series of vividly written
books based on his journalism, and Hamilton is the hero of one of them.

Hamilton had spent twenty-eight months as ADC and for a short
period as Roberts's Assistant Military Secretary, leading an intensely
interesting life under a stimulating chief. But as an ambitious officer who
loved the profession of soldiering, he felt an urgent need for the
refreshment of adventure. An opportunity beckoned in the Sudan, where
the ruler of the province, Major General Charles Gordon – one of the
popular heroes of the British Empire – was isolated and besieged in
Khartoum. Hamilton, before he went on leave, had talked to Sir Fred
Roberts about trying to join the Gordon Relief Expedition. Roberts
approved because of the obvious professional opportunity it provided for
his protégé.[15]

Egypt was crucial to Britain. The Suez Canal had been completed in
1869 and was substantially owned by the British Government. Since the
Canal offered the easiest sea route to India, the political and economic
stability of Egypt was obviously a matter of great concern. Egypt was an
ill-governed autocracy ruled by a hereditary *Khedive*; its finances were
rocky; and insurrection was always a possibility. Britain, France and Italy
were all worried about the fragility of the Egyptian government, and
Britain eventually took the lead in doing something about it, which meant
a British military presence. In 1882, General Sir Garnet Wolseley led an
Army into the country, and after the successful battle of Tel-el-Kebir, the
British Army occupied Egypt. An official with the bureaucratic title of
the British Consul General and Diplomatic Agent was installed ostensibly
as an adviser to the *Khedive*, but he occupied such a strong position that
the British virtually ruled the country.

The vast barren province of the Sudan to the south was within the
Egyptian sphere of influence, but the British were reluctant to move to
occupy it because of the substantial commitment this would entail from
the British Army. It was full of unruly Arab tribes and was a rich source

of slaves for illicit export. Although he was nominally the ruler of the province, the British Governor, Major General Charles Gordon, spent virtually no time there. Gordon, appointed in 1874, was a colourful adventurer with the same rash ambition and energy as many other pioneers of the British Empire. Since 1881 the Sudan had been in the throes of a dangerous insurrection by huge numbers of Arab tribesmen of different races, under a fanatical religious leader called the Mahdi. Powerful Islamic movements had arisen intermittently since the time of the Prophet, and they have never been stronger than during the twenty-first century. The uprising in the Sudan during the 1880s was typically the outcome of genuine religious frenzy. Two British expeditions to quell it and arrest the Mahdi had been defeated with great bloodshed. Meanwhile, the tribes had captured 20,000 rifles, ten artillery pieces and large quantities of ammunition. In early 1884 Gordon himself led another expedition, but was soon isolated in Khartoum, with nothing approaching the military strength needed to fight his way out.

This was a heated situation that had a direct effect on Britain's prestige, and an indirect but serious influence on Britain's control of Egypt. The obvious response to Gordon's situation was to mount a major military expedition to rescue him immediately. This was a political decision and Gladstone, the British Prime Minister, procrastinated rather than face the £20 million or so that the British taxpayer would have to pay. Unfortunately, Gladstone put off the decision for too long. Meanwhile public opinion in Britain increased in fervour; and informed and uninformed speculation about all aspects of the expedition produced much comment in the London press. Eventually, the expedition was mounted under the command of General (by now Lord) Wolseley. Gordon had been finally cut off in May 1884; Wolseley did not leave London until early September; and because of the difficulties of organizing the expedition, it only moved out in mid-October. After Gordon had been isolated in Khartoum, any organized expedition would have been very hard pressed to reach him in time. But, in the event, a five-month delay was simply too long. The first cause of the delay was Gladstone's indecision, but the second was the enormous logistical challenge of mounting the enterprise.

Wolseley was at the time Britain's most famous military leader and had gained his reputation by winning a number of small wars in Africa and Canada by commanding his troops 'from the saddle'. Extremely popular with the public and in some ways an original thinker, he was known as 'Britain's only General', although he was in effect *primus inter pares*, because Roberts was known as 'Britain's only other General'. Wolseley, like Roberts, was Irish. But the two had different temperaments. It is apparent from Wolseley's journal of the expedition that he was introspective and pessimistic, and complained sourly about everybody and everything that he encountered. Gladstone was particularly favoured by the General's unrelenting wrath.[16] Wolseley had for long surrounded himself with a body of selected subordinates, known as the 'Wolseley Ring'. Roberts in India had done a similar thing, surrounding himself with a 'Roberts Ring'. The British Army had not yet established a General Staff system, yet commanders in the field always needed the support of staff officers. This is what encouraged the growth of the 'Ring' system, which operated as an informal type of General Staff. The Wolseley and Roberts Rings roundly disliked each other, although the two Generals themselves had cordial relations.

Some of Wolseley's sourness may have been due to the daunting task with which he was confronted. Khartoum lies in the middle of a desert, 1,000 miles south as the crow flies from the mouth of the Nile: but it involved a 1,650 mile journey by water because of the way in which the river meanders. Two routes to Khartoum were possible. (See **Map 2.**) The one favoured by most informed opinion was via Suakim, a small port on the Red Sea that was easy to reach from the Suez Canal; and Khartoum lies an apparently manageable distance west of Suakim. But as Wolseley soon realized, he could not lay his hands on nearly enough camels to transport his army 250 miles across the waterless desert to Berber on the Nile, and from there upstream to Khartoum.[17] A railway from Suakim would have taken much time to build, and it would have been vulnerable to marauding tribes, as happened when a railway was partially laid after Wolseley's main expedition had failed.[18] This left the route up the Nile. It was immensely long and fraught with difficulties, the greatest of which were the six cataracts between the mouth of the Nile and Khartoum. They are extremely rough patches of water with rocks and rapids that rushed downstream, some of them several miles in length, and mostly impassable by boats unless they are emptied and manhandled upstream.

73

Wolseley's force was tiny, though he judged that its quality would prove decisive against the large numbers of undisciplined Dervish tribesmen. He had a total of 7,200 men from high-class Regular British battalions, plus some Egyptian units. But the tactical plan was controversial and in Hamilton's opinion unsound, because the distances were large, the Commander-in-Chief was isolated, communications were poor, and the plan disregarded the basic principle of concentration of force. Wolseley's plan divided his Army: 5,400 men were to be transported up the river in large rowing boats called whalers, which could be emptied and pulled upstream on the cataracts, while the remaining 1,800 men were organized into a desert force, an extraordinary hotchpotch drawn from sub-units of elite British troops, mounted on camels. This smaller formation was selected from regiments that carried a higher social cachet: probably a reflection of the Commander-in-Chief's snobbery. The desert force would, in theory, be able to charge forward at the last stage of the advance and relieve Khartoum.

Hamilton, as he had planned, interrupted his journey to Britain, managed to disembark and with great difficulty made his way to Cairo. In contrast, most of the large number of officers on Hamilton's troopship who also planned to join the expedition were discouraged by the problem of getting from Suez to Cairo. And, like Hamilton, they also realized that the expedition was going to be run by the Wolseley Ring, who would not welcome officers from India, where Roberts was becoming an increasingly important commander. In Cairo, Hamilton was delighted to find the 1st Gordon Highlanders, the sister battalion to the one in which he had carried out his regimental soldiering in India. The Commanding Officer was not optimistic that Hamilton would be accepted by Army Headquarters, again because of the Wolseley Ring. But, because the Gordons were short of officers, Hamilton was allowed to join them. He had no campaigning kit with him, but he quickly collected a private soldier's outfit of kilt, hose, khaki tunic and Glengarry cap from the battalion Quartermaster. Despite another difficulty that could have kept him guarding the line of communication – a difficulty solved by the personal intervention of Sir EvelynWood (who remembered Majuba) – Captain Hamilton was soon commanding a company of 1st Gordons in the river force, and was off to the War.

There were serious problems with the command of the expedition. Wolseley himself was with neither of the columns, but was stuck in a headquarters on the river far in the rear of his two forces, with only tenuous telegraph connections to them. The Commander-in-Chief was therefore unable to control the forces directly, as he had been accustomed to do during his earlier campaigns, and his inability to do this was to cause many problems. His Chief of Staff, Major General Buller, was brave and popular with troops, but he was headstrong, argumentative and intellectually limited; even Wolseley complained about him.[19] Buller was ultimately given command of the desert column, but by then the expedition had effectively failed. Tragically and unexpectedly, the original two column commanders were both killed. Major General Earle lost his life in action in the Battle of Kirbekan, in which Hamilton played a part. The officer who then took command of the river column was an administrator and a weak leader. The commander of the desert column, Brigadier General Stewart, a highly promising soldier, also later lost his life and his successor was an intelligence officer with no command experience. Both these replacements lacked drive, which was the quality needed above everything else for their columns to advance energetically.

Hamilton and his company moved slowly upstream, loaded in eleven whalers. They carried personal ammunition, supplies to repair the boats, and a four-month supply of rather miserable food: tins of bully beef, hardtack biscuits that were soon inhabited by weevils, and tea made with canned condensed milk. The desert column was much better fed.[20] Permitting such a difference in the rations provided to the two columns was a dereliction of duty on the part of Wolseley. Each of Hamilton's boats was more or less independent, and followed its own route; the whole company got together every ten days. The feelings of the men, as described by Hamilton, were 'as nearly as possible those of a party of Boy Scouts dressed up like Red Indians and let loose in a flotilla of canoes'.[21] At the cataracts the men had to wade waist-deep in water to haul the boats, but the soldiers treated the whole affair as a great adventure, and when the river column located a large party of Dervishes, they attacked them with skill and energy. This engagement took place on 10 February 1885, at Kirbekan, near the Fourth Cataract, about 500 miles by river north of Khartoum. By this time Hamilton's company had journeyed for four months and covered two-thirds of the distance to their final destination. But when the battle of Kirbekan was fought, Khartoum had already fallen.

Kirbekan lies up-river in the great bend in the Nile that loops to the east then south and west to reach Khartoum, a distance of about 300 miles. Not far from the eastern bank of the river, the Kirbekan ridge runs for half a mile to the east. On 10 February, 800 Dervish warriors were on top of the ridge, and with small-arms fire they were blocking the advance of the whalers of the river column. Major General Earle was on the spot and was not the type of leader who would be happy to engage in a defensive battle, but was determined to take the fight to the enemy. He quickly detached Hamilton's company and some Egyptian artillery as a fire group to keep enemy heads down. He then led his remaining infantry on a right-hand encircling sweep, with the soldiers in open order and using their rifles to good effect. He managed to attack the enemy from the rear and caught them unawares. They were soon wiped out, but the brave and resourceful Earle was killed by the last bullet fired on the battlefield. His tactics were based on those inculcated into British riflemen at Shorncliffe by Sir John Moore, in the years before the Peninsular War. These tactics were diametrically opposed to the defensive use of the 'infantry square', a drill that was still practised by the British Army at the end of the nineteenth century.

Hamilton's company buried the General under a palm tree, and Hamilton's description of the scene echoes the poignant note of *The Burial of Sir John Moore after Corunna*, written by the Irish clergyman Charles Wolfe near the end of his own brief life. Earle's desert grave stimulated Hamilton himself to write a twelve-line poem that does not appear in his two collections of verse. It is a graceful expression, worthy of Wordsworth, of emotion recollected in tranquillity:

> No rose blooms there, no laurel – no wild heather
> Or dark-leaved ivy drop their silvery dews
> For thee – no homely song-bird preens his feather
> O'er thy still heart . . .[22]

Earle's tactical flair and his leadership from the front made an indelible impression on Hamilton, and he based his own style of generalship on it.[23]

Before the end of December the desert column had branched off, leaving the river column to fight its own battle at Kirbekan. Some distance before the great loop in the Nile, the desert column now attempted to bound directly across the desert to Khartoum, a distance of less than 200 miles, in contrast to the 500 miles of the river route. They encountered nothing but difficulties. Stewart began to be anxious about his rear, and this caused him to divert part of his force to the Nile to protect his whole formation from hostile Dervish forces. The two separate parts of the desert column were eventually reassembled in the middle of January 1885, but the Mahdi correctly guessed what was happening and deployed large forces to block the British. The British fought a bloody and indecisive battle at Abu Klea on 17 January, using the tactics of defensive 'infantry squares'; and two days later, Stewart himself was wounded and died shortly afterwards. His successor had (as mentioned) never before commanded troops and Buller was sent forward to take over. But it was now too late – the impetus of the advance had evaporated – and, to make matters worse, Wolseley was for a time out of touch with his troops, to his intense frustration. On 26 January, Khartoum fell and Gordon was killed.

Wolseley did not consider that his failure to relieve Gordon had brought the campaign to a close, but he naturally had to telegraph London for further instructions. Again the Government prevaricated, but eventually agreed to continue the fight so long as Wolseley did not demand any further reinforcements. By this time the desert force was in no condition to continue to do battle and, on 20 February, it was ordered back. The river force, still fighting its way up the Nile, was also given the same orders. Wolseley despatched to London a substantial menu listing the reinforcements he needed to continue the campaign. The size of his demands, which came at the same time as a call for troops for another purpose – to build up strength to counter Russian threats against India – marked the end of the Nile campaign. The river column found that going down the cataracts was much easier than going up them. Unaccountably, the British Government in February 1885 ordered work to begin on the railway from Suakim. This was abandoned after eighteen miles of track had been laid, confirming Wolseley's earlier scepticism about the Suakim route. There was no further advance up the Nile to Khartoum until 1898, when a new expedition was commanded by a very different type of leader, General Kitchener.

Wolseley's campaign ended on an unpleasant note for the Gordon Highlanders, although their performance had throughout been exemplary. The London press was still full of stories about the expedition, and some were very uncomplimentary. Wolseley suspected that officers of the Gordons had been the source of some of the unfavourable rumours, and he therefore summoned the Commanding Officer to vent his displeasure. The Commander-in-Chief threatened that none of the officers of the battalion could expect any decorations or promotions as a result of the campaign.[24] This may have been due to a fit of ill-temper because Wolseley was by now a very disappointed man. However, Hamilton was spared, and as a reward for his services at Kirbekan he received the Distinguished Service Order (DSO), a decoration awarded to officers for action or good work in the field that ranked immediately below the Victoria Cross.

The 'Roberts Ring'

Hamilton was back in India in 1886, totally convinced that Roberts would have rescued Gordon.[25] The young officer had learned important lessons about command in war, perhaps realizing that the experience of defeat provides more plentiful lessons than the experience of victory.

Roberts had become Commander-in-Chief of the Indian Army in 1885, and Hamilton joined his headquarters and resumed his job as ADC. He was to hold staff appointments of increasing responsibility from 1886 to 1897, a period of eleven years when Hamilton was between the ages of thirty-three and forty-four.[26] This is a remarkable period of time to have been spent continuously in staff jobs: most unusual in the nineteenth century and inconceivable in the twentieth, after the British Army had established a General Staff system, when it became an article of faith that staff jobs should be alternated with command of troops, preferably on active service. Hamilton's long period on the staff in India gives a hint of the strength and cohesion of the Roberts Ring, particularly since he had not attended the Staff College, which was and is the customary route to staff appointments. Hamilton began his work on the staff in 1886 as a brevet major; was appointed brevet lieutenant colonel in 1887; and colonel in 1891 (after Roberts had waged an absurd war with the War Office over this promotion).

When Hamilton returned as ADC to Sir Fred Roberts, the General was a very exalted person. That same year Hamilton accompanied his chief to Burma, where Roberts was supervising the final annexation of that country. On their return, Hamilton's personal life took a sharp turn. The social life in Army Headquarters in India was lively, as Hamilton had earlier found in Madras and Ootacamund, and Hamilton's charm continued to work its usual magic. Before he went to Burma, he had met a beautiful, determined, rich and popular young Scots girl called Jean Muir; and before long he had proposed marriage. Although she was at the time unofficially engaged to an Austrian aristocrat, she soon learned to prefer the major in a marching regiment (as Hamilton described himself). In 1887 they had what was then known as a fashionable wedding, attended by the Viceroy and other leaders of Indian society. It was to be a happy fifty-four-year marriage, although she was to spend a good deal of time in Britain while he was in India and other places overseas.[27] They had no children, but after the First World War she adopted a boy and a girl. The boy, Harry, joined the army and sadly died of wounds in 1941.

On his return from Burma, Hamilton was given the key appointment of Assistant Adjutant General for Musketry at Army Headquarters. Here he came into his own. With the enthusiastic support of his chief, Hamilton's main aim was to prepare the infantry realistically for wartime conditions. He rewrote the whole of the Native Musketry Regulations; targets were painted with human figures not bulls-eyes; and the quantity of live ammunition for firing practice was increased. As a result, field firing improved dramatically:

> Markers hidden in deep trenches worked running or disappearing targets under a hail of bullets and when the attack closed in to 250 yards tossed out balls three feet in diameter made of canvas stretched over strips of bamboo, which bounded down the steep *glacis* upon the firing lines faster than even charging ghazis would have rushed. Units possessing fire discipline shot them to bits – others missed them clean.[28]

After Hamilton had spent two-and-a-half years in the job, the musketry efficiency of the Indian Army had been transformed, and his personal contribution to this had been widely recognized. Roberts (now Lord Roberts) left India in 1893, and was succeeded by General Sir George White, who had served with Hamilton in the Gordon Highlanders although of course as a much more senior officer. As soon as he arrived in India, White made Hamilton his Military Secretary, but soon afterwards Hamilton received a more interesting appointment. In 1895 a body of British soldiers was besieged by local tribes in the fort of Chitral, in the wild far northern border between Afghanistan and India (the region that is now Pakistan). An expedition was sent to the rescue and was faced with a very difficult task because of the forbidding mountainous territory. Hamilton's new job was Assistant Adjutant and Quartermaster General, a choice appointment for a colonel. As soon as he got to work, his immediate commander on the expedition's staff took a fall from his pony which put him out of commission. Hamilton was now confronted with the task of commanding the line of communication for 15,000 men through country that was barely accessible by heavy transport. Although this made great professional demands on him, the job was not a fighting command. And to make life more difficult, Hamilton had to mend some fences with Lord Roberts. Roberts had asked Hamilton to return to Britain to help him in writing his memoirs, which would carry the appointment of Assistant Military Secretary. This would have been of no value for Hamilton's future career, but he did not know how to refuse the wishes of his old chief. Jean Hamilton, who was then in England, had the delicate mission of explaining her husband's difficulty, and there were no bruised feelings.[29]

With Chitral relieved, the route to the fort was permanently manned and the expeditionary force returned. Hamilton was decorated for his good work, being made a Companion of the Bath (CB), an ancient order of chivalry that is still awarded mainly to officers in the armed services. Soon after this, he was offered and accepted an even better post, Deputy Quartermaster General of the Indian Army. This soon involved him in another spell of action. In the summer of 1897, yet another serious tribal uprising had erupted in the frontier region of India and Afghanistan, and three expeditions were despatched from India to quell it. The third and strongest of these was directed at the province of Tirah, another almost impassable mountainous region. White decided to send two complete divisions, and much to Hamilton's delight he was given command of a brigade, with the temporary rank of brigadier general. In October 1897 he was on his way, but another fall from a pony upset the arrangements. This time it was Hamilton who was thrown, and he had to relinquish his appointment because of a broken leg. After he had half-recovered, he was given the excellent job of commanding a reinforced brigade of seven battalions plus supporting troops. This formed the rearguard of the total force as it withdrew, and Hamilton did well, although his contribution was again good staff work rather than command in battle. An interesting sidelight from this episode is that Hamilton helped Winston Churchill, an ambitious young cavalry officer and war correspondent, to become attached to the expedition. This started a lifelong friendship that was later to pay two surprising dividends. In 1900, Churchill, still a war correspondent, accompanied Hamilton's Mounted Infantry in South Africa and through Churchill's despatches to his newspaper Hamilton began to become a household name in Britain. An even more significant event took place in 1915, when Churchill was civilian head of the Royal Navy and was partly responsible for Hamilton's appointment to command the Dardanelles expedition.

Hamilton's friendship with Sir George White had been a great stroke of good luck, comparable with his first encounter with Roberts: an encounter that had led to Hamilton's talents being recognized, to the immense benefit of his future career. Two prize appointments now came Hamilton's way. In 1898 he was offered the job of Quartermaster General in India, a prestigious and lucrative appointment; he was also nominated to be Commandant of the School of Musketry in Hythe, Kent.[30] This is the institution which Hamilton had attended as a junior officer and where he had been awarded the highest honours. He was anxious to return to Britain after his long service in India and he was anyway the natural choice for Hythe. He immediately accepted it although the job meant he would have to revert to the rank of colonel, and the appointment was not at all well paid. Hythe appeared at the time to be a natural stepping stone for him, even perhaps the culmination of his life's work. It was neither. Although he spent his time at Hythe productively in improving both musketry and infantry tactics, his time there was short. While he was at

Hythe he had another extraordinary stroke of good fortune because, when Hamilton arrived in Britain, there was much talk about troubles in South Africa: troubles which were to lead to the Second Boer War. Sir George White was soon sent to command the British Army in Natal, and in September 1899 Hamilton was on his way to join him as Assistant Adjutant General: something that would have been impossible had he taken the glittering job of Quartermaster General in India. A short time after joining White's staff, Hamilton graduated to active commands until the end of 1900. Then, after a year in England, he returned and spent the last six months of the war, initially as Chief of Staff to Lord Kitchener, Roberts's successor as Commander-in-Chief, and later in command of a large field force composed of mounted columns.

The obvious question raised by Hamilton's career so far is whether his long years as a staff officer had dulled his cutting edge by muting, even imperceptibly, his most aggressive martial qualities. A staff officer operates by executing with skill and energy the orders of his chief. In contrast, a commander in the field generates ideas with the support of his staff, and makes decisions. He really earns his pay by accepting responsibility for these decisions: an onerous but not necessarily time-consuming process.[31] Montgomery, one of the rare breed of great captains, could afford to spend much time making himself known to his troops, and always go to bed early, in the knowledge that the execution of his plans was now in the competent hands of selected staff officers. Do good staff officers make good generals? There is no definitive answer, but there is widespread opinion that they do not. Outstanding Anglo-American staff officers in the Second World War – Bedell Smith, de Guingand, Morgan – never became commanders. And outstanding Allied commanders – MacArthur, Patton, Montgomery, Slim – had never held important staff appointments. Eisenhower was the exception because he had made his name as a staff officer, but it is debatable whether he was an outstanding battlefield general.

Staff duties fall into three categories: G (General Staff, concerned with operations and intelligence); A (Adjutant's branch, which concentrates on manning and training); and Q (Quartermaster's branch, which controls supplies and logistics). Of the three, the G branch is the senior and makes the greatest demands on ideas, judgement, and an experienced 'feel' for strategy and tactics. (In the old German Army, a chief of staff carried equal operational responsibility with his commander.) In contrast, the A and Q branches are devoted mainly to administration; the problems of administration can be vast in modern armies that often fight over long distances and operate on a moving battlefield. However, in the Indian Army during the nineteenth century, there was much bureaucracy in the A and Q branches and the pace of work was slow. India was sometimes described unkindly as the 'sloth belt'.

Long years of service in the A and Q carry two prolonged dangers. The first is a very gradual erosion of the instinct to scrutinize the things that other people say, in a probing and questioning frame of mind. In the Second World War, Churchill constantly disputed the advice of his Chiefs of Staff because he was passionately anxious that their advice should be sound. Churchill's ruthless questioning made him unpopular with his subordinates. He was, however, totally justified because men's lives were always at risk. But Churchill was never a staff officer, and staff officers only too often believe what they are told. They accept the broad parameters drawn up by their chiefs, and just get on with their complicated job of executing orders. The second danger is the spectre of diminished alertness, a reduced consciousness of the importance of time, inevitably leading to slower reactions. Generals who have to take responsibility for life and death often have to act with great speed.

There was no sign that Hamilton at this stage of his career had succumbed to these dangers, which would have tamed his natural impetuosity. However, they were capable of casting an extended shadow, and I shall revisit these points in Chapter 10, which is devoted to the Dardanelles campaign. In that chapter, the first point will be considered in the context of Hamilton's relationship with Kitchener, Secretary of State for War and civilian head of the Army. In his dealings with Kitchener, Hamilton invariably did as he was told and did not bring his critical faculties to bear. The second point will be discussed when Colonel (later General) Mustafa Kemal's instantaneous reactions to his opponents' moves are described. Kemal became Hamilton's most dangerous opponent and a man who eventually graduated from being an aggressive tactician to be Turkey's leading general and finally the father of his country.

Notes

1 General Sir Ian Hamilton, *Listening for the Drums* (London: Faber & Faber, 1944), p.151. Details of Hamilton's early years with Roberts come from pp.150–71.
2 David James, *Lord Roberts* (London: Hollis and Carter, 1950), pp.181–97, which gives a good description of Roberts's command of the Madras Army.
3 Hamilton, *Listening for the Drums*, p.169.
4 General Sir Ian Hamilton, *The Commander* (Major Anthony Farrar-Hockley, ed.) (London: Hollis & Carter, 1957), p. 92.
5 Hamilton, *Listening for the Drums*, pp.150–1.
6 Anon. (Ian Hamilton), *A Jaunt in a Junk. A Ten Days' Cruise in Indian Seas* (London: Kegan, Paul, Trench & Co., 1884).
7 Hamilton, *Listening for the Drums*, pp.157–8.
8 Ibid.
9 Ian Hamilton, *The Ballad of Hádji and Other Poems* (London: Kegan Paul, Trench & Co., 1887). Reprinted by BiblioLife Reproduction Series, Breinigsville, PA, 2010.
10 Ian Hamilton, *Now and Then* (London: Methuen & Co., 1926).
11 Victor Sampson and Ian Hamilton, *Anti-Commando* (London: Faber & Faber, 1931).
12 Lieutenant General Sir Ian Hamilton, *A Staff Officer's Scrap-Book* (London: Edward Arnold; Volume 1, 1905; Volume 2, 1907).
13 General Sir Ian Hamilton, *Gallipoli Diary*, Volumes 1 & 2 (New York: George H. Doran, 1920).
14 General Sir Ian Hamilton, *The Soul and Body of an Army* (London: Edward Arnold, 1921); Sir Ian Hamilton, *The Friends of England* (London: George Allen & Unwin, 1923); Hamilton, *The Commander* (Major Anthony Farrar-Hockley, ed.)
15 Hamilton, *Listening for the Drums*, p.171.
16 Lord Wolseley, *In Relief of Gordon. Lord Wolseley's Campaign Journal of the Khartoum Relief Expedition, 1884-1885* (Adrian Preston, ed.) (London: Hutchinson, 1967), pp.180–1 (one example of many).
17 Ibid., pp.117–18.
18 Ibid., pp.212, 214, 219.
19 Ibid., pp.158, 162, 166.
20 Hamilton, *Listening for the Drums*, p.176.
21 Ibid., p.175.
22 Ibid., p.180.
23 Hamilton, *The Commander*, pp.76–80.
24 Wolseley, *In Relief of Gordon*, p.232.
25 Hamilton, *Listening for the Drums*, p.184.
26 Brigadier General C. F. Aspinall-Oglander, 'Ian Standish Monteith Hamilton', in *Military Lives* (from the *Dictionary of National Biography*) (Hew Strachan, ed.) (Oxford: Oxford University Press, 2002), pp.195–201.
27 Ian Hamilton, *Jean* (London: Faber & Faber, 1942).
28 Hamilton, *Listening for the Drums*, p.211.
29 Ian Hamilton (the General's nephew), *The Happy Warrior: A Life of General Sir Ian Hamilton* (London: Cassell, 1966), pp.104–19.

30 Ibid., p.240.

31 This brings to mind a well-known anecdote. Hindenburg, who had been brought out of retirement in 1914, won the mighty Battle of Tannenberg within a month of the beginning of the First World War. But not too long afterwards, it began to be rumoured that the plan of the battle had been the work of two subordinates, Ludendorff, the Chief of Staff, and Hoffmann, the Chief of Operations. At a reception after the war, a brave lady (almost certainly in her cups) asked the ancient warrior directly: 'Tell me, Field Marshal, who really won the Battle of Tannenberg? Was it you, or was it General Ludendorff, or was it really Colonel Hoffmann?' She received the cool but realistic reply: 'Madame, I do not really know who won the Battle of Tannenberg, but if the battle had been lost I know who would have lost it.'

CHAPTER 6

'The Last of the Gentlemen's Wars' and How it Degenerated

T he Second Boer War was a delayed continuation of the conflict fought in 1880 and 1881 that had ended in the continued independence of the Boer republics: in effect a British defeat. This happened eighteen years before the Second War exploded into military action in October 1899. The Second Boer War lasted for thirty-one months, an astonishingly long period that calls for some explanation. In numbers of soldiers on the ground and in the saddle – not to speak of the horses, mules and oxen; the artillery; the ammunition, food, fodder, medical supplies, clothing and other war materials needed to support the armies – the numerical superiority of the British was soon so huge that it is difficult to comprehend how the war lasted so long. This chapter will try and explain why. Chapter 7 will then address the question of how a conflict that began with eight months of tough but honourable battles – in which each side looked after its own and also its antagonists' casualties – managed to degenerate into a second and longer period which was neither a traditional military conflict nor a 'gentlemen's war'. In this second phase, large numbers of civilians were dispossessed, and through neglect suffered inadequate shelter, shortage of food and, for many women and children, disease and death.

Much had taken place during the eighteen years between the two wars. The Boers in the Transvaal and the Orange Free State remained in their attitudes as obdurately conservative as ever, although the Transvaal economy had been transformed by the discovery of gold in 1886. But in the Cape Colony, two uncompromising Englishmen confronted the Boer republics with hostility. The first was Rhodes, the Prime Minister of the Cape and multi-millionaire businessman, who controlled virtually the whole world's supply of diamonds from his headquarters in Kimberley, where the stones had been discovered in large quantities in 1870. The second was Milner, who was appointed in 1897 as British High Commissioner in Cape Town. Rhodes and Milner were determined to form a single colony that would include the two Boer republics. Rhodes was even more ambitious in his resolve to turn the eastern half of the African continent into a mighty swathe of British territory: an area that would be internally linked by a railway that was planned to run from the Cape to Cairo. Rhodes is one of the few men to have a country named after him, although the name Rhodesia was blown away by the 'winds of change' in the 1960s and it became two new countries, Zambia and Zimbabwe.

The inflexible attitudes of the two Englishmen were matched by the comparably inflexible attitude of Paul Kruger, the President of the Transvaal, an old Boer who had taken part in the Great Trek and therefore had long memories. He had an ally in Marthinus Steyn, President of the Free State, although Steyn was a more amenable character than Kruger. However, the two republics demonstrated Afrikaner solidarity, so that the imminent confrontation would be between both small Boer republics and the mighty British Empire.

The change that had created the greatest problem for Kruger was the direct result of the discovery of gold. The prospectors lured by the possibility of making quick fortunes inflated the size of the Transvaal population. These *uitlanders* – foreigners from Britain, Australia, Canada, Germany, America and Holland in search of gold – totalled 100,000 by 1896, more than the number of Afrikaner inhabitants. The gold had been discovered in the Witwatersrand (commonly called the Rand), a series of ridges running east to west, sixty miles long and twenty-five miles wide, between and some way to the west of the old capital of Pretoria and the rapidly growing commercial capital of Johannesburg. A difficulty that the prospectors soon encountered was that the gold was embedded in small quantities in solid rock, which meant that expensive capital equipment was needed to extract it. Large companies that had invested in mining and drilling equipment – mainly with European proprietors who were often owners of the highly profitable diamond enterprises in Kimberley – soon descended like cuckoos into the Afrikaner nest. The Rand rapidly became the source of twenty per cent of the world's gold production.

The *uitlanders* were regarded by the Boers as hostile intruders; the Great Trek had after all been an escape from the cultural influence of the British in the Cape Colony. What made the situation even worse for the Afrikaners was that the gold mines drew black labourers away from the Boer farms, which meant that African wages could no longer remain at rock-bottom levels. Kruger's response was to make life difficult for the *uitlanders* by making them pay high taxes, and disenfranchising them by stipulating that they had to live for fourteen years in the Transvaal before they received the vote. Kruger also made overtures to foreign powers, notably Germany which was openly antagonistic to the British Empire.

This naturally caused resentment and fury among British politicians in both the Cape Colony and London. At the end of 1895, a Kimberley physician called Jameson led a madcap expedition by 520 men, armed with rifles, machine guns and one field piece, into the Transvaal in the hope of raising an *uitlander* rebellion. Jameson and his absurdly hopeful invaders were soon rounded up near Johannesburg, with sixty-five killed and wounded. They were all jailed in Pretoria and handed over to British authorities for trial and punishment. The raid had been supported tacitly by the governments in both Cape Town and London, and the failure cost Rhodes his job as Prime Minister of the Cape Colony. Another direct result of the raid – something that posed a clear threat to the British – was that Kruger purchased 37,000 Mauser rifles from Germany, plus substantial supplies of ammunition; twenty-two artillery pieces (including eight large guns) from France; and Pom-Pom heavy machine guns (from Britain!) This ordnance was to have a serious impact on the war to come. When Milner arrived in South Africa, he petitioned Queen Victoria to protest personally to Kruger about the second-class citizenship of the *uitlanders*: a move that persuaded a reluctant Kruger to agree to attend a conference in Bloemfontein, capital of the Free State, arranged by President Steyn. And although the old President of the Transvaal made a concession by offering to reduce the period before the *uitlanders* could receive the vote, the British were not in a compromising mood. Kruger banged the conference table and proclaimed that the British would only be satisfied if they absorbed the two Boer republics. He was of course totally correct. Steyn now also decided to order a supply of Mauser rifles from Germany.

The situation was clearly becoming heated. London ordered 10,000 British troops from India to sail to Natal, with many more reinforcements to follow. Kruger, now quite unable to restrain his wrath, took the initiative, and issued an ultimatum to the British to move troops away from the frontiers of the two republics, and withdraw the 10,000 men from India who were now in Natal. This ultimatum was a relief to the British, who had no intention of succumbing because they visualized the possibility of a quick victory, without any danger of their being branded as aggressors. Not for the first time, the British seriously miscalculated. The Boer ultimatum expired on 11 October 1899.

As mentioned, the war that now erupted went through two distinct phases. The first was a period of eight months of conventional and vigorous military action, with many casualties, especially among the British. This episode was well described as 'The Last of the Gentlemen's Wars', a reflection of the chivalry that was often, although not invariably, seen on the battlefield.[1] This first phase ended in June 1900 when the British occupied Pretoria, in the confident expectation that the war was now over. But much to their surprise it was not. The second phase lasted for twenty-three months of mobile and maddeningly indecisive guerrilla warfare. The hardships endured by the Boer commandos during this period, and the prolonged neglect – although not purposeful cruelty – suffered by their families now in British hands, resulted in general exhaustion and the capitulation of the fighting Boers in May 1902. But the Boer commandos only surrendered on the basis of a majority vote and not a unanimous one, and much resentment remained. It was to resurface in 1914 in a revolt in support of Britain's German enemies, led by Christiaan de Wet, one of the two most aggressive and tactically skilful of the commando leaders. This later insurgency was paradoxically against the Boer leaders in South Africa, which was by now a substantially self-governing colony within the British Empire.

In October 1899, before the British moved forward to grapple with the enemy, the Boer commandos had mounted their ponies and with no delay made three incursions into British territory. The first was into the northern Cape Province, where they laid siege on two places: the small town of Mafeking and the larger town of Kimberley, centre of the diamond industry. The second was a minor and fairly ineffective invasion of the central Cape Province, undertaken in the vain hope of raising an Afrikaner uprising against the British. The third was an aggressive invasion of Natal where, by 2 November 1899, they managed to surround the garrison town of Ladysmith, locking up all the British troops in the province, including the 10,000 reinforcements who had recently arrived from India. These successes were a precursor of what was shortly to come. In fact, the first four months of the war saw a succession of Boer victories that were devastating to British arms and prestige. There were several underlying reasons why the Boers did so well, and these factors continued to operate throughout the war, and went a long way to explain the remarkable performance of the Boers in keeping the British Empire at bay until May 1902.

The first factor was a matter of sheer numbers. When the war began, the 40,000 Boers in the commandos outnumbered the British troops by almost two to one. As the war progressed, the balance of numbers tipped overwhelmingly in the British favour, yet the mobility of the Boer commandos made it possible for them to achieve local superiority in many battles. The raw numbers of British troops did not always count in their favour against Boer mobility and marksmanship. Small Boer mobile forces, like ants, often received the full attention of five times as many British horsemen trying to find them. But the pursuers soon learned the value of encirclement, a manoeuvre that always demanded large numbers of men.

The second factor was a reflection of the traditional aphorism that, in war, moral factors outweigh material ones in the ratio of three to one. The Boers opened hostilities by taking the initiative, and this tended always to be their general stance vis-à-vis the British. Throughout the conflict they were defending their own land, and they did so with crusading zeal. They were also boosted by the moral and material support they were receiving from a number of European countries who regarded them as

90

underdogs who were fighting aggressors. Small contingents of at least fifteen different nationalities fought on the Boer side.[2]

The third factor was a matter of skill that also provided a psychological advantage. The Boers remained to the end masters of the technique of fighting a war on the veldt. The best evidence of this superiority is that the British soon began to emulate them by developing mounted infantry tactics, and it was only when they did this that they began to achieve major success. A crucial contribution to the Boers' fighting powers was that some of the commando leaders quickly emerged as masters of the art of war, notably Koos de la Rey of the Transvaal and Christiaan de Wet of the Free State. They provided a sharp contrast to most British generals, who had a lot to learn. Hamilton was an exception in his ability to adapt rapidly to the new conditions.

The last point was the superior design of the Boer military hardware. The Boers' Mauser rifles were more than a match for the British Lee-Metfords and Lee-Enfields. All three weapons operated with magazines, the rounds being fed into the chamber by bolt action. The British rifles had an external and detachable magazine holding ten rounds; the Mausers had a five-round magazine within the wooden body of the rifle. But the Mausers had the advantage that cartridges were fed into the magazines using a clip of five rounds, which made for very fast re-loading. In contrast, the British weapons had to be reloaded one round at a time. The Boers therefore benefited from a higher rate of fire as well as from the generally superior marksmanship of the individual riflemen (as had been observed at Majuba). And the Boer artillery and Pom-Pom machine guns were extremely effective engines of destruction. The largest pieces, with a barrel diameter of 155mm, were essentially static siege guns, with a different role from the lighter and more mobile 15- and 13-pounder field pieces used by the British, which fired much smaller shells. Siege guns, nicknamed 'Long Toms', were deadly for the job of bombarding Mafeking, Kimberley and Ladysmith, and the guns were regarded by the garrisons as a real menace although there were not enough of them to blast the small towns to rubble.

Two Encounters and Three Lessons
Lieutenant General Sir George White was the commander in Natal, based

in Ladysmith, and had 13,000 men, including the reinforcements from India. Hamilton was one of White's staff officers, and he almost immediately emerged as a forceful commander of troops. White's initial move was to send forces north to anticipate the arrival of the Boers. Ladysmith is in southern Natal, and the Boers were some distance away: a hundred miles from the Transvaal and forty miles from the Free State. (See **Map 3**.) White therefore had some time to prepare, and he immediately sent out two strong forces to 'advance to contact', to prepare for the likely arrival of the Boers. Major General Sir W. Penn Symons was despatched to occupy the small town of Dundee, forty miles to the north-east of Ladysmith. Symons's force was a reinforced brigade: four infantry battalions, a cavalry regiment and three artillery batteries, numbering in total 5,000 men. Dundee was overlooked by two hills, Impati in the north and Talana in the north-east, and the ensuing battle was dominated by these.[3] Impati is the higher of the two hills, but Talana – the scene of the action – is only 600 feet high.

The morning of 20 October 1899 dawned damp misty and numbers of Boers were soon spotted on Talana Hill. At 0600 hours, much to the British surprise, the Boers began to shell Dundee erratically with a large siege cannon and some 75mm field guns. The British suffered some casualties and noticeable damage, but within twenty minutes the British batteries moved sharply into action and began to respond to the Boer gunfire. Symons was now eating his breakfast, but he immediately interrupted it to formulate a plan to dislodge and, he hoped, annihilate, the enemy. He thought it important to move quickly to catch the Boers before large reinforcements arrived, but his thinking was on strictly conventional lines, with his plan for a direct infantry assault on Talana Hill, followed by a cavalry charge to cut off the enemy's retreat. In the event, the cavalry jumped the gun and moved prematurely. Meanwhile, what came as an extremely unpleasant surprise to the long lines of British infantry, who were advancing in close order – which made them highly vulnerable to small-arms fire – was the ferocity of the Boers' defensive response. The British infantry were mainly short-service troops, and were jolted into some disarray by the fire of the Mausers. However, they pulled themselves together and made slow progress towards the top of the hill. At an early stage of the battle, Symons, who had made his presence felt by a large red flag carried by his ADC, received an agonizing wound that led to his death two days later. A lack of firm leadership now made itself felt, since by now the cavalry had disappeared. And when the British infantry got to the top of the hill, they were caught by 'friendly' fire from the British artillery and suffered terrible casualties. The capture of Talana Hill was a pyrrhic victory because the Boers had given the British a bloody nose and quietly crept away. The Boers had suffered few losses, while the numbers of British soldiers killed and wounded totalled 254. The British cavalry had by this time vanished into Boer territory and a large number of them were soon forced to surrender. The defence of Ladysmith had begun very badly.

Meanwhile, another substantial British force was moving on Elandslaagte, a station on the railway fifteen miles north-east of Ladysmith, where the Boers were rumoured to have cut the line that carried on to Dundee.[4] Ian Hamilton, now a local major general, was deputy commander, and because of his high rank he was able to make a personal impact on the battle, which was a tactical victory since there were more Boer casualties than British ones, although it was not a strategic one. A British tactical victory was a rare occurrence at this stage of the war. Hamilton's chief in the field was Major General John French, a thrusting cavalryman who had just arrived in South Africa and who was to prove an energetic and successful commander throughout the war. As a Field Marshal he was to lead the British Expeditionary Force that went to France in 1914. French's chief staff officer in 1899 bore another name to conjure with – Major Douglas Haig – the officer who was to succeed French at the end of 1915, to become the highly controversial British Commander-in-Chief in France and Flanders during the last three years of the First World War. French deployed 3,500 men at Elandslaagte, more than three times the Boer force opposing him. This was a promising superiority in numbers but, on the assumption that the infantry made a successful assault, the problem was how to cut off the Boers' retreat. The failure to do this had been the British mistake at Talana.

A mile south-east of Elandslaagte station, there is a 300-foot high feature, two miles long, that stretches to the south-east. This is two connected ridges in the form of a horseshoe at a right angle to the railway, and was the defensive position occupied by the Boer commandos.

93

French's plan was that Hamilton, commanding two-and-a-half infantry battalions, should lead the assault. The 1st Battalion Devonshire Regiment would advance frontally, and then halt to provide covering fire to support a right-flanking attack by the 2nd Battalion Gordon Highlanders and the half-battalion of 1st Manchester Regiment that Hamilton had in his command. Five squadrons of the Imperial Light Horse (ILH) joined them, as mounted infantry. The ILH had been raised in Natal from *uitlanders* from Johannesburg, educated and patriotic volunteers whose families had come from Britain. It was to become one of the most successful fighting units during the war. The driving force behind the Regiment and its Second-in-Command was Major Adrian Woolls-Sampson, a descendant of a line of British army officers who had settled in the Cape Province. He was in his mid-forties and had been a prospector, explorer, big game hunter, volunteer soldier, and colonial administrator. Hamilton later described him as having all the qualities needed by the commander of an irregular force: he was hard, brave and energetic; a crack shot; and he had an excellent 'feel' for ground.[5] The ILH was the British equivalent of a Boer commando, and it became the model for other British mounted infantry units.

Before the attack, Hamilton gave his men clear instructions to advance in open formation with the men three yards apart, and to use their rifles effectively. The lessons of the 1885 battle of Kirbekan (where General Earle had been killed) – especially the lesson that troops should advance in open formation – had made an indelible impression on Hamilton. He was also to revisit them later, when he trained troops during his brief tenure at the School of Musketry.[6] The 1st Devons moved forward to within 900 yards of the hill. But the assault that next took place from the British right faltered because of the Boer rifle fire and also – an augury of future warfare – because the attackers encountered a belt of barbed wire. This was the moment when Hamilton personally intervened to rally his men. The colonel of the ILH had by now been struck down, but Woolls-Sampson immediately assumed control and advanced, heroically leading his men, until he was himself badly wounded.[7] The weather was now closing in and there was heavy rain before the end of the battle. But the infantry had soon done its job and taken the second ridge, despite a fierce Boer counter-attack. It was now the turn of the cavalry: and French had made sure that it was ready. His two cavalry regiments made three bloody charges with lance and sabre and left a trail of Boer dead and wounded. They also left a legacy of fear. In all future battles during the war, the Boers continued to fight effectively using their Mausers and artillery, but they always dreaded the close assault of British cavalry and infantry: the loud swishing sound of the long bayonets being drawn from their scabbards and then the metallic click of the 'fix bayonets' always caused them to waver. At Elandslaagte, the British force lost 263 men; and the Boers suffered 425 casualties, of whom 200 became prisoners. The whole encounter was a model, but one that was not repeated very often:

> As was quickly recognized by the Great German General Staff, Elandslaagte stands out by its technique, by its precise and symmetrical form, a head and shoulder above the welter of scraps, scoops, regrettable incidents which slowly, slowly—very slowly— during the next two and a half years, were to besprinkle a vast sub-continent with blood.[8]

Three Victoria Crosses were awarded. In addition to these, two other men, both officers, were nominated for this great award but both were out of luck. The two were Woolls-Sampson and Hamilton himself (who had, as mentioned earlier, also been put forward for it after Majuba). This time the excuse was that while commanding a brigade he had too high a rank, because the Victoria Cross is a reward – and an important incentive for valour – for regimental officers and men at the 'sharp end'.

Talana and Elandslaagte were extremely instructive despite the fact that they were strategic reverses for the British: the advancing Boer forces soon drove the two outnumbered detachments back into Ladysmith. Three clear lessons emerged from these early encounters, although the ingrained conservatism of the British Army meant that the lessons were only slowly absorbed. The first lesson was that the Boers had to be taken seriously: they could no longer be regarded – as they had been by many British Regular soldiers – as ill-educated, badly led and untrained amateurs. Second, the British needed more than large numbers of men to defeat the Boers: they had to revise their tactics radically to achieve any success against an elusive, aggressive and skilled opponent. The third lesson applies to all wars, but was particularly relevant to the two Boer wars because of the incompetence of the early British leadership. Defeating the Boers meant that the colonels and generals in the field had to maintain a firm grip on their units and formations, since any perceptible weakness in the British control of the battle would be relentlessly exploited by their adversaries.

'Fortified Towns are Now Liable to Destruction'[9]
Ladysmith is a small town surrounded by hills. In 1899 it was a rail junction and garrison town, half-jokingly called the 'Aldershot of Natal'. It was then more unattractive than it is today. Besides being hot, it was dusty and crowded, and typhoid stalked the white and the black inhabitants. Being besieged in a fortress was regarded by senior officers of the British army as a dangerous contingency, and this doctrine had been taught at the Staff College, which used Hamley's classic *Operations of War* as a textbook (the quotation above comes from it). General White was therefore only too conscious of the danger of allowing his force to be trapped, but he had the normal British attitude towards the Boers: they were not considered to be serious opponents and could easily be smashed by the British force in Ladysmith. This was another serious misjudgement. White, if he had been wiser, could have fought his way south to cross the Tugela River to reach the veldt, where he would have been able to manoeuvre to counter the Boers' incursions and eventually defeat them in the field.

But White sacrificed this opportunity, or rather he was forced back into the town and had no alternative other than to defend it. Ladysmith had by now become crowded, with bell tents everywhere, and three months' supplies being accumulated for 13,000 troops; and more than 5,000 civilians, both black and white, plus 3,000 horses. White was in his mid-sixties and had been the Commander-in-Chief in India before he was appointed to head the British Army in Natal. He went there because Natal was likely to become a major centre of operations. White had won the Victoria Cross in Afghanistan a short time before his junior comrade in the Gordon Highlanders, Ian Hamilton, heard his first shots fired in anger. White, despite his long experience, did not have the flair and energy of his predecessor in India, Lord Roberts. In particular, when he was under

96

pressure he vacillated and lacked 'grip'. He was not alone in having such weaknesses.

Forty miles north of Ladysmith, the British force in Dundee was being shelled by a 'Long Tom' on Impati Hill. Many men were killed and wounded, and there was a great deal of destruction. Major General Yule, who had succeeded Symons in command of the force, was also elderly. He showed himself to be a ditherer and was in a welter of confusion until, in response to an order from White, he began to withdraw his troops from the town. They departed precipitately and left their wounded behind, including the dying Symons. They also abandoned forty days' supplies of ammunition and food, which the Boers who descended on the town soon began to loot enthusiastically. The Boers could easily have attacked the retreating British and defeated them, but they were too cautious and perhaps too inexperienced to do so. Yule's column eventually reached the supposed safety of Ladysmith and staggered into the garrison, hungry and unkempt: a condition that did not signal good morale.

White had been too busy to think about the lessons of Talana and Elandslaagte: respect for the Boers; the need for adaptable tactics; and that commanders are totally ineffective unless they exercise firm control and are psychologically on top of the battlefield. These lessons were soon painfully reinforced by two further battles fought a few miles north of Ladysmith.[10] The first was at Rietfontein where, on 24 October, a British brigade was crushingly defeated. The second was at Nicholson's Nek where, on 30 October, a number of British battalions were thrown back in humiliating disarray, with Boer artillery fire pursuing them into Ladysmith. British losses totalled 1,272 men, including 954 prisoners.

White had lost his balance when the ring closed around Ladysmith on 2 November. The British garrison, which had now crept up to more than 13,700 men, was no longer in a position to take the initiative against the Boers. Ladysmith under siege exacted two penalties: the emasculation of the defending force; and the great and urgent effort that had to be made by the troops sent to relieve the town. This became the major task of the Commander-in-Chief of the British Army in South Africa, who arrived in Cape Town on 31 October. He was General Sir Redvers Buller, the officer who had not greatly distinguished himself in the Gordon Relief Expedition. At the time of his arrival, accompanied by 50,000 men, the small British garrisons at Mafeking and Kimberley were already under siege, and Buller sent more than half his force, under Lieutenant General Lord Methuen, north to relieve them. Before long this British force was halted by strong Boer defences and the front had stabilized. Meanwhile White had got his substantial force surrounded at Ladysmith – despite Buller's specific instruction that he should not allow this to happen – which meant that the relief of Ladysmith had to be Buller's priority, and the town and the routes leading to it from the south became the major scene of operations. Buller deployed 19,500 troops in the advance.

Hamilton had accompanied White to Natal (as mentioned) as a senior staff officer. But in no time he was given a field command, and his performance at Elandslaagte – the leadership, energy and tactical sense that he demonstrated – showed him to be an outstandingly reliable subordinate. He was one of three senior officers in Ladysmith of whom much more would be heard in the future; the others were Major General Sir Archibald Hunter and Colonel Sir Henry Rawlinson. (French, the other man with a future, had got out of the town on one of the last trains.) On 26 October, when he was back in Ladysmith, Hamilton – aggressive as ever – developed a practicable plan for a four-battalion assault on a Boer laager that would have been virtually undefended. But White was unwilling to take the risk and, to Hamilton's frustration, he cancelled the order. Hamilton did less well at Nicholson's Nek, although he played only a subsidiary role. The plan, which turned into such a disaster, was drawn up by White, who took responsibility for it.

The siege of Ladysmith was to last for four months, from early November 1899 to early March 1900. During the siege the town never became a scene of furious activity; on the contrary there was a rather pervasive atmosphere of boredom, even apathy.[11] Church parades were held, and even occasional cricket matches. The defensive line for most of its length was two miles from the town itself, and by the standards of later wars it was relatively thin, being constructed of trenches, stone sangars and a few forts. There was a virtually continuous line from the north of the town to the south-east; then it turned south-west and finally bent east-west at Caesar's Camp and Wagon Hill. This southern sector, which the Boers called the *Platrand*, was Ian Hamilton's direct responsibility, and its defences were less well planned and constructed than those in the north. To the west of the town the line was even thinner, because little enemy activity was expected there.

Despite the sleepiness of the town, life was by no means easy for the besieged garrison. It was under regular but erratic fire from five large Boer guns sited on hills four or more miles away. They had earlier been spotted, and when they emitted puffs of smoke, alarms were sounded for people in the town to take shelter. Boer gunfire caused a good deal of destruction but did not take many lives. The worst effect of the 'Long Toms' was that people in the town began to live on their nerves, fearful of where the next shell would land. The enemy guns outranged the British field guns, although the garrison had two heavier pieces which were capable of replying to the Boers, one of these a naval weapon. Another hardship was dwindling reserves of food. There was nothing approaching starvation, and plans had been made to feed the garrison for three months, but the extension of the siege beyond this period meant reduced rations. Typhoid was also a continuous grumbling problem, causing much sickness and occasional deaths.

The worst problem in Ladysmith was the demeanour of Sir George White, who was for much of the time frozen into immobility. To make matters worse, a number of his senior staff officers operated according to the richly detailed British Army Standing Orders, and never demonstrated an ability or inclination for aggressive improvisation. White's mental detachment from his command was widely criticized by the officers of the garrison, particularly by Colonel Rawlinson, who had the ear of two senior commanders who arrived in South Africa in January 1900, Lord Roberts and Lord Kitchener. (Rawlinson was to become an Army Commander in the First World War.)

It was Rawlinson who managed to persuade a reluctant White to authorize two raids on the continuously troublesome Boer guns. On 8 December 1899, 600 men of the ILH, led by Major General Hunter in person, triumphantly disabled two of these large pieces of ordnance and got away. On 11 December, 500 men of the 2nd Battalion Rifle Brigade knocked out a single dangerous gun, but they did not get away unharmed, and suffered sixty-one casualties, mainly wounded. These were the only occasions when the defenders made serious efforts to control the battle. They spent the rest of the period of the siege in waiting for the long delayed progress of Buller's relief column; or else in defending themselves against Boer attacks. The garrison remained physically isolated, although it kept fairly regular contact with Buller via the flashing of heliograph mirrors. This was a device that could not be used in bad weather, but in the South African summer it was a serviceable method of getting messages through.

The initiative was now passing to the besiegers. On the night of 6/7 January 1900, the British were surprised by a major assault from the south which overcame the weak defences on the *Platrand*, the ridge between Caesar's Camp and Wagon Hill, although it was beaten back by the British troops to the right and left. On that ridge the defensive line relied on stone sangars without connecting trenches, and the fields of fire in front of the line had not been cleared of obstructions. The Boer attacks came near to complete success, and the greatest heroism was shown by both attackers and defenders. Among the British in the forefront of the action was Ian Hamilton, who continued to be at his best when the bullets were flying. The British line was eventually secured as heavy rain was beginning to fall. The defenders lost 424 men, including 175 killed, leaving a shockingly bloody expanse of mangled bodies. The state of the defences had been Hamilton's personal responsibility but he had spent little time in planning and supervising the work. The episode therefore provided an unusual insight into his strengths and weaknesses at this stage of his career. His general attitude was always aggressive rather than defensive; impulsive rather than reflective; and more attuned to responding to enemy action than to drawing up contingency plans for events that might or might not happen. These negatives were unimportant when Hamilton was conducting offensive operations, which he was doing for most of the Second Boer War, especially when he was personally leading his men as if he had temporarily reverted to being a battalion or even a company commander. However, when he was required to operate at a high level of command, as was to happen at Gallipoli, his duties demanded that much of his time should have been spent *thinking*. His greatest responsibility should have been to consider different eventualities in a generally uncertain environment, and to try to detect what was happening 'on the other side of the hill'. At Gallipoli the problems that had arisen at Ladysmith were going to recur.

While the inactivity in the town continued to irritate some of the officers and men of the garrison, Buller's relief expedition was beginning to hit serious road blocks. These blocks were the Tugela River, a strongly-flowing stream that runs from west to east; and beyond its northern bank, a range of substantial hills and valleys. This was topography that provided natural advantages for the defenders, particularly for defenders like the Boers who had a natural 'feel' for the shape of ground and had a flair for selecting the best firing positions for their small arms and artillery. For Buller, the thirty miles from the Tugela to Ladysmith were going to be a surprisingly long distance.

Buller made his first serious move at the village and river crossing of Colenso.[12] The British assault followed two days of bombardment, which naturally alerted the Boers to what was about to happen: Buller's troops attacked on 15 December 1899, six weeks after Ladysmith was first besieged. The Transvaal commandos, under thirty-seven year-old Louis Botha, a leader who was soon to become one of the most prominent military and political figures in the Boer hierarchy, occupied a four-mile line of well-positioned fire trenches just north of the river. These trenches covered the three possible fords – known in South Africa as *drifts* – which the British planned to cross to get to the northern bank. Buller divided his force and made a two-pronged frontal attack, each prong composed of an infantry brigade. The men attacked two sharp loops in the river. Their commanders did not anticipate – although they should have done – that the men in each loop would immediately come under Boer fire from three different directions: left, front and right. When the attackers began to suffer heavy casualties, an unexpected and indeed unlikely disaster immediately followed. The commander of the artillery pushed a dozen 15-pounder guns into the front line, anticipating that the Boers would soon be on the run and could be pursued by gunfire. But the Boers did not run away, the British were pushed back, and the guns were isolated. Volunteers made desperate efforts to bring them back and five men received Victoria Crosses for their almost fruitless bravery; two guns were saved. The heroes included Lord Roberts's only son, whose Victoria Cross was posthumous. The old Field Marshal therefore had to carry a heavy shadow of grief when he sailed for South Africa, because when the Government in London heard the outcome of the battle – a defeat for the British at a cost of 1,138 casualties, compared with forty Boers – they decided to replace Buller as Commander-in-Chief. A gloomy cable Buller had sent to London about Colenso confirmed the wisdom of the decision that he should go. The Government immediately brought Roberts away from his Irish command and sent him to the War. Buller received the news stoically and continued his job of attempting to fight his way north. In Ladysmith itself, the garrison had been encouraged to hear the sound of the guns at Colenso and expected Buller's men to arrive within hours. But hope soon turned to disappointment when the disheartening news about the battle was flashed through to the beleaguered garrison by heliograph.

By mid-January 1900, Buller's force had been built up to 30,000 men, and he found a crossing place over the Tugela thirty miles west of Colenso. But the problem was that the road from there to Ladysmith goes through a defile between two mighty hills: Tabanyama to the west and Spion Kop to the east. One or both of these peaks had to be captured if the British Army was going to advance. Buller again split his strength and delegated the crossing to half his force, which he put under the command of Lieutenant General Sir Charles Warren, who set out on 16 January. Warren soon demonstrated his main characteristic, which was sloth. By the time he had secured the river crossing and made a frontal attack on Tabanyama, the Boers were entrenched there and repulsed the British, with the loss of 470 men.

He then made an effort to take Spion Kop, a feature that stretches for three miles, south-west to north-east, rising to 1,500 feet, slightly higher than Tabanyama. On the night of 23/24 January, Warren sent 1,900 of his men to swarm up the steep western slope, but they could not haul any field guns up with them, and they also left behind most of their entrenching tools. The British reached what they thought was the summit and had the greatest difficulty digging into the rocky soil, although they managed a single long shallow trench. When the sun rose, they found to their horror that they were not on the peak after all, but the Boers were. These hardy farmers had climbed up the eastern face, which was anyway much easier going than the opposite side. The Boers, who were fewer than 400 men under Botha, did not stop punishing the British all day with their small-arms fire, reinforced by constant shelling from their artillery below the hill. And although some reinforcements managed to get up the western face, they were only strong enough to help the British detachment survive: there was no question of their overwhelming the Boers.

It was a deadly and unrelenting encounter, and at the end of the afternoon the British were ready to withdraw: a few white flags were appearing. Ammunition and water were running short and it was almost impossible to communicate with Warren. The British detachment started retiring; but, strangely enough, so did the Boers, who also seemed to have had enough. However, Botha drove them back, and when they got to the top of the hill they found it unoccupied, except for the dead and dying. The Boer victory was fortuitous. The long British trench later became the grave of the many fallen British soldiers.

The dreadful day had cost the British between 1,800 and 2,000 men: the precise number was never known. But their casualties were ten times as high as the Boers'. The battle bore a startling resemblance to Majuba in three respects: in the shape of the battle site; in the general course of the conflict, with the British not using their full strength and the Boers making an unexpected appearance from the more accessible side of the mountain; and in the overwhelming disparity in the casualties suffered by the two sides, a tribute to the continued superiority of Boer marksmanship. A weird coincidence was that three men who were later to make an impact on the world were on Spion Kop when the bullets were flying, and survived unscathed. They were Louis Botha, the Boer commander; Winston Churchill, then a war correspondent; and Mohandas Gandhi, at the time the leader of a group of volunteer stretcher bearers.

Although Buller was not the cleverest of generals, he never lost the affection of his men, who were still prepared to follow him. Much of his troubles had anyway been caused by the inadequacy of his subordinates. Fortune now began to smile on him in two ways. First – an early example of interdiction – the numbers of Boers facing him were thinning out as some of the commandos had to move west to shore up the Boer defences against Lord Roberts's advance from Cape Town. Second, Buller had learned from his mistakes. When he next attempted to cross the Tugela, he employed all his troops as a single command and moved his point of attack from place to place to disperse the opposition: a tactic that Haig was to employ on a much expanded scale in 1918. Buller also used his artillery in a way that was extensively developed during the First World War: he employed a creeping barrage, by which a moving curtain of fire fell a hundred yards ahead of the advancing infantry. The British began their assault on 21 February 1900, and Buller entered Ladysmith on 1 March. There was less jubilation in the town than there was in London, where the population was overcome with joy that the British Empire had emerged intact from its trials. But General White's career did not survive: he was incapacitated by illness and, when he recovered, his career stalled; as a consolation prize he became the Governor of Gibraltar. However, Hunter, Rawlinson and Hamilton all went on to higher things. The call came first to Hamilton, who was despatched to join Lord Roberts in Bloemfontein, the newly-captured capital of the Orange Free State. This led the way to the greatest professional opportunity of Hamilton's career.

Notes

1 This is the title of an informative and well-written memoir by a British subaltern, who was to become one of the leading exponents of armoured warfare in the First World War and later a leading military analyst and commentator. J. F. C. Fuller, *The Last of the Gentlemen's Wars* (London: Faber & Faber, 1937).

2 Louis Changuion, Frik Jacobs and Paul Alberts, *Suffering of War* (Bloemfontein, South Africa: Kraal Publishers, for the Museum of the Boer Republics, 2003), p.243.

3 Thomas Pakenham, *The Boer War* (London: Weidenfeld & Nicolson, 1979), pp.125–32.

4 Ibid., pp.133–41.

5 Victor Sampson and Ian Hamilton, *Anti-Commando* (London: Faber & Faber, 1931), pp.33–121.

6 Ibid., pp.112–13.

7 Ibid., p.114.

8 Ibid., p.107.

9 Major General Edward Bruce Hamley, *The Operations of War, Explained and Illustrated* (Edinburgh and London: Blackwood, 1878), p.309.

10 Pakenham, *The Boer War*, pp.142–55.

11 Ibid., pp.261–76.

12 Ibid., pp.224–41, 277–307, 343–70; also Tabitha Jackson, *The Boer War* (London: Macmillan – Channel 4 Books, 1999), pp.64–7, 69–79, 91–4.

92nd (Gordon Highlanders) on battalion parade in India, *circa* 1880. Most of the men are in home service dress – scarlet doublet, kilt and Glengarry – worn during the cool weather in India. The soldiers in the front rank are pioneers, many with luxuriant beards. The soldiers to the left of the second rank are dressed in drill order – short white jackets. There are four mounted officers. The remaining officers are viewing the parade from the higher balcony of the building behind the parade ground. (National Army Museum (NAM) negative 29041)

Lieutenant Ian Hamilton, *circa* 1880. From photograph 3.

Officers, 92nd (Gordon Highlanders), *circa* 1880, wearing hot weather uniform. Lieutenant Hamilton is the right-hand figure in the front row. In the back row, the first officer is Major White, who became the General Officer Commanding the British Army in Natal, 1899–1900, and Hamilton's chief at Ladysmith; and the third figure from the right is Major Hay, who commanded the Gordons (and was Hamilton's superior) during the battle of Majuba Hill, 1881. (NAM negative 126417)

Officers, 92nd (Gordon Highlanders), *circa* 1880, wearing cool weather uniform, many in serviceable locally-made tunics. Hamilton is standing fourth from the left, wearing a light uniform. (NAM negative 6182)

Gateway in an Indian fort, *circa* 1878. Officers and men of the 92nd (Gordon Highlanders). This fort may have been Dera Ishmael Khan. (NAM negative 6212)

Peiwar Kotal, general view, 1878. This is an overall image and shows three soldiers and a dog in the foreground. This photograph demonstrates the difficulty of the terrain: the scene of Roberts's first major victory. (NAM negative 126418))

Peiwar Kotal, view with troops, 1878. The soldiers are advancing, presumably as reinforcements. (NAM negative 126421)

Majuba Hill, 1881. This view from the east shows the easier route taken by the Boer attackers. The British were unaware of this relatively easy approach. (NAM negative 126531)

The Gordon Relief Expedition, 1888–89. This photograph shows the unloading of whalers from railway trucks onto the river at Assuit. (NAM negative 126538)

Tirah Expedition, 1898. Gordon Highlanders with piled arms. The weapons are Lee-Metford bolt-action magazine rifles, used between 1888 and 1898. (NAM negative 126631)

Lieutenant General Hamilton commanding 'from the saddle,' during the advance from Bloemfontein, 1900. (NAM negative 124517)

Lieutenant General Hamilton and Major General Smith-Dorrien (Commander of 19 Brigade), planning the advance on Pretoria, 1900. (NAM negative 124504)

Sir Alfred Milner, Governor of Cape Province (in plain clothes); Field Marshal Lord Roberts, Commander-in-Chief (with arm in sling); and commanders and staff officers, 1900. Hamilton is at the right of the seated figures. The standing officers include, at number six from left, Colonel Henry Wilson (later Field Marshal and CIGS, who was assassinated in 1922); number seven is Lord Stanley (later the Earl of Derby, who succeeded Kitchener as Secretary of State for War in 1916); number eight is Colonel Sir Henry Rawlinson (later General and Army Commander in the First World War and subsequently Commander-in-Chief in India). (NAM negative 85379)

General Hamilton and
Vice Admiral de Robeck,
on board ship off the
Gallipoli Peninsula,
1915. (Imperial War
Museum (IWM)
negative Q13503)

Major General Hunter-Weston and
staff officers, Gallipoli, 1915. (IWM
negative Q13307)

View of V Beach from the *River Clyde*, 1915. This unusual panoramic view shows the improvised bridge of boats from the ship to the shore. (IWM negative Q25129)

SS *River Clyde*, 1915. This photograph shows the sally-ports cut into the starboard side of the hull. (IWM *negative* Q20244)

W Beach, 1915, 'Lancashire Landing.' (IWM negative Q13910)

Y Beach, 1915. This was where the British landing was for many hours insecure; this was not totally due to the difficult terrain. (IWM negative Q14831)

Anzac Cove, 1915. This photograph shows the formidable cliffs. The sharp hill one-third of the way along the skyline is the Sphinx. (IWM negative Q13824)

Lone Pine. This feature was in the forward line of the ANZAC position and the scene of bitter fighting. Colonel Mustafa Kemal commanded the Turkish troops in this sector. This is a post-war photograph, with a British Military Cemetery on the right. (IWM negative Q13886)

ANZAC soldiers charging with the bayonet. This is something that rarely happened at Gallipoli, where the fighting was generally at close quarters. (IWM negative Q13659)

A typical trench, probably in the ANZAC sector. The proximity to the Turkish positions is indicated by the trench periscopes. The officer on the right is in the Royal Naval Division. (He was probably a visitor since his division was mostly engaged at Cape Helles.) (IWM negative Q13426)

60-pounder gun. This was one of the twelve heavy artillery pieces that the British employed on the Peninsula. (IWM negative Q13340)

The problem of water supply. This endless difficulty was generally handled by filtering the water and filling cans (often cleaned petrol tins), which were then transported by mules to the front line. (IWM negative Q13448)

Suvla Bay, the salt lake, from the south. This photograph was taken after the landing and shows the flat terrain that made for an easy assault. (IWM negative Q14318)

Cape Helles, W Beach, shortly before the evacuation. This photograph was taken from a British hospital and shows Achi Baba Hill, six miles away. This was the original objective, and was still maddeningly out of reach. (IWM negative Q13546)

Lord Kitchener and Lieutenant General Birdwood, November 1915. This photograph was taken during Kitchener's visit of inspection, when he decided that the Gallipoli Peninsula would be evacuated. (IWM negative Q13596)

CHAPTER 7

Learning from Their Own Mistakes

Bismarck, the German statesman whose attitude to life was coolly pragmatic, is supposed to have said that foolish men learn from their own mistakes; wise men learn from mistakes made by other people. But he was not British. In South Africa the British were compelled to learn from their own mistakes, and it was a hard process. Buller arrived in Cape Town as Commander-in-Chief on 31 October 1899, and could do little to arrest the procession of military reverses. He was faced with demands from west and east, and made the wise decision to concentrate his own effort on the Natal front in the east, because of the imminent threat to Ladysmith with its important British garrison. Lieutenant General Lord Methuen in the western Cape Province was ordered to advance on Kimberley and Mafeking with more than 30,000 men.[1] The distances that were to be fought over were very large. Kimberley is 500 miles north-east of Cape Town as the crow flies, and a greater distance by rail because the line loops in a large salient toward the east. Mafeking is a further 200 miles north of Kimberley. Bloemfontein, capital of the Free State and an important step in the path of the British advance to the Transvaal, is 100 miles east of Kimberley; and the final objective, Pretoria, is 300 miles north-east of Bloemfontein. Taking account of the bends in the railway line, Pretoria is 1,000 miles from Cape Town. (See **Map 3**.)

By the end of November, Methuen's men were approaching Kimberley, travelling partly on foot and partly by rail. Seventy miles short of the town, at Orange River Station, Methuen was organizing a relief column, which was soon to hit substantial Boer opposition. Meanwhile, trouble was brewing in the central Cape Province, where Boers had captured the rail junction of Stormberg, fifty miles south of the Orange River which separates the Free State from the Cape Province. On 11 December, the local British commander, Lieutenant General Gatacre, badly mishandled his response to the Boer attack. His 3,000 men outnumbered the enemy, but orders within his force were misunderstood, and 600 men were left isolated on a hill south of the station, from which Gatacre's remaining troops were retiring. The total British losses were 698 men: some killed and wounded but most captured.

Meanwhile, Methuen's advancing spearhead of 13,000 men had got to the junction of the Modder and Riet rivers, twenty-five miles south of Kimberley. The Boers were acutely conscious of the danger to their force besieging Kimberley. They, therefore, prepared to meet the British and assembled 3,000 men from three commandos, two from the Free State and one from the Transvaal, under the overall leadership of the Free State commando leader, Piet Cronje. Koos de la Rey, who was to become the outstanding military leader from the Transvaal, and maybe the best of all the Boers, had developed a tactical method that would be decisively important in defeating Methuen's force. The Boers avoided the high ground and dug fire trenches in the low ground, in front of hills where any existed. At the Modder, where there are no hills, they dug trenches in both banks of the Riet River, a tributary that joins the Modder nearby. Both rivers have steep banks and are thick with mud: hence the name Modder River. The Boer trenches were occupied by a substantial number of riflemen reinforced by field guns.

The Modder River battle on 28 November was an exhausting long-range infantry duel that lasted for ten hours. Two British brigades were ordered to advance but were immediately pinned down, despite the personal intervention of Methuen who, like Penn Symons and Hamilton, believed in leading by example. On their left flank the British had some success, but the end result of the encounter was no more than the maintenance of the status quo, although there were 460 British casualties (and as usual many fewer Boers: a total of eighty). The Boers drew back after the battle, but the British were in no fit state to follow them.

The battle of Magersfontein on 11/12 December was even more painful for the British. The Boer trench line extended for four miles in front of Magersfontein Hill, which is fifteen miles north-east of where the Modder River battle had been fought. By this time, the celebrated Highland Brigade, under Major General Andrew Wauchope, was to bear the brunt of the assault; and also the casualties. On the night of 11 December, the Scotsmen advanced in large, close formations to avoid straying and getting lost in the darkness. But as dawn was breaking and they were opening out into line to assault the enemy, whose trenches were only 400 yards away, they received a torrent of small-arms and artillery fire. The result was carnage. Wauchope, who also believed in leading from the front, lost his life. The situation became worse later in the day when the wounded and the unwounded, pinned down by enemy fire, were badly blistered by the sun, especially on their legs below their kilts. Again the disparity of casualties was heavily balanced against the British, with 902 men killed or wounded, compared with 236 Boers. After Magersfontein, there was no question of Methuen advancing further towards Kimberley. And it is not surprising that in Britain, the short period that witnessed the disasters of Stormberg, Magersfontein and Colenso immediately became known as Black Week.

By this time Lord Roberts was on his way to South Africa; he landed at Cape Town on 16 January 1900.[2] The most important appointment he made was his Chief of Staff (and later successor) Lord Kitchener. Kitchener had made his name in 1898 when he had organized and led the expedition up the Nile to revenge Gordon: an expedition that had crushed the power of the Dervishes at the Battle of Omdurman, near Khartoum. Roberts, with his long experience of commanding 'from the saddle', had a formidable range of military talent: the magic gift of leadership, accompanied by a sound strategic sense and a finely-tuned feel for tactics. Kitchener had an inflexible will and a good strategic judgement, but he had flaws: he was a poor delegator and an indifferent tactician. His main personal quality was that he radiated power, an air of command that some observers thought was typified by the size of his moustache, 'the virility symbol of the British Empire' (although Kitchener's own uncertain sexuality was never discussed).

Roberts brought two specific gifts to his command in South Africa:

his demonstrable 'grip', and a huge increase in the number of troops: 150,000 reinforcements were in South Africa at the time of Roberts's first encounter with the Boers at Magersfontein. These new levies included volunteer units from Britain and irregular (newly raised, mainly mounted) corps from Britain, South Africa, Canada, Australia and New Zealand. It was obvious to Roberts that the Boers' advantages on the battlefield were mobility and musketry. He addressed the first of these problems immediately, by raising mounted infantry, soldiers who would travel to the scene of action on horses or ponies, but thereafter fight as infantrymen. Roberts's mounted infantry units were intended to be a match for the Boer commandos, but with the sinewy cohesion of British military discipline. Forming mounted infantry units meant that British infantry soldiers had to learn how to ride, which would take time. This important new type of military formation was to provide Ian Hamilton with the opportunity to make his name.

Roberts quickly made his presence felt. After the Field Marshal's first victories at Kimberley and Paardeberg (shortly to be described), the young war correspondent Winston Churchill caught a glimpse of the old warrior in Bloemfontein:

> The conversation stops abruptly. Everyone looks round. Strolling across the middle of the square, quite alone, was a very small grey-haired gentleman, with extremely broad shoulders and a most unbending back. He wore a staff cap with a broad red band and a heavy gold-laced peak, brown riding boots, a tightly-fastened belt, and no medals, orders, or insignia of any kind. But no one doubted his identity for an instant, and I knew that I was looking at the Queen's greatest subject, the commander who had in the brief space of a month revolutionized the fortunes of war, had turned disaster into victory, and something like despair into almost inordinate triumph.[3]

Roberts and Kitchener took three weeks to formulate their strategic plan, which was to seize the initiative and to take the war to the Boers. They concentrated on the western route, from Cape Town to Kimberley, then to Bloemfontein, and finally to Pretoria. This represented a planned advance of 1,000 miles, with the railway playing an important role in transporting the British force. The immediate relief of Mafeking would have splintered the British effort, so Roberts intended to detach a minor force to make for Mafeking at a later stage in the advance. He also decided to leave Buller in Natal to make what progress he could, by aggressive action and by keeping the Boers defending their positions and away from the British advance in the west.

By 15 February, Roberts's men were in Magersfontein. They had been forced along, spending alternative days riding by train and marching. Cronje thought he was well prepared, and set himself up for a repetition of the bitter battle that had been fought there two months before. But Roberts's tactics caught him by surprise: the British ability to move rapidly on the battlefield was quite unexpected. French, now commanding a new Cavalry Division, drove his men hard to encircle the Boers from the east, and a direct infantry assault in tandem with the cavalry attack caused the Boer morale to crumble. Kimberley was surrounded and the siege soon came to an end, with the Boer besiegers making their escape. This was not before time, because conditions in the town had become extremely unpleasant due to sickness, shelling and shortage of food. It was worst for the children and for the black workers in the diamond mines that had not been operating during the siege. But even after the fall of Kimberley the Boers never stopped resisting. De Wet, whose reputation as a commando leader in the war was to become second only to de la Rey's, attacked the main British supply train south of Kimberley, and the army lost 180 ox-drawn wagons packed with supplies. Roberts and Kitchener had been to a large degree the cause of this catastrophe because they had earlier changed the system of transporting supplies, taking the responsibility away from units and centralizing everything. This was to relieve battalions and regiments of the labour-intensive work of carrying supplies so that they could devote themselves to the fighting, but Roberts and Kitchener failed to make sure that the bulky and vulnerable accumulations of stores needed by the fighting units were well enough protected.

Roberts shrugged off this setback. Nevertheless the Boer force under Cronje's overall command got away, and French's cavalry was by now too exhausted and outnumbered for a vigorous pursuit, although they managed to shadow the Boers from a distance. The Free State general led more than 4,000 men. With them were their families and black servants, which meant that he could no longer exploit the Boers' natural advantage of mobility. The marching speed of the force was reduced to the pace of the ox-drawn wagons, and the commandos and their families plodded east, moving south of the Modder River and then crossing to the north bank at Paardeberg Hill, where they camped. They were twenty-five miles east of Kimberley and seventy-five miles short of Bloemfontein. The plum was about to fall into British hands, because they now had both larger numbers and greater speed than their antagonists.

Unfortunately, Roberts was now stricken by a distressing ailment prevalent among men who spend long hours in the saddle, haemorrhoids, and his doctors kept him in Kimberley. On 18 February the command was passed to Kitchener, whose 'grip' was a good deal less secure than Roberts's. The British were now south of the Modder, and the problem that Kitchener faced was how to advance north, forcing a crossing of the river, a difficult job because of the steepness of its banks. Even if the crossing were successful, the British troops would confront a five-mile shallow trench line manned by Boer marksmen. Kitchener, unaccompanied by any senior staff officers, ascended a hill overlooking the river, and after a quick inspection of the Boer positions through his field glasses, developed a plan virtually 'off the cuff'. In his haste he made two costly mistakes. First, he decided to attack rather than besiege the Boers. A siege would have been effective, because French's cavalry was by now well to the north-east watching the Boer camp, and it would have been virtually impossible for Cronje and his substantial force with their slow transport to escape to Bloemfontein. Kitchener's second error was to embark on a direct frontal assault, something that was to degenerate into a series of uncoordinated attacks. To the west, a brigade commanded by Brigadier General Horace Smith-Dorrien got across the river and occupied high ground, but was unable to attack from there without support from the rest of the army. Meanwhile, the other infantry attacks were bloodily repulsed. One was launched into an elbow loop in the river but was immediately assailed by fire from three sides, as had happened to Buller's infantry at Colenso. Kitchener was wrong-footed, and charged around the fringes of the battlefield in a search for an alternative plan, reportedly exhausting a number of horses through his frantic but futile activity. The day's work cost the British 1,300 casualties.

Roberts rejoined the army the next day and was not pleased by what he saw. He stopped further infantry attacks and decided to wait it out for some days, bombarding the Boer camp with all his artillery. Finally, as he had done so successfully at Kimberley, he despatched French's cavalry to encircle the Boers from the east. The British cavalry's aggressiveness together with the heavy fire of the British artillery, not to speak of the British six-to-one superiority in numbers, persuaded Cronje that further resistance would yield nothing except further loss of life. The photograph of the large and unkempt Boer leader surrendering to the diminutive but immaculate Field Marshal, and Roberts's courteous comments on his opponents' bravery, were quickly circulated throughout the world. The two commanders then had breakfast together, before Cronje and his wife were sent into exile for the rest of the war. It was 27 February – the anniversary of Majuba – and Roberts shortly afterwards marched his men on to Bloemfontein, which the Boers had by then begun to evacuate. It was not a smooth progress because of an unfortunate brush with the Boer rearguards at Poplar Grove on 7 March. In this, French's Cavalry Division was stopped in its tracks by small numbers of enemy riflemen in improvised positions and suffered 213 casualties. Bloemfontein fell on 13 March, but recriminations continued between Roberts and French, who was well known for his 'short fuse'. French's performance at Poplar Grove increased Roberts's doubts about the value of cavalry in its conventional role and fed his growing faith in mounted infantry.

Across the Veldt with the Mounted Infantry
It was Lord Roberts who, not surprisingly, had summoned Hamilton to join him. But after Roberts's devoted protégé had left the rigours of Ladysmith, he needed to build up his strength and recover from a lingering bout of typhoid. He arrived in Bloemfontein in mid-March 1900, shortly after the town had been occupied by the British, following the defeat of the Boers at Paardeberg. Hamilton was by now a local (i.e. temporary) major general and before long was promoted local lieutenant general; he was forty-seven-years of age. The challenging job he was given was to command an important but experimental formation, planned

specifically to fight the Boer commandos head-on. This was the Mounted Infantry Division, with three brigades: 2 Mounted Infantry, 2 Cavalry, and 19 Infantry, plus a substantial force of artillery.[4] The fighting strength of the Division was 11,000 men, 4,600 horses, 8,000 mules, thirty-eight cannon, and a number of machine guns. Two Mounted Infantry Brigade was composed of four regiments, each commanded by an experienced British lieutenant colonel, and the men came from Britain, South Africa, Australia, New Zealand, and British men domiciled in Ceylon and Burma. (Each individual unit was described as a mounted infantry corps, but the word regiment is a less confusing name for it.) Two Cavalry Brigade was made up of three crack Regular cavalry regiments from the British Army. And 19 Brigade comprised three British Regular battalions with a long fighting history, plus the City Imperial Volunteers (CIV). Each of the mounted infantry regiments and infantry battalions contained 1,000 men; and each cavalry regiment had 400. Altogether the Division had the makings of a formidable fighting force. The CIV comprised 1,600 men (a battalion, an artillery battery and some mounted infantry) and was raised by business firms in the City of London. It was soon to make a name for itself.

Since mounted infantry was a relatively new concept, the regiments needed time to become efficient on their own, and to deploy as parts of a brigade and as elements in turn of a larger formation. Hamilton had five weeks to do the job before the Division was on the move. Meanwhile, the British force in Bloemfontein remained in the town for six weeks. The reason for this delay was a typhoid epidemic caused by the British troops drinking water from the Modder River that had been contaminated by human and animal carcasses. The death toll was shockingly high: more than fifty men a day. There was also a serious outbreak of that malady so often associated with armies, venereal disease. To provide urgently needed medical help, many volunteer doctors, nurses, and hospital orderlies began to arrive; they included Dr Arthur Conan Doyle, by now a rich man as a result of the success of his Sherlock Holmes stories. While the hospitals and medical staff were very busily occupied, Roberts and his officers used the time to re-equip and reorganize the British force for the next phase of the advance.

The Field Marshal planned to move forward on a narrow front, following a direct route from Bloemfontein to Pretoria, relying as far as possible on the railway although it had been severed in a number of places. The distance is 300 miles, and after Pretoria, a further 200 miles to the frontier between the Transvaal and Portuguese East Africa. The main thrust would be by 65,000 men, in three columns under Roberts's overall direct command: French's Cavalry Division on the western flank, Roberts's own force of 40,000 men in the centre, and Hamilton's Mounted Infantry Division thirty miles away to the east. Five more distant independent forces also remained actively pursuing Boer commandos: three in the west and two in the east. In the west, the most distant column was directed at Mafeking, to relieve the garrison in cooperation with a northern force from Rhodesia. A nearer column was Methuen's, which was ordered to join the main advance at Kroonstad (the capital of the Free State after the loss of Bloemfontein), which was 130 miles along Roberts's main route to Pretoria. In the east, the larger of the two columns was Buller's, making its lumbering advance through Natal and eventually across the Vaal River.[5] In addition there was a strong garrison of Militia (i.e. trained reserve) battalions in the Cape Colony. In total, Roberts commanded 200,000 men, the largest British army that had ever gone to war: and five times the fighting strength of the Boers. This disparity gives some idea of the Boers' fighting prowess, and the respect in which they were held by the British.

With such a number of men under arms, leadership was of supreme importance. Roberts was ruthless in getting rid of incompetent officers. Buller and Methuen were retained under sufferance, although in effect demoted, but there was no mercy for White after the relief of Ladysmith, or Gatacre after his defeat at Stormberg. On the other hand, many of the officers whom Roberts promoted as column commanders or as staff officers went on to build outstanding careers, such as the following dozen whose names were later to become famous: Allenby, Byng, de Lisle, French, Haig, Hamilton, Hunter, Plumer, Rawlinson, Robertson, Smith-Dorrien, and Wilson. Roberts always had a fine eye for talent.

Roberts followed the well-established military principle of maintenance of the aim, the aim in this case being the direct defeat of the Boer republics. Having as he hoped defeated the Free State, his next objective was Pretoria. Although he was acutely conscious that commando attacks on his line of communication would be much worse than mosquito bites, he had to look upon this problem as of secondary importance. In the end, however, these attacks were to lead to a British response that took a number of unfortunate forms – farm burning, concentration camps and blockhouse lines – innovations that left such painful memories of the long, final guerrilla phase of the war.

Shortly after the fall of Bloemfontein, the Presidents of the two Boer republics held a council of war at Kroonstad.[6] Both leaders agreed to take steps to rally support from a number of European countries, although such endeavours were going to be more hopeful than realistic. A matter of more urgent moment was that Christiaan de Wet, Cronje's successor in command of the Free State commandos, made the decision – against the objections of his political masters – to send his men back to their homes, with the stipulation that they had to return by 25 March. This concession had two purposes: to give the men some rest after their months of hard campaigning and, perhaps more importantly, to ensure that those who returned really wanted to continue the fight. The commandos had always been plagued by men melting away to return to their farms, which after all had provided their family livelihood. Roberts had offered an amnesty to any Boers who surrendered and formally signed an oath not to take up arms against the British: a significant attraction to the faint-hearted. De Wet and the dedicated warriors who returned from their ten days' leave were not tempted by any offer of amnesty. De Wet also decided to reduce the size of the wagon trains, so that the commandos would in the future become even more mobile than before. They would be flying columns: experienced, strongly motivated, agile, and deadly behind the sights of a rifle.

On 31 March, twenty miles from Bloemfontein, de Wet's commando of 1,500 men skilfully ambushed two Royal Horse Artillery batteries at a place near the town's waterworks now called Sannas Pos (earlier known as Sanna's Post). After a vicious fight, the Boers captured 428 prisoners, 117 wagons and seven guns. On 3 April, 800 Boers who had three field guns with them, attacked a British garrison near Reddersberg. After a twenty-four hour fight the British surrendered, with the loss of 600 men, the vast majority being captured. These unfortunate episodes naturally worried senior British officers, but they did not shake Roberts's resolve. His main force began to move north on 3 May, although Hamilton's Mounted Infantry Division had begun to lead the way on 22 April. The three brigade commanders in this division were seasoned campaigners, and the commander of 19 Infantry Brigade was later to become a general of some importance. He was Brigadier General (soon to be promoted major general) Horace Smith-Dorrien, the same brigadier who had crossed the Modder early in the battle of Paardeberg.

Hamilton and Smith-Dorrien made an interesting comparison. As I have earlier emphasized, Hamilton was rather a complex man. The two occasions on which he had been recommended for the Victoria Cross say enough about his personal valour, but nothing about his personal qualities of imagination and charm. Winston Churchill, who got to know him during the advance to Pretoria, observed Hamilton's effectiveness as a decision-maker and leader 'from the saddle', and Churchill's evaluation was uncannily accurate:

> His highly nervous temperament animating what appears a frail body imparts to all his movements a kind of feverish energy. Two qualities of his mind stand forward prominently from the rest. He is a singularly good and rapid judge of character. He takes a very independent view on all subjects, sometimes with a slight bias towards or affection for their radical and democratic aspects, but never or hardly ever influenced by the set of people with whom he lives. To his strong personal charm as a companion, to his temper never ruffled or vexed either by internal irritation or the stir and contrariness of events, his friends and those who have served under him will bear witness. He has a most happy gift of expression, a fine taste in words, and an acute perception of the curious which he has preserved from his literary days.[7]

Churchill also pays tribute to Hamilton's vision and understanding of broader issues, an important point that will shortly be discussed further.

Smith-Dorrien was five years younger than Hamilton and was a more down-to-earth character: a peppery officer who nevertheless had sound judgement and robust common sense. His command of bad language made him the envy of the men in the ranks. The Second Boer War was his fifth campaign.[8] (It was Hamilton's sixth.) Unlike Hamilton, he had spent most of his service commanding troops and had few staff jobs, although he had passed through the Staff College. In 1914, when Sir John French took the British Expeditionary Force to France, his two immediate subordinates and corps commanders were Lieutenant General Haig and General Grierson. Grierson died before any shots were fired, and the War Office appointed Smith-Dorrien as his replacement, although French held a long-standing grudge against him. As a result, although Smith-Dorrien did outstanding work during the Retreat from Mons during the first month of the war and in the later fighting in 1914, French found an excuse to sack him in May 1915. Like General White, defender of Ladysmith, Smith-Dorrien's last appointment was as Governor of Gibraltar. His judgement was certainly sound enough to carry conviction in his appraisal of Hamilton in South Africa when 19 Brigade became part of the Mounted Infantry Division:

> From now on I enjoyed every moment of the campaign. He was a delightful leader to follow, always definite and clear in his instructions, always ready to listen and willing to adopt suggestions, and, what is more important, always ready to go for the enemy and extremely quick at seizing a tactical advantage, and, with it all, always in a good temper.[9]

This makes an interesting comparison with Churchill's measure of Hamilton, quoted above. Churchill's judgement of Hamilton's personality is persuasive, as is Smith-Dorrien's view of his tactical ability and his way of doing business on the battlefield: they were both based on *direct personal experience*. Churchill was also positive about Hamilton's breadth of vision – his ability to think in strategic terms – although this is something that must have come from no more than the conversations they had, since Hamilton was not involved in broad military policy, which was the exclusive concern of Roberts and Kitchener. The point that was relevant to Hamilton's future was whether he was more than an effective tactician. Was his ceiling higher than the command of a division? When in 1915 Churchill gave the nod to Kitchener's decision to appoint Hamilton to lead the Dardanelles Expedition, both Kitchener and

Churchill must have been persuaded that Hamilton had the vision needed by a man who was to hold an important politico-military appointment. Were they right? This is why Chapters 8 and 9 will devote attention to scrutinizing Hamilton's career between the end of the Second Boer War and 1915, for indications that he possessed the broad intellectual capacity needed for a commander to be successful in the big job he was given to assault the Dardanelles.

The British army that advanced from Bloemfontein was not a juggernaut, but it was strong, flexible, confident, and well-led.[10] The Mounted Infantry Division operated aggressively on the right flank, and on occasion during the march it ranged outwards toward the east in search of the commandos. During the first phase of the advance, the 130 miles to Kroonstad, Hamilton 'bumped' the enemy on four occasions. The most serious of these was the action at the Sand River on 10 May, where the Boers holding a hill in some strength were attacked frontally by the infantry and encircled by the cavalry around the Boers' right flank. This and the other sharp encounters did not impede the Division's progress, and they caused far fewer casualties than the British had suffered at Boer hands in earlier engagements. The army reached Kroonstad on 16 May, and stopped for a few days to replenish supplies and wait for damage to the railway line from Bloemfontein to be repaired.

The Mounted Infantry Division was moving forward again on 22 May. In the valley town of Heilbron they found the enemy, but for once the Boers were too exhausted to strike first. The commando was made up of 1,000 weary men, five guns and – surprisingly, in view of de Wet's decision to travel light – sixty wagons. They had arrived just before the British and were promptly shelled and directly attacked, with Hamilton as usual in the middle of the action. The Boers got away, but Hamilton's men captured fifteen wagons and seventeen prisoners, suffering no casualties. The fortunes of war were beginning to move in the British direction.

The next engagement, at Doornkop, was to be of greater strategic importance.[11] On 24 May, the Mounted Infantry Division was ordered to move from the right to the left flank of the British army, and Hamilton started working with French and his Cavalry Division, a co-operation that had been so successful at Elandslaagte. On 26 May, Hamilton and French crossed the Vaal to enter the Transvaal, where President Kruger was still running his government. After the Division spent twenty-four-hours bringing supplies up to the troops:

> Forward again. That day Hamilton marched his men 18 miles – ('10 miles', say the text-books on war, 'is a good march for a division with baggage', and our force, carrying its own supplies, had ten times the baggage of a European division!) – and succeeded besides in dragging his weary transport with him.[12]

Hamilton's and French's Divisions were now approaching the Rand and were about to encounter the last Boer defensive line before Johannesburg, the centre of the gold-mining industry. This was the cauldron in which the antipathy between the Boers and the *uitlanders* had been fermented and which had been the basic cause of the war. By this time 21 Infantry Brigade had joined Hamilton's force. It was commanded by a namesake, Major General Bruce Hamilton, whose father had been the redoubtable 'Tiger' Hamilton, the Commanding Officer of the 12th (Suffolk) Regiment which Ian Hamilton had joined from Sandhurst. The two infantry brigades were now formed into a division under Smith-Dorrien, although Hamilton remained in overall command.

Eight miles west of Johannesburg, 8,000 Boers were located occupying one of the ridges of the Rand running east to west, parallel to and just south of the railway, at the town of Florida. At the western end of this ridge is a hill called Doornkop, which was to give its name to the battle. French (who was the senior) and Hamilton worked out a plan for an assault to go in on the afternoon of 29 May.[13] They ordered a direct infantry attack from the south by Smith-Dorrien's newly-formed Division, with heavy artillery support, while French's cavalry and 2 Cavalry Brigade (from Hamilton's own division) were to sweep around the left of Doornkop and envelop the Boers' right flank. The British had by now learned lessons about effective infantry tactics against Boer sharpshooters, and the men were well spread out – covering a distance of almost two miles per brigade, or half a mile per battalion – and making as much use as they could of the broken rocky ground. Bruce Hamilton on the left had to take great care to keep his men in touch with Smith-Dorrien's on his right, so as to maintain a continuous infantry line. Smith-Dorrien hit the strongest opposition. The ground was found to be less steep than had appeared from a distance, but the grass in front of the Boer positions had been burned black, so that the khaki uniforms of the British made them easy targets. Despite losing 250 men killed and wounded, the British infantry carried the day; French's cavalry made little contribution. The way was now clear for the advance to Johannesburg.

It was still a 'Gentlemen's War', and Ian Hamilton had a friendly conversation with a group of Boer prisoners, one of whom had besieged Ladysmith. He said that his comrades should have attacked the *Platrand* – Hamilton's own sector of the defensive perimeter – earlier than they did, but had been restrained by their cautious commander. This was an excellent analysis and we do not know how Hamilton responded to it. A poignant feature of the Battle of Doornkop was the loss, on the British right, of ninety-seven men of the 1st Gordon Highlanders, almost forty per cent of the total British casualty roll. Hamilton addressed the Gordons in a touching speech, describing his personal connection with the Regiment. The funeral of their dead was marked by the heart-rending pipe music 'The Flowers of the Forest', something played only too often in Highland regiments.

The occupation of Johannesburg was a virtual walkover, but this was not quite the case with Pretoria.[14] The British army remained in Johannesburg for two days to wait for a minimal quantity of supplies, and on 3 June began a fifty-mile march north to Pretoria. There was Boer opposition in the outskirts of the town, but cavalry and mounted infantry moved against it, and the defenders also received a good deal of attention from the British artillery. Late on 4 June all resistance stopped. The next day, after a train crammed with Boer fighters and their horses had steamed eastward under the frustrated eyes of the British, Roberts formally took over the town and liberated the 3,000 British prisoners of war who had been held in and around it. A grand military procession followed; it lasted for three hours, undoubtedly impressing the inhabitants. President Kruger had gone away some days before, together with gold from the republic's treasury valued at a million pounds sterling, and established himself in the small town of Machadodorp, 140 miles east of Pretoria. He eventually made his way to Europe, and never returned. He died in Switzerland in

1904. Roberts had taken a substantial risk in pressing on so hard with limited supplies, having assumed that Johannesburg and Pretoria would fall quickly. But he had benefited from the psychological advantage of his virtually uninterrupted advance from Cape Town, and he and Kitchener might have been forgiven for thinking that the war was over.

One immediate problem was that the British occupation of Pretoria did not mean the surrender of the Boer commandos, and there were 7,000 men from the Transvaal still at large. Although Louis Botha, one of the two most important Boer leaders, made a tentative approach to discuss peace terms, this approach was soon halted when news arrived of the aggressive and successful activity of de Wet and his men from the Free State (described below.)[15] Roberts therefore made a quick decision to go after the Transvaal commandos and led three divisions east along the railway leading to Portuguese East Africa. The 'sharp end 'of the British army was by now seriously under-strength because of the need to garrison the conquered territory and also because of casualties from sickness and enemy action. The divisions that Roberts now led towards the enemy totalled only 16,000 men, barely half their nominal strength.

On 11 January 1900, about twenty miles from Pretoria, the British hit a force of 5,000 Boers occupying a group of steep hills running north to south and straddling the railway. The feature immediately south of the railway is called Diamond Hill, because of a large gemstone that had supposedly once been found there. Roberts planned to encircle the Boer position, with French's Cavalry Division moving around from the north; Hamilton's mounted infantry in the south sweeping well beyond the hill; and with the 11th Infantry Division advancing in the centre, just south of the railway. But the Boers reacted strongly to the British moves, and Hamilton was forced to attack Diamond Hill directly from the south. His men were well spread out and used natural cover, but they were only partially successful. Although a number of Boers fled, a further effort was going to be needed the next day to finish the job. The next morning, Hamilton was unfortunately put out of commission by a serious bruise on his shoulder from a hit from an enemy shrapnel ball. At this time, Churchill, officially a civilian, played a small but dramatic part in the battle.

The young war correspondent managed to swarm up the south face of the hill on his own and occupy a crevice where he was unseen by the Boers at the top. From there he signalled to Hamilton's men with his handkerchief tied to the end of his stick.[16] Whether or not Churchill's signal helped guide the attackers forward, they soon got to the plateau at the top of the hill, and were accompanied by some field guns, and also shortly afterwards by Hamilton himself. The British and Boers faced one another from a distance of a mile, but the outnumbered Boers soon decided to use the cover of night to withdraw. On 13 January Hamilton's men went after them and occupied the railway station at Elandsfontein. The battle was now at an end, at the cost of 180 British casualties. It was an indecisive affair, and after three days of rest and reorganization, Hamilton's Division was off as a flying column in the pursuit of various elusive Boers. This was to be how the British were now going to conduct the war, with the Boer commandos making their presence felt in individual places across the broad swathe of the country, and the British responding, often too late. In these circumstances a British victory was going to be a prolonged and painful process.

The Second Phase of the War: A Double Degeneration
At the time when Roberts's army seemed close to victory in the Transvaal, the Free State was unexpectedly exploding into a new surge of Boer activity. The aggressive, strongly-motivated Free State commandos now had a strength of about 8,000, under the leadership of skilful men, the most important of whom was Christiaan de Wet. In such a large country, and with mobility limited to the speed of a horse, the commando raiders were always going to possess an advantage, because when news of their actions had been received by the British, the pursuers were nearly always going to be too late to catch their quarry. Thus, at a purely tactical level, the war was about to degenerate into a hit-and-run affair with no decisive military conclusion. Degeneration was soon however to carry a more sinister meaning. Roberts's and later Kitchener's response to the Boers' aggressiveness – the British Army's system of burning Boer farms and putting women and children in concentration camps – was seen before long by many observers in South Africa and Europe, including in Britain, as a morally deplorable development. It had the echo of the 'Highland

Clearances' of eighteenth century Scotland. However, it is difficult to think of an alternative policy that would have coped with the exceptionally difficult circumstances in South Africa. Nevertheless, the British generals deserve the harshest blame for allowing the camps to be run with such gross inefficiency.

The British army had crossed the Vaal River on 27 May and annexed the Free State the next day, renaming it the Orange River Colony.[17] The immediate response of the Free State commandos was three astonishingly successful raids on the newly established British military posts between Kroonstad and the Vaal. On 4 June, Christiaan de Wet, with only 800 men and a handful of supplies, ambushed and plundered a British convoy at Heilbron. Then on 6 June, at Roodewal, he repeated the treatment on a larger scale, defeating in the process a whole British battalion. Even before these actions, Christiaan de Wet's brother Piet had carried out a raid at Lindley. Here he surrounded and captured an entire British yeomanry regiment composed of officers and men from the upper crust of Irish society. This caused both distress and glee in Ireland, which had always been a divided society. These three raids netted a bag of more than 1,000 British troops and mountains of supplies. The Boer losses were negligible, and the Boer morale was immensely boosted.

After Roberts and Kitchener had finished their business at Pretoria and Diamond Hill, which they hoped would write finis to the war, they turned to the local troubles in the Orange River Colony. Their plan, which was constructed ad hoc and rather precipitately, was to organize a number of columns, each made up of 2,000 to 4,000 men, with the job of sweeping the veldt in search of the enemy. Hamilton commanded one of these; he was unlucky and in fact fooled on one occasion, which will be described below. The only force – a very substantial one – that fulfilled expectations was a group of five columns under the overall command of Lieutenant General Hunter, one of the few officers who had emerged from Ladysmith with an enhanced reputation.

Hunter's success came in the mountains to the east of the Orange River Colony, a chain abutting the frontier with the neutral native state of Basutoland.[18] A triangle of mountains encloses a saucer also triangular in shape, with each side about ten miles long and the small town of Fouriesburg in the middle of it. The saucer is called the Brandwater Basin, and within it Hunter's men cornered a very substantial force from the Orange River Colony, including President Steyn (former ruler of the Free State) and Christiaan de Wet. The Boers immediately saw their danger and prepared for a siege, although 1,800 men escaped, led not unexpectedly by de Wet accompanied by the former President. Six wagon tracks led through the mountains into the Basin, and Hunter mustered enough strength to force five of these (taking the calculated risk, which paid off, to leave the sixth one uncovered). The British had a good deal of artillery and Hunter's aggressiveness closed the trap, after a number of sticky close-quarter firefights in the cold winter weather. On 29 July the Boers laid down their arms, at a place later and appropriately called Surrender Hill; 4,300 prisoners came into British hands, a larger haul than Roberts had collected at Paardeberg. Hunter's casualties totalled 275 men, mostly wounded; for once the disparity between the losses suffered by the two sides very much favoured the British. By 10 August Hunter was on his way north to continue making (unfortunately abortive) sweeps against the elusive enemy.

De Wet's next coup was a defensive one, but in its way quite remarkable. On 18 August, he was leading his commando of 250 men and had been harried by British columns into the Transvaal. His only refuge would be to return to the Orange River Colony, but he faced a serious problem, the Magaliesberg, a forty-mile stretch of mountains that runs west from Pretoria before bending slightly north. He could have crossed this mountain range through one of a number of passes, but they had of course all been blocked by the British. Hamilton's column was positioned at the entrance to the largest of these passes, the Olifant's Nek. Undeterred, de Wet saw a route of escape: up the nearest mountain itself. He stopped at a native hut and spoke to its black inhabitant, a 'Kaffir' (not a politically incorrect word to use in 1900), and pointed to the mountain. The rest of the story is told by de Wet himself:

> 'Right before us, can a man cross there?' 'No, baas, you cannot!' the Kaffir answered. 'Has a man never ridden across here?' 'Yes, baas,' replied the Kaffir, 'long ago.' 'Do baboons walk across?' 'Yes, baboons do, but not a man.' 'Come on!' I said to my burghers. 'This is our only way, and where a baboon can cross, we can cross.' With us was one, Adriaan Matthijsen, a corporal who came from

the district of Bethlehem, and was a sort of jocular character. He looked up at the mountains, 2,000 feet above him, and sighed: 'O Red Sea!'[19]

The British who were blocking the passes were left frustrated and de Wet was to continue to be a source of irritation to his opponents for the rest of the war.

The occupation of Pretoria did not give Roberts and Kitchener their eagerly expected victory, and the commandos, as slippery and enterprising as ever, continued to keep it from their grasp. This caused a hardening of British attitudes, and the war entered a dark phase that was to last until its conclusion in May 1902. The British generals began to instruct their men to burn the farms and dispossess the families of the Boers who were still fighting, and also to destroy their possessions and kill their livestock. This policy was reminiscent of the village burning used with few scruples but considerable effectiveness as a means of subduing rebellious tribes on the North-West Frontier of India.[20] By this time, Buller had at last advanced through Natal into the Transvaal, and on 27 August he fought a successful battle at Belfast, 100 miles east of Pretoria. Part of Roberts's main force participated in this battle, since the Field Marshal was now advancing to the frontier of Portuguese East Africa, more than100 miles beyond Belfast. It was at Belfast that Roberts and Kitchener formally decided on the policy of farm-burning, although it had occasionally been carried out before then, in particular by Hunter during his advance to the Brandwater Basin.

Although most British officers viewed the 'scorched earth' policy as militarily necessary, Hamilton kept his hands clean: 'To burn a farm or a haystack is, according to my ethics, utterly heathen and damnable. I never authorized such an act, and I'd sooner have stood a Court Martial than do so.'[21]Anyway the farm-burning was to a large extent counter-productive. With their homes nothing but burnt shells, which meant that they had nowhere to return to, the Boers fighting in the commandos had an extra reason to continue the struggle. Indeed, the British policy increased the Boers' determination to resist, just as the devastation of German cities from the aerial bombing during the Second World War had a corresponding effect.

When the Boer women and children lost their homes, the British army was forced to take responsibility for looking after them. This was the reason for the setting up of concentration camps (as they were to be named after the war). There were eventually forty-six such camps, housing more than 93,000 whites and 24,000 blacks. On the surface they appeared to be well-ordered establishments, with neat lines of tents and each camp supervised by British army doctors and nurses. They were, however, run with hideous incompetence, with inadequate food and even worse healthcare. The inevitable outcomes were general under-nourishment, widespread disease, and a toll of premature deaths. During the 1930s the phrase 'concentration camps' was adopted in Nazi Germany to describe the villages of insanitary wooden barracks surrounded by barbed wire and policed by armed men who were light on the trigger, where Jews and other 'undesirables' were sent to be worked to death and huge numbers eventually murdered. Although the British concentration camps were a disgrace and deserved the condemnation they received, they could not be compared in horror with the German ones.

Roberts left South Africa at the end of 1900 and handed over command to Kitchener on 29 November. Kitchener relied more heavily than his predecessor on the farm-burning and concentration camps. The old Field Marshal returned a hero, after successfully winning the war (in the opinion of most British people, although very few Boers agreed). He received the thanks of a grateful nation and a cash award of £100,000 (worth at least £5,000,000 or $8,000,000 in today's money). He was appointed to the Horse Guards to replace Lord Wolseley as Commander-in-Chief of the British Army, an anachronistic job that was abolished in 1904 as part of a programme of army reform. Hamilton received a knighthood and the permanent rank of major general and went back with Roberts as his Military Secretary, although he was to return in October 1901 to become Chief of Staff to Lord Kitchener. By then the emphasis of the British army was on the building and manning of blockhouses, an appropriate policy for an officer like Kitchener who had started his career as a Royal Engineer. These were set up to watch for marauding commandos and restrict their movement, and were built along railways and eventually in lines across the country.

The blockhouses were primitive structures built to hold up to a dozen sweating soldiers. Most were constructed of corrugated iron but some were made from stone blocks; and although they were not meant to last, a few still stand today. They were uncomfortable because the corrugated iron was baked by the South African sun. However, they were eminently practicable, and over time they were extended across the veldt at intervals of up to a mile, with adjacent blockhouses in sight of one another and connected with thin wire; surprisingly this wire was effective in stopping a horse.[22] This cumbrous system managed to corral the commandos by fencing them into enormous open areas where they could in due course be mopped up by columns of mounted infantry. The first blockhouses were built as early as January 1901. A large number had been thrown up by October, when 10,000 square miles in the Transvaal and northern Orange River Colony and 4,200 square miles around Bloemfontein had been declared 'protected areas'. This was only the beginning. By the end of the war there were 8,000 blockhouses guarded by 50,000 white troops and 16,000 African scouts. Although de Wet believed that the value of the blockhouses did not justify the effort and cost of putting them up, this system slowly worked. By October 1901, 2,000 commandos were being rounded up every month. At the same time Kitchener boosted the number of his troops by arming 10,000 black Africans, a development that horrified the Boers. And at long last he realized the folly of the concentration camps and ordered that the dispossessed families should be left to be cared for by the commandos.

The British were getting the upper hand when Ian Hamilton returned to Pretoria in October 1901, as Kitchener's Chief of Staff. Ninety columns were now roaming the country, and the blockhouse network was confining the commandos to narrower and narrower areas in which they could operate. The numbers of fighting Boers were dwindling although their spirit remained as strong as ever, something that made them such formidable opponents. As Chief of Staff, Hamilton was a square peg in a round hole, although Kitchener welcomed him 'as a hero-worshipping friend, whose sensitiveness, refinement and charm satisfied a craving in his nature'.[23] But Kitchener had no use for a Chief of Staff. He carried everything in his head. This had potentially dangerous consequences, as had been apparent at Paardeberg, and was later to be during the First World War.

At Pretoria, the military command system seemed to be working on its own; everything was determined on the spot without informed and thoughtful discussions of alternative courses of action. At 0530 hours every morning, some junior staff officers marked a large map with information on the movements of the various columns, and others would arrange the telegrams that had come in, to be scrutinized and acted on by the Commander-in-Chief. Then the Military Secretary would write down brief instructions to the various columns and departments, at Kitchener's dictation.[24] In this way Kitchener carried out both jobs of developing and executing his plans, an unusual and rather dangerous way of conducting a war.

And so the conflict wound down. The Boers, exhausted but unbroken, agreed to peace terms that offered a promise of self-government in the future. These were approved by a majority vote, and the statesmanship of Louis Botha led the country before too long on a prosperous path. However, the recalcitrant de Wet was only temporarily satisfied, and he was to lead a rebellion in 1914 when the British went to war with Germany. In early April Hamilton had been given the command of a number of columns in the field. But he was back with Kitchener at the end of May and participated at the Peace Conference. Since he then considered himself eligible for a brief rest, he returned to Britain via Japan and the United States. He was slated for a senior staff appointment on his return to London.

Notes

1 Rayne Kruger, *Goodbye Dolly Gray* (Philadelphia &New York: Lippincott, 1960), pp.121–4; also Thomas Pakenham, *The Boer War* (London: Weidenfeld & Nicolson, 1979) , pp.193–200, 201–6.
2 Tabitha Jackson, *The Boer War* (London: Macmillan – Channel 4 Books, 1999), pp.85–91.
3 Winston Churchill, *The Boer War: Ian Hamilton's March* (Norwalk, CT: The Easton Press, 2007), p.26. (Churchill's book was originally published in 1900.)
4 Ibid., pp.177–80.
5 David James, *Lord Roberts* (London: Hollis and Carter, 1954), pp.315–20.
6 Pakenham, *The Boer War*, pp.386–95.
7 Churchill, *The Boer War: Ian Hamilton's March*, p.68.

8 Brigadier General C. Ballard, *Smith-Dorrien* (London: Constable, 1931), pp.ix–x.
9 General Sir Horace Smith-Dorrien, *Memories of Forty-Eight Years' Service* (London: John Murray, 1925), p.182.
10 Churchill, *The Boer War: Ian Hamilton's March*, pp.91–101.
11 Ibid., pp.102–7.
12 Ibid., pp.108–9.
13 Ibid., pp.109–17; also Smith-Dorrien, *Memories of Forty-Eight Years Service*, pp.205–10.
14 Churchill, *The Boer War: Ian Hamilton's March*. pp.129–34.
15 Ibid., pp.164–75.
16 General Sir Ian Hamilton, *Listening for the Drums* (London: Faber& Faber, 1944), p.248.
17 Pakenham, *The Boer War*, pp.434–7.
18 Ibid., pp.438–45; also Archie Hunter, *Kitchener's Sword-Arm: The Life and Campaigns of General Sir Archibald Hunter* (New York: Sarpedon, 1996), pp.150–68.
19 Christiaan Rudolf de Wet, *The Three Years War* (London: Archibald, Constable, 1902), p.187.
20 Pakenham, *The Boer War*, pp.440–1, 493–5, 509–10, 548.
21 Victor Sampson and Ian Hamilton, *Anti-Commando* (London: Faber & Faber, 1931), p.27.
22 Pakenham, *The Boer War*, pp.536–7, 546–7.
23 Philip Magnus, *Kitchener, Portrait of an Imperialist* (London: John Murray, 1958), p.182.
24 Sir Ian Hamilton, *The Commander* (Major Anthony Farrar-Hockley, ed.) (London: Hollis & Carter, 1957), p.101.

CHAPTER 8

Observer of a Distant War

Lord Roberts returned to England on 2 January 1901 and received a tumultuous reception from the Royal family, the Government and the British population.[1] He soon afterwards started his new job as Commander-in-Chief of the Army, an official recognition of the position he had earned as Britain's number one soldier. Hamilton had accompanied his old chief, and now became his Military Secretary. This meant that he was his senior confidential assistant as well as the staff officer who played an important role in arranging officers' appointments throughout the Army.

The office of Commander-in-Chief of the British Army was not at this time as powerful as that in the Indian Army, although the Indian Army was smaller and its operations were restricted to the sub-continent and southern Asia. The responsibility of the Commander-in-Chief in Britain had been gradually eroded during the years of Queen Victoria's reign, when her cousin the Duke of Cambridge – whose whiskers the infant Ian Hamilton had tweaked – was Commander-in-Chief for thirty-nine years ending in 1895, a period of profound and continuous resistance to change. He was a figure who might have come out of Gilbert and Sullivan and once said 'I don't believe in brains'. It is not surprising that the Army suffered painful failings at home and abroad, and the decline in the importance of the Commander-in-Chief of the Army was accompanied by a growth in the influence of the political head, the Secretary of State for War, which meant continued tension between the top man in the Army and the senior politician in overall control. Reorganization continued during Roberts's time at the War Office, and this was to reach an inevitable conclusion when the office of Commander-in-Chief was abolished in 1904. In a democracy, politicians are generally the winners.

Before Roberts's arrival at the War Office, a scheme had been set up to divide the country into six separate military districts, called commands, each comprising an Army Corps of three divisions, which were nominal rather than real because the divisions were invariably under-strength. Two of these corps formed the foundation of the British Expeditionary Force (BEF) that went to France in 1914. In 1905, Hamilton was himself to be appointed General Officer Commanding one of these districts, Southern Command.

Further reforms followed immediately after Roberts's arrival, and he was as energetic a reformer as he had been in India decades before. His new programme of reforms introduced improved weapons for the infantry, cavalry and artillery; more efficient transport; simpler and more serviceable uniforms throughout the Army; and advances in military education and training. Most importantly, the life of the men in the ranks was made more comfortable and rewarding, with better barracks and canteens where soldiers could spend their free time. While all these reforms were in progress, Roberts conducted large-scale military exercises, and personally spent as much time as he had always done in inspecting garrisons and making his presence felt by the men in the ranks.

As mentioned in Chapter 7, Hamilton returned to South Africa in November 1901 as Chief of Staff to Kitchener; this was not a very fruitful period in his career. Then, for a couple of months at the end of the war, he commanded a splendid force of 17,000 men organized in sixteen mounted columns that took a leading part in sweeping back the last of the Boer commandos. The war ended in May 1902, and in July he was back in London and rejoined Roberts, as a lieutenant general (three stars in modern terminology).

In September, he accompanied Roberts and French to the annual manoeuvres of the German Army, an experience that was to provide lessons for the future, particularly for French, who was to be given the job of commanding the BEF. Despite the formidable reputation of the Germany Army, Roberts and the two generals did not gain a high opinion of German 'drill, tactics, dress and equipment'. [2] The Japanese Army was closely modelled on the German Army, so that the German deficiencies should also have applied to the Japanese. But this was certainly not the case. In 1904 (as will be recounted), Hamilton saw the Japanese Army in action and he was greatly impressed by all aspects of it. But this experience did not make him feel any less negative about the German Army.

Hamilton, who still spoke the German language well, returned to Germany to observe manoeuvres in 1906 and 1909. His focus was on the tactics employed, and in 1906 he was critical of the German reliance on detailed planning, which seemed to him to restrict individual initiative:

> I also enlarged on the defects of the qualities of forethought and preparation, pointing out that where everything was always perfectly prearranged, sterilization of the virtue of initiative might ensue. Few Germans are capable of improvising anything on the spur of the moment.[3]

Hamilton's strictures help explain the ad hoc nature of the preparations for the Gallipoli expedition, a hastiness that was driven by a lack of dedication by Hamilton and his staff to rigorous planning, as well as by indifferent military intelligence and time pressure. It is strange that Hamilton's conclusions about the German Army seem to contradict the experience of the Russo-Japanese war – a Japanese success substantially based on meticulous strategic preparation – in contrast to the Russian failure, which was the outcome of improvisation, in particular the Russian attempts at response to the aggressive and meticulously planned moves by the Japanese.

In 1903 Hamilton was promoted to Quartermaster General, although this appointment prompted a question in the House of Commons by a Scottish member who saw it as an example of favouritism on behalf of a leading member of the Roberts Ring. But Roberts's position was too strong for him to be fazed by the criticism. Hamilton, at the age of fifty, was now one of the senior officers who had the future of the British Army in their hands: an appointment that had been due to his long and faithful service to Lord Roberts in India, and his brief but impressive performance in the field in South Africa.

One of his significant contributions during his time as Quartermaster

General was his testimony before the Commission on the War in South Africa, which met between October 1902 and July 1903. He also sent a long memorandum that was sceptical about the value of cavalry except as mounted infantry. In common with many other successful leaders in South Africa, he saw no future value in cavalry armed only with cold steel, an opinion that did not greatly please French and Haig, who were dyed-in-the-wool cavalrymen. But significantly, the cavalry soldiers who went to France in 1914 as part of the BEF were armed with the same Short Magazine Lee-Enfield rifles that were used by the infantry, and during the First Battle of Ypres, the soldiers in the cavalry regiments fought very effectively in a static role in the trenches.

Serving in London appealed greatly to Hamilton and his wife, after the long years he had spent overseas. But he retained his sense of adventure, and a unique opportunity came his way in early 1904. His appointment as Quartermaster General expired at the end of January, and at this very time a war was about to break out in the Far East between Russia and Japan. Britain and Japan had signed a treaty of alliance in 1902, and a senior British officer was to be accredited to the Japanese Army for a year as an observer. This seemed an entirely appropriate appointment for Hamilton. The changes in the War Office (discussed below) produced problems, and it was left to Lord Roberts to recommend Hamilton for the job, but as a representative of the Indian Army rather than the British Army, and when he joined the Japanese he sent his official despatches to India. This arrangement was only fixed after Hamilton had already embarked on his journey: at his own expense.[4] The Russo-Japanese War was to be an experience even more pregnant with lessons than the German manoeuvres two years before. The time that he spent with the Japanese Army in Manchuria is the main concern of this chapter. When he returned to the War Office from the Far East in 1905, Roberts had gone, and so had the office of Commander-in-Chief.

Following the extremely negative report of the Commission on the War in South Africa, a heavyweight three-man committee was set up under Lord Esher. It was charged with pointing the way to future action and worked with total dedication. It reported in early 1904 and recommended a complete reorganization of the War Office. An Army Staff was established, which was something that Roberts had always wanted but had been unable to set up. A new Army Council of seven men – three civilians and four senior officers – was appointed to run the affairs of the Army. The Chief of the General Staff, later named Chief of the Imperial General Staff (CIGS), would become the Government's main military adviser and conduit of instructions from the Government to the Army. These measures meant that the British Army would be better prepared for war in 1914 than it had been in 1899.

The First Large Twentieth Century War

The Russo-Japanese War was fought essentially for the control of Port Arthur, the naval base at the extreme south-west tip of Manchuria. Because of Port Arthur, Southern Manchuria was to be the seat of the war. The Korean Peninsula projects south from Manchuria and separates the Korea Bay (part of the Yellow Sea) to the west, and the Sea of Japan to the east, bodies of water that were to witness two mighty naval battles – and Japanese victories – between the Russian and Japanese fleets. These navies may have been evenly matched in size, but Japanese leadership was far superior.

The name of the Chinese province of Manchuria came from the Imperial Manchu Dynasty, the Qing Dynasty. The province was shaped like an enormous chevron pointing east, following the frontiers as they existed in 1904. The left or northern arm was 900 miles from west to east; and the right or southern arm was the same length, and stretched from Port Arthur in the south-east to the eastern tip of the province. The area between the two arms of the chevron enclosed the Gobi Desert of Mongolia. From the extreme north of Manchuria to its southern coast on the Korea Bay, the distance was more than 1,000 miles.

It is a large province, but one that at the time of the war was sparsely populated, the local tribes numbering only about twelve million people. Manchuria is an attractive place, with conical mountains and hills covered in evergreen trees and separated by numerous valleys, with rivers and swamps full of fish. The lowlands were at the time meticulously cultivated by peasant farmers who grew millet grass for fodder, and a variety of vegetables. The millet had some tactical importance in the fighting because it grew high enough to conceal Japanese infantry, who were on average not much more than five feet three inches tall. The glades and uncultivated land are made beautiful in summer by a wealth of wild flowers like those that also grow in Europe. Manchuria, which is on the same latitude as southern Europe and the northern United States, is hot and often very rainy in the summer, and in the winter months cold, wet and snowy. Because of the mountainous terrain it is a country easier to defend than attack, despite the large amount of space for manoeuvre. During the course of the war the Russians were the defenders and the Japanese the attackers, but the Japanese nevertheless won all the battles, because they planned their strategy with great care to ensure local superiority, and also because the Japanese troops were agile enough to swarm over the mountains and ravines. Hamilton described a flanking attack by a Japanese regiment at the Battle of Chaotao on 19 July 1904 that succeeded to perfection despite a precipitous terrain that would have proved impossible for European soldiers.[5]

Port Arthur was enormously important to Russia because it was ice-free, unlike Vladivostok, the major Pacific port on the east coast of the gigantic province of Siberia. During the latter part of the nineteenth century, Russia began to encroach on Manchuria and managed to seize Port Arthur, which had been in the hands of the Japanese until international pressure forced them to evacuate it in 1895. Although Russia had increasing ambitions, these were supported by less power than appeared at first glance. The Russian Empire had the advantages of a population of 150 million, four and a half million trained soldiers who could be mobilized for a major war, and a country that occupied one-sixth of the world's land mass, but there were cracks in the foundations: massive inequality, a ruling house whose arbitrary power was widely resented, political instability, and tensions between the social classes that were to lead to revolutions in 1905 and 1917. Directly relevant to the Russian position in Manchuria was the difficult situation of the troops sent to the province, soldiers who had to be sustained by the single-track Trans-Siberian Railway. This was a line 5,800 miles long from Moscow to Vladivostok that for long periods of the year carried only three trains a week. The Russian forces in Manchuria were on a limb and generally short of supplies. The original line cut across Manchuria, and a 400-mile branch was built to connect it with Port Arthur in the south-west. This was to be Russia's artery during the whole of the war that broke out in 1904.

134

While Russia was making moves in Manchuria Japan had successfully encroached on Korea which, like Manchuria, had been a Chinese province. The southern tip of Korea is 150 miles across the sea from Japan, which makes Korea the only reliable route for transporting men and supplies from Japan to the Asian mainland. Japan's generals planned to make Korea their main base in the war that was on the horizon. They foresaw this war because Russia's eastward expansion was threatening Korea, something that gradually drove Japan toward a confrontation, a process that started with diplomatic protests and eventually led to military action. Japan made repeated diplomatic approaches to St Petersburg, but these negotiations – which embraced *ten* draft treaties between August 1903 and February 1904 – were all abortive. Talks were finally broken off on 6 February 1904. On this date, the Japanese Army and Navy sprang immediately out of the starting gate, in the same way as they were to do on 7 December 1941. The Japanese forces were as well prepared for war in 1904 as they were to be in 1941, and on both occasions their antagonists were not. In 1904–05, the Japanese retained the initiative for the whole course of the war, and this was the key reason for their successes in battle. But in the Second World War, the distances were greater and the conflict more prolonged, and this allowed time for the sleeping American giant to wake up and mobilize its unparalleled resources.

How did Japan – this little-known and isolated group of islands in the north Pacific – develop into such a powerful, skilled and ambitious nation? Following the arrival of Commodore Perry in Tokyo Bay in 1853, the Japanese began immediately to Westernize. The autocratic and centralized government of the country drove the process forward, and the speed and success of this were to be among the most striking phenomena of nineteenth century history. An early and very important step on the path to modernization was the creation of an army and a navy based on European models. For their army, the Japanese went to the countries they considered to have the strongest armies in the world, France and Germany. The Germans were to exert the stronger influence on Japanese strategy, tactics, and military organization (even uniforms), and followers of Germany in the Japanese Army became known as 'Kaisermen' or 'High-Korrar' (in Japanese English a description of the high-collar uniforms of German Army officers).[6] Japan went to Britain for guidance from the Royal Navy, universally recognized as the pre-eminent naval force in the world.

The Japanese did not copy their European guides slavishly. The First World War was to demonstrate that the French and German Armies and the Royal Navy all had major flaws. The Japanese were clever enough to learn at an early stage how to model themselves on foreign strengths while avoiding weaknesses: 'It is only in the close and eager application of copying that we light upon the shortcomings of our models.'[7] Very importantly, the Japanese military leadership recognized the superiority of the raw material of its Army. The soldiers in the ranks were tough, self-reliant peasants imbued with a strong military spirit:

> We can turn a Japanese peasant into a first-class soldier in three weeks, and the Germans cannot make their pudding-headed yokels into soldiers under three years.[8]

The Japanese logistical 'tail' was organized on Oriental lines, using a system whose effectiveness was soon to be demonstrated in Manchuria. The Japanese Army was recruited by conscription, and the way the system recruited coolies made for efficiency not only at the 'sharp end' of battle but also in the long and tenuous line of communication.

By the late 1870s the Japanese Army was firmly established on Western lines, with a comprehensive system of educating officers, despatching at least ten picked men abroad every year to learn the military practices of the French and German armies. The soldiers in the ranks, conscripted for three years with a later period in reserve service, were carefully divided into two groups. Only the best men were selected to be front-line warriors, and these were intensively trained. In the 1880s recruits for the fighting units were universally illiterate; by 1904 they could all read and the majority could also write.[9] The rest of the recruits became military coolies, or uniformed labourers. They did not feel in any way inferior. Being soldiers in uniform, they considered they were following an honourable calling.[10] At the beginning of the Russo-Japanese War, Japan could put in the field 270,000 front-line troops, plus 200,000 military coolies. The coolies played a vital logistical role, working in cooperation with locally-recruited coolies from Korea and Manchuria. A typical example of the system in practical operation was the formation of small detachments of three coolies whose job was to pull a cart filled with 250 pounds of rice, the Army's staple food: a daily pound of rice per man. Hamilton subsisted for much of the time on the soldiers' rations, and he was always hungry.

The Japanese military force was organized into armies of three or four divisions, each army totalling plus or minus 40,000 men, a formation roughly equivalent to an army corps in France and Germany. Hamilton was attached to a force that was to play a major role in the war, the First Army, commanded by General Kuroki. To understand Hamilton's movements as he rode with his Japanese hosts over the landscape of Manchuria, I need to describe in the barest outline the military engagements fought during the sixteen-month conflict. There were six major battles – two at sea (the Yellow Sea and Tsushima), and four on land (the Yalu River, Liao Yang, Mukden, and the eventual capture of Port Arthur). These, and a number of smaller engagements, were all Japanese victories.

Although Hamilton was a close and informed observer of the details of the land fighting, he was not interested in the war at sea, which was as important as the war on land. The conflict was after all fought for the control of the naval base and fortress of Port Arthur. Moreover Japan, being an island nation, had to rely on its sea power to protect the flow of reinforcements and supplies to the seat of war. This meant that Russian domination of the seas around Korea was unthinkable. And appropriately the war was brought to an end by the crushing Russian defeat at the sea battle of Tsushima.

On 6 February 1904 – the day when the diplomatic negotiations had been broken off – a Japanese division prepared to land in north-west Korea with the intention of marching south-west down Manchuria to besiege Port Arthur. It made very slow progress because of the poor condition of the roads. The Second Army of four divisions was soon afterwards sent out to reinforce the original Port Arthur detachment, and attacks on the port and fortress began in earnest during April. The siege was long and bitter, but Port Arthur eventually succumbed in January 1905, largely through the fire support provided by the ships of Admiral Togo. He was to become the outstanding figure of the war and soon to be renowned all over the world.

On 8 February the Japanese fleet, under Togo, moved swiftly and aggressively to blockade Port Arthur, in anticipation of the arrival of the Japanese Army that was on the march. Togo's intention was to lure the Russian fleet out to sea, where it would meet the guns of the Japanese navy. He had also laid beds of electro-mechanical mines in the approaches to the harbour, powerful self-triggering explosive devices, and a remarkable innovation that would be widely copied in Europe. The Russian commanders in Port Arthur were sluggish and unresponsive, but they eventually made two forays, on 13 April and 15 May. During these, the Japanese mines sent three major Russian ironclads to the bottom, with most of their crews, and one of them took the admiral in command down with it. This series of engagements in the Yellow Sea was the first Japanese naval victory. It was both a tactical and a strategic defeat for the Russians, because what remained of their fleet did not dare to emerge again from its anchorage in Port Arthur.

The force marching on Port Arthur represented less than a third of the Japanese Army's fighting strength.[11] The strategic plan, developed over a period of years before the war, laid down that the greater proportion of the army was to be directed north-east following the line of the railway, to put pressure on – and if possible crush – the main Russian army. This was the primary strategic objective; the secondary one was to keep Russian reinforcements far away from Port Arthur.

The Japanese Army was familiar with the terrain of Manchuria. In addition, it took military intelligence seriously. This provided insights into the Russian strength and dispositions, while the Russians had no accurate idea about what lay on 'the other side of the hill'. In fact they vastly over-estimated the size of the Japanese army.[12] In contrast, the Japanese had a good idea of the size of the total Russian field force which numbered only 80,000 men, excluding garrison troops. This meant that the Japanese possessed the first important requirement for success: superiority in numbers. They also had more artillery than the Russians, and employed it better.

Three major battles (shown in **Map 4**) were fought during the advance north-east. In these the Japanese maintained the initiative from first to last, and the Russians were forced to respond and as often as not were caught wrong-footed by their single-minded and aggressive antagonists.

The senior Russian commanders, forced to defend their positions against an enemy whose size and dispositions were little understood, succumbed to a strange and prolonged lethargy. These three battles were, first, the Japanese crossing of the Yalu, the river that separates Korea from Manchuria, an operation carried out between 26 April and 1 May with great panache and success. The second battle, fought over the period 26 August to 4 September, was the larger engagement at Liao Yang, 200 miles north-east of Port Arthur along the railway. The third was the decisive battle of Mukden, fifty miles north-east of Liao Yang. This was a prolonged affair that began on 18 February 1905 and resulted in a long Russian retreat during March. Mukden, followed shortly afterwards by the annihilating naval battle of Tsushima, brought the war to an end. But now is the time to move back to May 1904, immediately after the crossing of the Yalu, because this is when and where Hamilton arrived on the scene.

General Kuroki Carries the Honour of Japan
Hamilton had arrived in Tokyo on 16 March 1904 and lodged at the British Legation until 4 May. He spent this long interlude in meetings with Japanese generals and political leaders, and he also began to gather impressions of the Japanese Army. He was warmly welcomed, although there was a subtle veil between him and the Japanese generals that got in the way of total frankness in their conversations. This was to a limited extent due to the problem of language, although many leading Japanese spoke English, German, or French. A greater problem was that the Japanese kept their plans very close to their chests, a feature of their 'impenetrable secretiveness', in Hamilton's words. He knew nothing about the Japanese strategy for the war until he saw some of the results of it on the battlefield where General Kuroki's First Army had crossed the Yalu, to open the main route from Korea into Manchuria.

Hamilton eventually left Tokyo by sea and then marched overland to reach the headquarters of the First Army at Fenghuancheng on 27 May. From there he made a number of visits to the Yalu River, where the battle had been fought between 26 April and 1 May. On his arrival he assembled the three younger British officers who were also attached as observers and sent them to the individual divisions of the First Army, while he remained with Army Headquarters. Before the battle, Japanese intelligence estimated that the Russians could only spare 6,000 men to defend the Yalu, while the Japanese First Army had 35,000. The Japanese preponderance of strength made the crossing of the Yalu a viable operation of war.[13]

The Yalu River flows in a number of streams through flat land from north-east to south-west, eventually to enter the Yellow Sea on the west coast of Korea. The terrain north of the river is mountainous, and from there the Yalu is joined by a second river, the Aiho, which runs through a cleft in the mountains and flows first east and then south to where the two rivers meet. To the immediate east of this junction is a feature called Tiger Hill, one that was to play an important part in the battle. The Russian defensive position stretched for twenty-five miles west from the eastern bank of the Aiho, an astonishingly wide frontage for the small force that was all that the Russians were able to muster.

The Japanese plan of attack had been worked out in Tokyo, an indication of how the Japanese viewed its importance. It was going to be the first clash in history between a Japanese army and a European army, and the prestige of the Japanese Empire was at stake. Kuroki followed the plan carefully except in one respect, in which caution held him back. The plan had called for a sweeping right-flanking assault, but Kuroki curtailed the extent of this sweep because he wanted to guarantee the strength of the centre of his line. This meant that the attack was going to be more directly frontal than enveloping.

Although Hamilton would not disagree openly with his Japanese allies, he was privately critical of Kuroki's caution. Hamilton temperamentally admired military flair and he was certain that Marlborough, Napoleon, and Lee would have acted differently. But the Japanese were fighting a twentieth century war and they were working out ways of carrying it out on scientific principles – accurate intelligence, careful planning, excellent armaments, superior strength, total secrecy, moving only when ready – principles to which the British made modest concessions only during the last year of the Second Boer War when Kitchener, an engineer, organized the system of blockhouses that made a decisive contribution to victory. The six astonishingly successful Japanese battles during 1904–05 provided plausible evidence that they were wise to adopt the scientific approach, what Hamilton called (with a hint of disapproval) 'making all things absolutely safe'.[14] The method also worked well for the Japanese at the beginning of the Second World War, although they were finally defeated because their enemies learned to do it much better. The Japanese had grossly underestimated the military resources that their enemies would be able to mobilize by 1943, and which grew exponentially in 1944 and 1945.

Kuroki intended to cross the Yalu to reach the east bank of the Aiho, in accordance with the plan of a right-flanking assault although, as described, this had now been modified to limit the extent of the right-hand sweep. Where the crossing was to take place, the Yalu flows between islands and only in places is it a single stream, occasionally 400 yards wide. The first parties of Japanese began crossing in boats just before dawn on 26 April. Kuroki now surveyed the ground carefully and decided that a number of bridges had to be constructed to get his Army across. With the most impressive engineering skills, the Japanese built ten bridges in record time, using improvised trestles and pontoons. Meanwhile, despite the fact that the Russians could see quite a lot of what was going on, they were astonishingly unresponsive, except at Tiger Hill. This important feature had been captured quickly by the Japanese, but was then recaptured by the Russians before it was finally and permanently back in Japanese hands. It dominated the southern part of the battlefield.

The Japanese now began to deploy their artillery. They did this with great care to keep their movements hidden from the Russians. The guns were concentrated on an island in the river called Kinteito, 4,000 yards from the nearest Russian positions on the west bank of the Aiho near its junction with the Yalu. Hamilton described in exquisite detail the artillery duel that was about to begin. The Japanese were unwilling to reveal the positions of their guns; and no Japanese gun was fired – something that would of course have revealed its location – until the first rounds had come from the Russian guns.

The Russians made no effort to conceal their artillery or their infantry trenches, which were to make them all splendid targets for Japanese guns. Kuroki had available – and he immediately concentrated – ninety-two artillery pieces. These were seventy-two field guns and twenty howitzers of 120mm caliber, a vastly heavier weight of artillery than the Russians possessed. On the night of 29-30 April, the Japanese guns were massed on Kinteito Island, and were admirably entrenched and concealed from the enemy. They were hidden in folds in the ground, and trees were transplanted to spots that would conceal the muzzle flashes. Poles were erected and strung together with cables, with branches hanging from them. The gun pits were connected with trenches, and saps – trenches pushed forward – went down to the river to collect water to spread on the dust raised by the gunfire, again for reasons of concealment. Bomb-proof shelters were constructed for the gunners and for the ammunition reserves and communications.

The Japanese artillery set up two observation posts (OPs) on hills some distance to the rear; they had an excellent view of the Russian positions and good telephone communications with the guns. The OPs and the gun lines had maps marked with identically numbered grid squares, so that fire control was simple. Artillerymen today will not be in any way surprised by the Japanese system, but it was a real innovation in 1904, when so much gunfire was over open sights. The targets were not registered before the battle because of secrecy, but telephone orders to correct the fall of shot only needed brief messages, which were translated into switches – rapid changes – of range and direction that were passed to the guns in the gun lines themselves. I have left to last the most striking feature of the artillery preparations. The whole sophisticated affair, with its concealed guns, elaborate trench network, and well-chosen OPs and admirable fire control, was constructed in total secrecy *during the course of a single night*.[15] This brings me to another characteristic of the Japanese troops: they dug like men possessed (as the British army later learned to do during the reconquest of Burma).

All remained quiet until the Russian guns opened fire on the Japanese river crossings. Then, within seconds, the Russians received a bombardment of demonic intensity, a weight of explosive that opened the door for the advance of the Japanese infantry. Within thirty minutes, the Russian guns had all been silenced, and a Russian general had been killed by the Japanese artillery fire.

Meanwhile Kuroki had made a feint attack to menace the substantial town of Antung, eight miles west of the river crossing. The Russians took the bait and moved half their total force to protect this threat to their right. However, the main Japanese assault came on the Russian *left* across the

Aihu, and this culminated in a triumphant Japanese charge up a hill, on which small specks in Prussian blue uniforms were seen from a distance planting the flag of the Rising Sun. Guns were now brought up and the troops in the Japanese centre surged forward. The Russians were forced to retreat, although a rearguard on their right was captured after it had been trapped in a narrow valley flanked by precipitous hills, where they had put up a brave but hopeless fight.

Hamilton criticized the way in which the Russians fought their battle, although he was the first to recognize the bravery of the Russian soldiers. In particular he thought that the Russian artillery had been mishandled. It should have been sited where the guns could not have been seen by the Japanese, and from there they could have given great help to the Russian infantry by indirect fire. When Hamilton walked over the battlefield, he noticed:

> Not one single missile of any description came within 300 yards of the Japanese howitzers, whose shooting was carried out, therefore, as calmly as if they had been at practice camp. It was equally good too. On one spot, fifteen yards by fourteen yards, where a Russian battery had been, I counted eight craters made by their high explosive shells.[16]

He was also appalled by the way in which the Russian infantry trenches were constructed without head cover or loopholes or any attempt at camouflage. And he was shocked by the indifferent musketry of the Russian troops. They had been taught to fire in volleys, sixty to seventy rifles at a time, without much effort at aiming at their targets. The British infantry had abandoned volley firing at the end of the 1870s.[17]

The Battle of the Yalu confirmed Hamilton's high opinion of the men in the Japanese ranks, although he was critical of their infantry tactics of advancing shoulder-to-shoulder, something that made them particularly vulnerable to enfilade fire.[18] And he was not in any way surprised that there were indelible Prussian fingerprints all over the deployment of the Japanese troops:

> In frontage, extension, depth, brigade reserves, divisional reserves and army reserves, the arrangements were exactly those of a German army corps attacking a skeleton enemy.[19]

The butcher's bill showed a preponderance of Russian casualties over Japanese ones, with Russian total losses of 1,900 (including 1,300 killed), and the Japanese total of 900 (including 160 killed).[20] This ratio of Russian to Japanese losses is striking. The virtually universal pattern in warfare is that attackers lose more men than defenders, for the simple reason that attackers are in the open and vulnerable to defensive fire while defenders are normally protected in sheltered positions. The smaller number of Japanese casualties at the Yalu speaks directly to the planning of the battle, notably the exceptionally effective use of the artillery, the bridging work of the engineers, Kuroki's feint on the Russian right, and at all stages his 'grip' on the proceedings.

The crossing of the Yalu was a small battle by the standard of many later ones. But it was a significant strategic victory because it opened the door for the Japanese invasion of Manchuria. Tactically it was a model of efficiency and economy, and was a considerable tribute to the planning of the Japanese generals and their staff. The jury is out on whether the more imaginative approach favoured by Hamilton would have worked better. This is a matter that would have a bearing on the assault on Gallipoli.

General Oyama in Command
With the crossing into Manchuria now totally secure, the Japanese High Command began to carry out its strategic plan to advance north-east along the railway to put pressure on the Russian army. The Japanese assembled four armies, including Kuroki's, so that their order of battle (ORBAT) began to resemble that of a typical large formation in the First World War. The Chief of the General Staff, General (soon to be Field Marshal) Oyama, was made Commander-in-Chief and was to become in time almost as celebrated as Admiral Togo.

Montgomery studied the Russo-Japanese War late in his career and developed a high opinion of Oyama: 'a most able soldier; he was bold and encouraged his army commanders to use their initiative within the broad limits of his directives.'[21] When Hamilton was in Tokyo before he left for Korea, he had met Oyama, who came from an old aristocratic family. He did not find Oyama a 'studious, scientific, professional soldier,' but he had a legendary reputation for courage and in particular for imperturbability. Hamilton illustrated this with a well-known story from Oyama's military career. Some years before, he had been in command of a force fighting the Chinese at Port Arthur, and had been urged to send reinforcements to a part of his line that was being fiercely attacked. Oyama made no response at all. He was at the time near the front line and his eye caught the dead body of a Chinese soldier who was being protected by his dog, which was quite inconsolable. Oyama went up to the dog and spent some time trying to pacify it and gave it some of his own rations from his haversack. When the dog had become less fretful, Oyama quietly ordered his last reserve to be deployed to where it was needed. He had used the episode of the Chinaman and his dog 'to gain time to think over the situation quietly'.[22]

As Hamilton got to know Kuroki better during the months after the crossing of the Yalu, he became increasingly impressed by his same qualities of calmness, thoughtfulness and imperturbability: a combination of traits that ran like a red thread through the personalities of the leading Japanese commanders. At his OP during the first assaults at the Battle of Liao Yang, Kuroki lay on the ground and took a nap, using as a pillow his cigar box covered with his handkerchief.

After the Battle of the Yalu, Hamilton talked to General Fujii, the First Army Chief of Staff, who wanted to discuss the performance of the Japanese Army. Hamilton was pleased to be asked, and mentioned the close infantry formations, which made the troops vulnerable to enfilade fire. This point was noted and something was done about it by the middle of July. But there was less response to Hamilton's comments on the artillery: first, the poor quality of the gun horses; second, what Hamilton considered over-reliance on the telephone at the expense of visual signalling with heliographs and lamps, which was important when soldiers were on the move; and third, the rather untidy fire discipline, despite the stunning accuracy of the fire itself.[23] As the Japanese had learned to do with the German Army, they took advice seriously, but only acted on points they considered really important. They rejected those that would have been expensive and troublesome to implement if the existing systems were working reasonably well. As might be expected of a contemplative man, Fujii spent his spare time with a fishing rod in his hand.

The First Army now began to receive reinforcements, which entailed a hiatus of almost two months before the Army was again on the march. The number of troops was increased to 42,000 and later this number was further boosted. Kuroki and his men set out north-east on 26 June. On the long march to Liao Yang, where the next big battle was to be fought between 23 August and 4 September, the First Army engaged the Russians four times. These were the capture of the Motienling Pass in late June, the Battles of Chaotao on 17–19 July, and Yoshirei on 31 July, and the first phase of Liao Yang, named the Battle of the Twenty-Sixth of August.

On the way to Chaotao, during the first week in July a scratch force of three Japanese companies numbering 630 men defeated and put to flight 2,000 Russians, an almost precise reversal of the traditional doctrine that a three-to-one superiority was needed for a successful attack.[24] The Japanese were to repeat this performance on a larger scale when they invaded Malaya in December 1941. At Chaotao (as mentioned earlier) Hamilton saw the Japanese troops charging up and down formidable hills like mountain goats. Hamilton sometimes compared Japanese soldiers to the Gurkhas of Nepal, for whom Hamilton always felt great respect and affection, and who were equally agile. During the Battle of the Twenty-Sixth of August, Hamilton learned of a stupendous marching feat by a reserve regiment of Japanese infantry. They force-marched eighty-five miles in forty-eight hours, a performance that Hamilton found difficult to believe even after he had checked the distance on a map.[25] At Yoshirei, fought on a hot summer day, something was observed that could have been seen nowhere else: 'a curious palpitating tremor,' which turned out to be the Japanese soldiers in the firing line cooling themselves with their small hand-held fans.[26]

Hamilton described the terrain of the Battle of Liao Yang with a neat explanatory device, using an ordinary piece of legal-size writing paper:

> All the approaches to the position now held by the Russians were broken up into a wild jungle of peaks, ridges and ravines. It was a sort of country suitable for very young men and wild goats. Take a sheet of foolscap; crumple it up; pull it out again; multiply the scale by 50,000; then perhaps some adequate idea may be formed of the configuration of the terrain.[27]

The Russians had lost 30,000 men during the first six months of the war. However, traffic was now moving more quickly on the Trans-Siberian Railway to bring more troops to Manchuria. General Kuropatkin, the Russian commander of the fortified city of Liao Yang, who had more 'grip' and technical skill than the other Russian generals and admirals, resolved to use the 130,000 men and 400 guns now at his disposal to take a stand. He had received contradictory advice from his peers and subordinates, but he disregarded this, mainly because of instructions from St Petersburg that he had to stop the Japanese somewhere. Oyama, who now commanded three armies (plus the 100,000 men of what was now the Third Army detached to besiege Port Arthur), mustered 220,000 men and 600 guns to face Kuropatkin. The weather had been very wet during August, turning much of the ground into mud, but before the end of the month it had all dried out. With a total of 350,000 men who would shortly be locked in combat, Liao Yang was to be the biggest battle in history up to that time: twice the size of Gettysburg, fifty per cent larger than Sedan, and three times the size of Omdurman, measured in all cases by the number of men who fought. This meant that it was to be a very special experience for Hamilton.

Kuropatkin fought the battle by dividing his army into two separate forces, occupying initial positions sixteen miles south of the city. One was forward on his right and the other forward on his left, with a twelve-mile gap between them. The Russian lines bulged south and stretched for forty miles. For an army of 130,000 men this was a relatively wide frontage, certainly by the standard of the First World War, but it was demanded by the size of the front that the Russians had to cover. However, as Kuropatkin's army was pushed back to a second, and narrower, position, and then to a third position behind the second, the gap was closed. These two retirements had been planned and were well controlled.[28]

Oyama orchestrated his assault using his full panoply of force: the Second Army on the left, the Fourth Army in the centre and, on the eastern side of the initial gap, Kuroki's First Army. The first attack began on 23 August, and included Kuroki's battle of 26 August. The Russians were now pressed back to their second line. This was assaulted on 30 August, and as a result the Russians were driven back to their third line. A coordinated assault by three substantial armies was not a simple operation, but it was carried out successfully, partly as a result of informal co-operation between individual divisions, e.g. one division would borrow artillery support from the one next door in order to solve a specific tactical difficulty in the mountainous country. As mentioned, this is a point made by Montgomery. It reflected well-established German practice and had been widely followed during the Franco-Prussian War of 1870.[29]

Kuroki was given the difficult task of sweeping right to surround the Russian left, with the aim of capturing the railway north-east of Liao Yang. But the ground was rugged and the Russian opposition unexpectedly strong. Kuroki, with the same caution that had restricted the sweep of his right-flanking assault on the Yalu River, delayed his advance for fear that he would be encircled by the Russians. Oyama – another careful planner – strongly endorsed his decision.[30]

However, by 4 September Kuropatkin had decided to pull back his Army by rail to Mukden. The Battle was over, and as was to be expected, the Japanese attackers lost more men than the Russian defenders: 23,000 compared with 18,000. For the Japanese it was a substantial tactical victory, but not a strategic one because Kuropatkin, who had exercised great skill in controlling his defending troops, managed to extricate more than 110,000 men to fight another day. In sheer numbers on the ground, the Japanese had the relatively comfortable superiority of seventy per cent (220,000 compared with 130,000 men). But at the strategically more successful Battle of the Yalu, the superiority had been far higher, an overwhelming balance of almost six-to-one (35,000 compared with 6,000 men).

The Russian soldiers had as usual fought bravely, as Hamilton observed when he walked over the ground:

> Never have I seen such a scene. Such a mad jumble of arms and *accoutrements* mingled with the bodies of those who so lately bore them, arrested, cut short in the fury of their assault, and now, for all their terrible, menacing attitudes so very, very quiet. How silent; how ghastly; how lonely seemed this charnel house where I, a solitary European, beheld rank upon rank of brave Russians mown down by the embattled ranks of Asia.[31]

Preparation for the move up the railway and the attack on Mukden took the Japanese army many months. During this period, Hamilton made plans to return home, but he found time to visit briefly the Japanese besiegers of Port Arthur after the port had fallen on 1 January 1905. He was very impressed by the Japanese commander who had won the battle. The final and decisive Battle of Mukden began on 18 February. On 13 February, Hamilton had set sail from Yokohama to England.

Both the Russians and the Japanese were ready for peace, and in May the two sides were brought together by President Theodore Roosevelt and a Peace Conference was held in Portsmouth, New Hampshire. It was one of the first examples of the United States playing a role on the international scene. As a result of this Conference, Japan retained Port Arthur and gained control of the railway along which so much of the war had been fought. Japan's primacy in Korea was also confirmed. Before the end of the war, which had been such an unhappy experience for Russia, revolution broke out at St Petersburg and was brutally suppressed. Worse was to come in 1917.

An enlightening event occurred during Hamilton's return to Britain. Kitchener, Commander-in-Chief of the Indian Army, asked Hamilton to interrupt his journey to visit Indian Army Headquarters in Calcutta and sent a special ship to transport him from Rangoon. Hamilton had been the Indian Army Attaché to the Japanese Army, and had corresponded regularly with Kitchener from the seat of war, so that the request to go to Calcutta was not unexpected. Hamilton dined with the Viceroy, who was extremely interested in what had been learned about modern warfare. But when Hamilton spent a day watching a large formation of the Indian Army in a field exercise, he considered it a 'bow and arrow' affair:

> To speak to the Elders of the Army about trenches, barbed wire, attacks in depth, and the shooting of guns 'indirect' would be futile. As for any attempt to tell the cavalry that their opposite numbers at the battle of Liao Yang could only be used to cook rice for the infantry – that would have been to court the fate of Saint Sebastian.[32]

Kitchener and his Generals were not in the least interested in what Hamilton had to say, and his written critique was eventually lost in the dusty files of Indian Army bureaucracy. The 'bow and arrow' generals continued as before, in the certain knowledge that Kitchener had expressed no disapproval of how they carried out their business.

The Russo-Japanese War as a Precursor

The Russo-Japanese War was a big conflict measured by the numbers of troops on the ground. And it was remarkable because the Japanese always held the initiative and won every engagement. In the main these were battles of manoeuvre rather than battles of attrition like those in the First World War. Hamilton had no doubts beforehand that, despite the mountainous terrain of Manchuria, a war of movement was going to take place. The area of operations was wide, and the Japanese planned their battles in such a way that, when they were ready to fight, they could bring superior weight to bear. As Hamilton had anticipated from his experience in South Africa, traditional cavalry armed with lance and sabre played no role in the fighting, despite the fact that it was a war of movement. The Russian Army included Cossacks, but they were generally ineffective in their traditional role of scouting and guarding the fringes of the battleground.[33]

This chapter is concerned more with Hamilton than with the Russo-Japanese War per se, and this makes it important to focus on what Hamilton learned from it. During the years leading up to 1914, the leaders of the British Army were preparing for a major war on the European continent. Yet they spent more time studying the Second Boer War – a guerrilla conflict against skilled marksmen adept at moving quickly from place to place – than looking for lessons from the Russo-Japanese War, which was fought between what were then large conscript armies that employed traditional battlefield tactics. In its normal way, the British Army was preparing for the last war rather than the next one. Hamilton was in the unique position of bringing his experience of the war in Manchuria to bear on decision-making at the top levels of the British Army. However, how much did his experiences in the Russo-Japanese War actually influence him when he was promoted to supreme command at the Dardanelles? This is an important question for this biography, and I shall begin by summarizing what he actually did experience in Manchuria. His published writings tell a good deal about this.

What Hamilton Learned

Japanese commanders: Hamilton was struck by the imperturbability of the Japanese generals. In the German fashion, there was an emphatic difference between the staff officers – clever, conscientious and energetic doers – and the cool, objective decision-makers in command. But the difference between the two groups was even greater in Japan than in Germany, because the aura of detachment that characterized the generals was typical of the upper reaches of Japanese society:

> The Japanese mind seems readily to lend itself to the system of one man supporting all the weight, pomp, and responsibility of a position, whilst another man works free and untrammeled in the shadow afforded by that latent power.[34]

Planning and preparation: The punctilious planning that was such a feature of the Japanese Army – something carried out in Tokyo in major matters and in the field in less important ones – made an obvious contribution to the Army's success against the Russians. It was based on knowledge of the terrain (many senior officers had fought the Chinese in Manchuria), plus excellent military intelligence about the Russian Army. Nevertheless, as Hamilton says on a number of occasions, there was a downside; he was convinced that careful planning suppresses initiative:

> As far as I can grasp the characters of the subordinate Japanese officers, they seem to be extremely good at carrying out orders, but are not distinguished by any exceptional self-confidence when acting on their own initiative.[35]

He questioned Kuroki's decision at the Battle of the Yalu River to restrict the strength of his right-flanking attack so as not to weaken his centre. In Hamilton's view, a bolder commander would have reaped a greater reward through totally encircling the enemy force. But Hamilton, despite what he had seen of large armies in both Germany and Manchuria, seems not to have appreciated that as wars grew in scale, planning on scientific principles was becoming an increasingly insistent mantra. There was also a great penalty for failure if a risky venture turned sour (e.g. Greece in 1941, and Anzio and Arnhem in 1944). Yet in modern warfare, although there may no longer be opportunities for daring large-scale initiatives on the battlefield, there is often a role for men with maverick ideas (e.g. von Lettow-Vorbeck, Lawrence, Stirling, Wingate). And imaginative ideas for surprise and deception have become more important than ever, although they have to be planned with practised skill (e.g. the bogus plan that

Allenby got into Turkish hands in Palestine in 1918, the German right-flanking feint through Belgium in 1940, and the Anglo-American spoof plans to land in Sardinia in 1943 and at the Pas de Calais in 1944). At Gallipoli itself there were to be two spectacular examples, although they were not big enough to influence the final decision of the campaign. After the preliminary, and unsuccessful, naval assault had been brought to an end, a young officer in the Royal Naval Division, Bernard Freyberg, made a solitary, nocturnal two-mile swim to the beach at Bulair to light flares with the aim of persuading the Turks that the British would land there. Immediately after Freyberg's swim, the 29th Division landed at Cape Helles using the disguise provided by the old collier, the *River Clyde*.

The Japanese rank and file: Hamilton was justifiably impressed by the Japanese soldiers. I have mentioned his comments on the soldiers' agility in climbing up and down mountains; the furious energy of their digging; and their occasionally astonishing marching ability. These were a manifestation of the soldiers' physical strength, partly because the conscripts in the fighting ranks were all picked men. Hamilton often saw the soldiers bathing, something they did whenever they had any spare time and which made them, in Hamilton's opinion, the cleanest army in the world. Because of the admirable hygiene of the soldiers as well as the efficiency of the Japanese Army's medical services, it is not too surprising that deaths from disease were less than a quarter of those from enemy action. In contrast, the British army in the Second Boer War lost five times as many men from disease as from enemy bullets and shell fire.[36]

When they were naked he was always struck by their powerful muscles, which made them able to carry heavier loads than soldiers of any other nation. On the march, the Japanese carried kit weighing about two-thirds of their body weight: a pack with greatcoat, cloak, blanket, bivouac tent, spare boots, straw sandals, cooking pot, as well as rifle, bayonet and a large quantity of ammunition.[37] An attempt was made before the invasion of France in 1944 to make the British soldiers carry a ninety-five-pound load (roughly the amount carried by the Japanese), but they could not manage it and it had to be cut back to the sixty pounds to which the British infantry was accustomed.[38]

I have mentioned the Japanese tactic of advancing shoulder-to-shoulder which made them vulnerable to enfilade fire, a system that was changed partly on Hamilton's advice. He did not mention anywhere the Japanese soldiers' musketry, although he noticed more than once the poor shooting of the Russians due to their practice of volley-firing. He also said that the only soldiers who were actually better than the Japanese were the Regular long-service British infantry, most of whom were skilled at rapid and well-aimed musketry.[39]

The points I have made so far demonstrate that the qualities of the Japanese soldiers would have earned them a high place in comparison with troops from any other countries. Hamilton, with great sensitivity, also detected a powerful and deeply-rooted spiritual attribute of the Japanese that made them unique, something that was even more strongly evident during the Second World War. When the Samurai Warrior caste lost its feudal role during the process of Westernization, something of their ethos was subtly transferred to the soldiers in the new conscript Army. The result was that, in Hamilton's words, death in battle meant an assurance:

> of everlasting life in the memories of their fellow countrymen. This is a sentiment which appeals to the Japanese soldier. He cares, so far as I can see, nothing for the applause of crowds, or for banquets or feasts, and not very much indeed for any actually substantial reward; but to him the hope of fame after death is a very real thing.[40]

Strategy: It is noteworthy that, although Hamilton describes Japanese Army tactics fully and accurately, he pays very little attention to strategy. In the two large volumes of the *Staff Officer's Scrap-Book*, there was only one incidental reference to the Battle of the Yellow Sea; Tsushima is not mentioned at all. And in his graphic descriptions of the battles fought by the First Army, he makes little of the importance of the Japanese superiority in numbers and in artillery. To describe Hamilton's approach slightly pejoratively, his perspective was dominated by the fascinating detail of the worm's eye view.

In summary, Hamilton's description of the war is the work of a knowledgeable professional soldier, but there are gaps in the things that he noticed. And I believe that there is enough in what he says – and what he does not say – to indicate how his experiences in Manchuria would influence his command of the Dardanelles expedition. These appear in italics.

Forgotten Lessons from a Distant War

• The Russo-Japanese War had shown that *a 'native' army composed of hardy peasants but trained and organized on German principles, can become a formidable engine of war.* In Gallipoli such an army had the additional advantage of being commanded by senior German officers. There is no evidence that Hamilton sensed the close similarity between the immensely formidable Japanese Army in Manchuria and the Turks whom his Army was to face at Gallipoli.

• The Russo-Japanese War confirmed the widely accepted truth that *a successful attacking force must have a substantial superiority in numbers of men and artillery over the defenders*; this is normally assessed at three-to-one, and is especially true of mountainous terrain that favours defence, like Manchuria and Gallipoli. In the Battle of Liao Yang, which was not a complete success, the Japanese Army had seventy per cent greater numbers than the Russians. At the more successful Battle of the Yalu, the Japanese had six times as many men as their opponents. At Gallipoli, since little was known for sure before the landing about the size and disposition of the Turkish force, there was obviously no guarantee that the British would have enough men and guns. In fact, the British landing was made with *inferior* numbers of trained and fully-equipped troops. This contributed to the British beachheads being quickly contained by rapidly-arriving Turkish reserves, who accounted for most of the Turkish strength.

• The Japanese successes were based on careful planning, derived from knowledge of the ground and reliable military intelligence about the opposing forces. *The Gallipoli expedition was mounted at great speed, and as a result insufficient attention was given both to the terrain and to the enemy.* These were matters of enormous significance for the development of any plans that were to have a chance of succeeding.

• In all wars, strategy is more important than tactics. Hamilton's career was based on his personal bravery and his tactical experience, knowledge and insight. His most successful active service had been command 'from the saddle' of a division pursuing Boer commandos across the veldt. It is no surprise that in his comments on the Russo-Japanese War, *Hamilton concentrated substantially on tactical and not strategic considerations*. Nor is it surprising that at Gallipoli (again based on his published writings), Hamilton's focus was on the troops in contact with the enemy rather than the big picture.

These four ideas are potentially powerful. And if enough evidence exists to support them, a fifth idea must immediately follow:

• Despite Hamilton's ruses – Freyberg's epic swim and the *River Clyde's* splendid role as a Trojan Horse – and notwithstanding the unparalleled heroism of the assaulting infantry, *the Gallipoli expedition was doomed to failure before the actual assault took place*. There was not enough ingenuity in the initial plan, and not enough punch – in numbers and firepower – to carry the expedition to a successful conclusion.

Notes

1 David James, *Lord Roberts* (London: Hollis & Carter, 1954), pp.369–408.
2 Ibid., p.387.
3 General Sir Ian Hamilton, *The Friends of England* (London: George Allen & Unwin, 1923), p.230.
4 Ian Hamilton (the General's nephew), *The Happy Warrior. A Life of General Sir Ian Hamilton* (London: Cassell, 1966), pp.196–201.
5 Lieutenant General Sir Ian Hamilton, *A Staff Officer's Scrap-Book* (London: Edward Arnold; Volume 1, 1905), pp.293–5.
6 Ibid., p.177.
7 Ibid., p.150.
8 Ibid., p.204.
9 Lieutenant General Sir Ian Hamilton, *A Staff Officer's Scrap-Book* (London: Edward Arnold; Volume 2, 1907), pp. 9–10.
10 Ibid., p.7.
11 Brevet Major W. D. Bird, *Strategy of the Russo-Japanese War* (London: Hugh Rees, 1911), pp.98–9.

12 Hamilton, *A Staff Officer's Scrap-Book,* Volume 2, pp.7–8.
13 Bird, *Strategy of the Russo-Japanese War*, p.100.
14 Hamilton, *A Staff Officer's Scrap-Book*, Volume 1, p.134.
15 Ibid., pp.106–9.
16 Ibid., p.127.
17 Ibid., p.271.
18 Ibid., p.188.
19 Ibid., p.111.
20 Christopher Martin, *The Russo-Japanese War* (London: Abelard-Schuman, 1967), p.68.
21 Field Marshal Viscount Montgomery of Alamein, *A History of Warfare* (Cleveland, OH: The World Publishing Company, 1968), p.456.
22 Hamilton, *A Staff Officer's Scrap-Book*, Volume 1, pp.23–6.
23 Ibid., pp.188–9, 301.
24 Ibid., pp.238–9.
25 Hamilton, *A Staff Officer's Scrap-Book,* Volume 2, p.44.
26 Hamilton, *A Staff Officer's Scrap-Book*, Volume 1, p.326.
27 Hamilton, *A Staff Officer's Scrap-Book,* Volume 2, p.37.
28 Martin, *The Russo-Japanese War*, pp.103–8.
29 Hamilton, *A Staff Officer's Scrap-Book*, Volume 2, p.96.
30 Ibid., p.129.
31 Ibid., p.127.
32 Sir Ian Hamilton, *The Commander* (Major Anthony Farrar-Hockley, ed.) (London: Hollis & Carter, 1957), p.120.
33 Hamilton, *A Staff Officer's Scrap-Book*, Volume 1, p.131; also Volume 2, p.136.
34 Ibid., p.14.
35 Ibid., p.16.
36 William H. McNeill, *Plagues and People* (New York: Random House – Anchor Books, 1998), p.288.
37 Hamilton, *A Staff Officer's Scrap-Book,* Volume I, p.54.
38 Norman Scarfe, *Assault Division* (Stroud, Glos, UK: Spellmount, 2004), pp.12, 25.
39 Hamilton, *A Staff Officer's Scrap-Book*, Volume 1, p.4–5
40 Ibid., p.197.

CHAPTER 9

An Abortive War of Words

C hapter 8 described the changes at the War Office recommended by the Esher Committee when it made its report in early 1904. By the time that Hamilton returned from Japan in 1905 the post of Commander-in-Chief of the British Army had been abolished, and the new machinery to run Army affairs, the Army Council, was beginning to operate rather tentatively. However, none of the early Chiefs of the Imperial General Staff demonstrated enough 'grip' for effective leadership, and it took the powerful personality of Sir William Robertson, appointed in 1915, to command real authority. During his tenure he had the support of the Army, although he fought running battles with the Prime Minister, David Lloyd George, battles which the Prime Minister inevitably won, and Robertson was sacked in February 1918.

In view of the weakness of the early Chiefs, it took a politician to implement the much-needed programme of Army reform. He was Richard Burdon Haldane, a forty-nine-year-old lawyer, who in December 1905 became the political head of the Army, as the Secretary of State for War. Haldane was a member of the highly talented and reforming Liberal Party Government, led by Sir Henry Campbell-Bannerman, which had won the 1905 General Election with a landslide after ten years of Conservative Party rule. Haldane was a successful Scottish barrister, who had been educated at Edinburgh and Göttingen Universities, and who published scholarly works and also knew Germany well. During his tenure as Secretary of State for War, he occasionally attended the annual German

Army manoeuvres and also visited the German War Ministry. He was both a clear thinker and an effective executive, and he became, in the words of Douglas Haig, 'the greatest Secretary of State for War that England has ever had'.[1]

The annual British Army Budget at the time was £30 million, which accounted for twenty-one per cent of total national revenue. Even if this figure is inflated a hundred times to compensate for the fall in the value of sterling, £30 million was a small figure by today's standards. This was a reflection of British policy to keep down the size of the Army and use it to garrison the Empire, relying on the Royal Navy to provide the first line of defence of the British Isles. For its £30 million, the Army provided a proliferation of diverse formations and units. There was a jumble of regiments that had developed in their own ways over the course of their generally long histories, a diversity that strengthened regimental esprit de corps, which was considered a unique quality of the British Army. The whole force that came under Haldane had five components.

(1) The Regular Army comprised men who were serving with the Colours at home and abroad. At home, most units did not have enough soldiers in the ranks because the system of linked battalions meant that each overseas battalion, kept at full strength, was fed by drafts from the one at home.

(2) The Regular Army Reserve was made up of men who had 'served their time'. Since soldiers were recruited for seven years with the Colours and five in the Reserve, a substantial body of Reservists had been built up. These would fill the ranks of the under-strength Regular Army when a threat of war called for a general mobilization.

(3) The Militia was a cadre of part-time soldiers who received a month's annual training and were affiliated to Regular units, normally (in the infantry) providing a third battalion alongside the two Regular ones. The Militia was recruited for home service and there was no obligation to serve abroad, although the Militia Reserve (later replaced by a new more broadly-recruited Special Reserve) was liable for overseas service. Some young Militia officers who had failed to get into Sandhurst managed to capture

Regular commissions through what was called the Militia 'back door'. And many private soldiers were recruited into the Regulars, after they had seen something of soldiering in the Militia.

(4) The infantry Volunteers and Yeomanry cavalry were the largest body of men in total. They represented a confusing collection of regiments with a variety of idiosyncratic uniforms, and were raised in all parts of the country, with little central organization. They were often linked to county regiments, but were run by their commanding officers, who had a good deal of independence. The annual training was only two weeks, plus a few drills at other times, but many members did not even meet this small training commitment. Like the Militia, the Volunteers and Yeomanry were recruited exclusively for home service.

(5) A collection of independent Cadet Corps in schools and universities was mostly, although not always, affiliated to local regiments. These corps were officially recognized by Haldane as part of his reform programme. During the First World War, these training organizations met an important need by providing subaltern officers for the many units of Britain's New Army.

As Haldane viewed his personal empire, he formulated two guiding principles. The first was to identify the purpose for which the Army was going to be deployed, and this would determine the particular formations he planned to set up and fully prepare for war. These became the British Expeditionary Force that went to France in 1914. The second principle was to simplify and synthesize the various Reserve formations that in the event of war would take over home defence, and possibly provide support to the Regulars before too long. Haldane and his Army subordinates carried out much sensible rationalization, and their work was widely appreciated at the time and afterwards. But hidden problems remained, and these began to emerge during the controversy that shortly arose over the question of compulsory service. This is the main concern of this chapter.

Before beginning his reforms, Haldane located a few talented staff officers to advise him and help him execute his plans, and his number one assistant was Douglas Haig. Haig, a rich cavalry officer, had made his name as Chief of Staff of the Cavalry Division during the early part of the Second Boer War. He ended that war as a successful column commander before returning home, already in command of a crack cavalry regiment. Obviously a man with a future, Haig went to India in 1903 at Kitchener's request, to become Inspector General of Cavalry, and was soon afterwards promoted major general. Haldane brought him back in 1906 to be Director of Training on the General Staff and his most important aide.[2] Haig soon demonstrated great ability as a staff officer, something that raises again the question of whether excellent staff officers can also be excellent commanders. Despite his prowess on the staff, his performance in the First World War, commanding first a corps, then an army, and finally a group of armies as British Commander-in-Chief was, to say the least, controversial. Haig liked Hamilton, despite their difference of opinion on the future role of cavalry, discussed in Chapter 8. 'General Johnny Hamilton is a nice fellow,' Haig wrote to his sister.[3] Hamilton also became a favourite of Haldane, who later provided him with a high-profile outlet for his talents by enabling him to write a modest but very important piece of propaganda, entitled *Compulsory Service*.

Hamilton had a very good job waiting for him on his return from the Far East. He was appointed General Officer Commanding the Southern Command, one of the six military districts into which Britain was divided.[4] The original plan had been for each district to have an establishment of three divisions, but the usual problems of recruitment scaled this down. Southern Command was made up of the 3rd Division and six batteries of heavy artillery, plus the nominal rolls of reservists who would be mobilized if war threatened to bring their units up to full strength. The Southern Command cavalry came from the Yeomanry.[5] This important military district was, of course, part of a patchwork stitched together by a peaceable nation. In the normal way, training was based on an annual programme, with the scale of training mounting step by step, from improving the skill of individual soldiers, to work in sections, then platoons, and so on, culminating in the annual manoeuvres of the whole military district. Hamilton supervised the training in a general way, but this was really a job for the officers and NCOs of the individual units. Hamilton gave his accustomed emphasis to musketry.

He spent four years at Southern Command, and during that time, extra-curricular duties became a very important part of the job:

> Tidworth House, then the official residence, was admirably suited to the requirements of a commander and his wife who, with no financial cares, had a genius for entertaining. The Government found that the most popular way of entertaining foreign royalties and other distinguished visitors was to send them to Salisbury Plain to see the Army at work and enjoy the hospitality of the Hamiltons.[6]

Haldane was Hamilton's guest on numerous occasions 'to watch the growth in the standard of excellence in his organization.'[7] He was promoted full general (i.e. four stars) in 1907, and in 1909 was elevated to the most rarified grade of the Order of the Bath, the Grand Cross (GCB). When he left the Southern Command, Hamilton was appointed Adjutant General at the War Office, an appointment he held for a little over a year. It was during this time that Haldane invited him to write the book *Compulsory Service,* which was a means of giving wide publicity to the policies of Haldane's military reorganization.

Roberts Versus Haldane

Lord Roberts had retired precipitately (which for a field marshal meant going permanently on half-pay) when the office of Commander-in-Chief was abolished. However, energetic as ever, he threw himself into a crusade which he saw as a matter of great national importance: a scheme for compulsory military service. He became the figurehead and driving force of an organization called the National Service League that soon made its presence felt. It proposed a four-month or six-month training period (depending on the branch of the service) that would be compulsory for all physically-fit young men when they reached the appropriate age. During their brief service, these recruits would begin to understand the basics of military discipline, and learn something of the theory and practice of musketry. The system would before too long begin to generate a large and growing pool of Reserves who could be mobilized if a major war appeared likely.

Haldane decided to respond to Roberts by sponsoring a relatively short book for sale to the public. This was, as mentioned, a piece of advocacy entitled *Compulsory Service* (published in 1910), devoted to describing the army reorganization that Haldane had originated and executed so efficiently.[8] In parallel, he examined and essentially rejected any form of compulsory service: both the medium-length service enforced on the European Continent (e.g. the German two-year system), and the short-service proposal of the National Service League. Haldane wrote the introduction to the book, and the main text came from the pen of Ian Hamilton. Four main points were made by Haldane and amplified by Hamilton from his long professional experience.

First, the defence of Britain remained in the hands of the Royal Navy, but a substantial home-service force of part-time soldiers could be mobilized to meet any enemy army that managed to get through the naval cordon. This defence force was substantial enough to warn any invaders that they would have to employ large numbers of troops for any hope of success, numbers inevitably easy to detect by the Royal Navy and which would make them targets for its formidable guns.[9] To fill this home defence role, Haldane reorganized the Volunteers and Yeomanry into a body of impressive size, renamed the Territorial Force. This comprised fourteen infantry divisions and fourteen cavalry brigades, the organization being decentralized into the hands of county associations run by local bigwigs. The Militia seemed to Haldane an unnecessary duplication, and he amalgamated it into the larger Territorial organization. However, some members would not accept this and dropped out. The official strength of the Territorial Force was 302,000 men, but by 1913 it had only recruited 250,000, of whom only a small number had agreed to serve overseas.[10] In addition, in that year 30,000 had not fulfilled their modest annual training obligation. The Territorial Force was, therefore, not as impressive as it appeared on paper. It was below strength, only partially trained, and (as will be discussed below) not warmly regarded by the Regular Army.

Haldane's second point addressed the Regular Army. There was no change in the size of the Regular Army overseas: 113,000 men continued to be deployed on garrison duties. His third point was devoted to the Regular Army at home, numbering 129,000 men, plus a slightly larger number of Regular Reserve and Special Reserve, which would more than double the size of the Regular Army if war was declared. This home force had two tasks: (i) to train recruits and, through the system of linked battalions, to keep the overseas battalions up to strength; (ii) to provide a fully-manned and completely trained field force of 150,000 men, comprising six infantry divisions and an expanded cavalry division, with a full complement of artillery, engineers, and support services. It would be available to send overseas when war was declared, and each unit's Regular Army Reservists would be put back into uniform to fill the ranks. This Army was successfully built, and became in 1914 the British Expeditionary Force that went to France, and was by far the best field army that the British had ever sent overseas. However, in comparison to the French and German Armies, it was no more than an army in miniature, superb in quality but grossly deficient in quantity.

Haldane's fourth point was that compulsory service was in almost all circumstances rejected. At the end of Hamilton's contribution, there were shadowy references to a large future army, but in peacetime 'very little more than a paper affair', and one which would be a 'third line organization based on compulsion'. But this was clearly territory that Hamilton had not explored, and was not part of the master plan. [11]

The Haldane reorganization, despite its great merits, suffered from an astonishing weakness. In 1905, staff conversations had been secretly begun between the British and French Armies. [12] It was, therefore, increasingly likely that if France and Germany went to war, the British field force would fight alongside the French. Yet the French and German conscript armies were many times larger than the British, with the French Army estimated at eighty-three divisions and the German Army likely to be 110 divisions. [13] (The number of German divisions deployed in 1914 was even larger.) This disparity meant that Britain would be compelled to fight as a junior partner to the French. Despite the contribution of the Royal Navy during any large conflict – a contribution that was perhaps more appreciated in Britain than on the Continent – the small size of the British military force would become an immediate embarrassment to the British Government, and a source of serious and growing resentment on the part of the French. The French had a rich and valued ally in Britain, yet it was mostly French blood that was being spilt on the battlefield.

Haldane and Hamilton did not confront the unwelcome prospect of Britain having to provide a Continental-size force to support the French Army. This would probably have meant improving the training of the

Territorials and persuading or compelling them to serve overseas. It might also have demanded the recruitment of a large national army by voluntary service or – unmentionable word – by compulsion. After the balloon went up in 1914, all these things were to happen. There was another major and related problem that was barely anticipated. If the BEF was immediately committed to battle (which actually happened in 1914), and if it suffered horrendous casualties (which also happened), what cadre of experienced men would survive and be available to train the large national levies? This was a stubborn difficulty that was to dog the British Army throughout the First World War. In all too many cases involving organizing and training new units, the name of the game was improvisation, although this is something that the British have often done surprisingly well!

In *Compulsory Service*, despite the large and undetected deficiency in his case, Haldane the lawyer argued persuasively against Roberts's proposal. And Hamilton, the conscientious staff officer who accepted the parameters within which he had to develop his arguments, amplified Haldane's case with support from his own long experience as a soldier.

During the 1880s, Hamilton had strongly favoured the ancient system 'under which soldiers in the ranks served until they were pensioned'.[14] This system made them hardy, steady under fire, and strongly imbued with the regimental spirit. But this system was now defunct, and long service now meant seven years with the Colours and five with the Reserve. Nevertheless, in what Hamilton wrote, there was still an echo of his nostalgia for the Victorian Army in which he had served, as had his father before him. He describes a typical old warrior 'reviewed by his King, his broad chest glittering with medals . . . and a pleasant sense of voluntarily performed duty in his heart.'[15]

This was all antithetical to any type of compulsory service. Hamilton in particular deprecated the two-year German system because the type of robot-like discipline it inculcated robbed the soldiers of individual initiative.[16] And he saw from the Russian Army how compulsion actively discouraged voluntary enlistment.[17] He also reminded his readers that a brief experiment in the British Army to introduce three-year short service, aimed at young men who wanted to give the Army a trial, was abandoned after two years because too few men signed on for further service with the Colours.[18] An additional point that Hamilton appreciated, but did not emphasize, was that a large conscript Army would demand substantial numbers of professional officers and NCOs as instructors, which would reduce the effective size of the Regular Army.

After his experience in the Second Boer War, Hamilton felt able to appraise the military effectiveness of part-time soldiers. The Territorials were not highly regarded in Regular Army circles, the officers 'disowning them contemptuously as "dog shooters" '.[19] However, Hamilton had seen that many part-time soldiers had become efficient after they had served for some months on active service.[20] But old prejudices die hard and in 1914 Kitchener, the newly-appointed Secretary of State for War, decided to sideline the Territorials. It is an open question whether a large field army based on the Territorial Force would have performed better or worse in France and Flanders than Kitchener's New Armies, a body that had to be built from the ground up. The Territorials were already partially trained and equipped before the war began, and a small number of selected units did go to the Western Front before the end of 1914, and made a name for themselves. In addition to these, the substantial numbers who had by now agreed to serve overseas were sent to replace Regular units on garrison duty, so that the Regulars could be brought to the seat of war. The 29th Division that fought in Gallipoli was assembled in this way. Later in the war, Territorial units fought in the firing line in many places, and most performed well.

Hamilton attacked the idea of compulsory service from a number of different directions, but underlying all his arguments were two fundamental points. First, compulsory service would in all circumstances be more expensive than the Army's present arrangements, and it was therefore politically unacceptable. To governments that during the whole course of the nineteenth century and into the twentieth had been relentlessly cheese-paring, this financial argument carried enormous weight.[21] Haldane's reforms had been popular, not least because he had carried them out with a modest *reduction* in the Army's annual budget.[22]

Hamilton's second underlying point was that any conscript Army that was then visualized would be engaged in peacetime in totally defensive activity. It would serve exclusively in Britain since it would have made no practical sense to send four-month or six-month conscripts on garrison duty overseas. This home service would encourage 'defence-mindedness', something that would act as a serious brake on the initiative and enthusiasm of the British Army, an armed force 'formed, trained, inspired by the idea of the attack'.[23] As if echoing this point, Hamilton's final conclusion had an emotional overtone:

> If you wish to count your bayonets by the million, you must make up your mind to retrace the steps of Empire. If you wish to maintain the Empire you must encourage the voluntary spirit. The human heart is not a savings-bank; rich in proportion as nothing is drawn from it.[24]

The lines of dispute were now drawn up. Within four months, the National Service League joined battle by publishing a book of their own, a piece of advocacy arguing the opposite case to *Compulsory Service*. This riposte was entitled *Fallacies and Facts. An Answer to 'Compulsory Service'*. It had Lord Roberts's name on the title page as author, although he contributed only the first of the three sections of the book, entitled 'A Nation's Peril'.[25] The second, 'The Military and Naval Situation', was written by Leo Amery, the historian and politician who had already established a reputation and was to have a long career in politics. The third, 'The Argument from History', was the work of a Scottish history professor, John Adam Cramb.[26]

The book is full of knock-about arguments and counter-arguments trenchantly expressed, with the occasional barb of malice that makes for lively reading. The section written by Professor Cramb is persuasive although donnish, as might have been expected. But the contributions of Amery and Roberts are focused and powerful, and reveal a historical perspective that gives them a broad vision of the future, something lacking in *Compulsory Service*.

Amery, in making his most important point, went straight for the jugular:

> for our generation at least, only one potential opponent (is) in view. That opponent is Germany. The immense strides made by the German Navy in recent years, and the seriousness of the German challenge to our command of the sea, have already been referred to. But Germany is not only our greatest rival at sea. She is the

most formidable military power in the world. She can put
1,700,000 men into the field, keeping over 2,000,000 more for local
defence, for lines of communication, and for drafts.[27]

Amery also referred to Germany's likely ally Austria-Hungary, with a
field Army of 750,000 plus vast reserves. He also mentioned Italy, a
possible ally of Germany, a power that had 600,000 troops and (like
Austria-Hungary) considerable reserves.

Roberts, with his incomparable reputation, added weight to the case
by basing his argument on Britain's traditional policy of maintaining the
European balance of power, 'whilst we ourselves moved on our steady
path to Empire in other parts of the world.' Britain's ancient policy was
carried out by large financial subsidies to weaker European countries, to
match the endemic strength of the more powerful. But this had earlier
imposed a crushing financial burden on Britain, a burden that would be
insupportable in the twentieth century. Roberts shared the Regular Army's
scepticism about the value of the Territorial Force; and he saw clearly that
there were simply too few men in the projected Regular field force for
the job that they would have to perform.[28] To Roberts there was only one
answer to Britain's military dilemma. This was to build a large reserve of
men who would receive more training than the Territorial Force: training
that they would be compelled by law to undergo.

There is no doubt in hindsight that the logic and vision of Roberts and
Amery and the National Service League put them on the side of the
angels. Some younger officers, notably Henry Rawlinson and Henry
Wilson – men who would build important careers during the First World
War – supported compulsory service, and Wilson wrote to Roberts to
endorse his case, which made him unpopular in some circles.[29] But it was
unfortunately true that although the published reviews generally thought
that the war of words had ended in Roberts's favour, this did not in any
way affect the outcome.[30] Compulsory service was politically and
financially impossible, and a government that enacted it would have been
thrown out of office. Legislation to bring it about was not passed until
early 1916, when Britain was already a year and a half into the greatest
war she had ever fought. In 1910 Haldane may not have been acutely
conscious of the possibility of a European war, but to Haldane's
subordinates on the General Staff such a war was an imminent spectre.

The evidence for this was the continuing Anglo-French staff talks that were devoted to planning for just such an eventuality.

Hamilton's opposition to compulsory service – which was a matter of principle and not opportunism – was naturally a bitter blow to Roberts. But he was a big man despite his small stature, and in his book he continued to express his affection and respect for Hamilton, although he had been compelled to disagree so sharply with him.[31] In 1910, while Hamilton was at work on his book, he accompanied Roberts, as General in Waiting, to various European countries to visit their sovereigns to announce officially that King George V had succeeded his father, King Edward VII.[32]

The Ticking of the Clock
During the whole period since Hamilton had returned from the Russo-Japanese War, the clock had been ticking steadily, measuring the hours before a major conflict broke out between France and Germany. Such a conflagration would inevitably involve Britain, and this was the contingency against which Roberts and Amery had so eloquently urged the Government to prepare.

After the publication of *Compulsory Service* in 1910, and after only a year as Adjutant General, Hamilton left for Malta for his last peacetime command. He became General Officer Commanding the British Army in the Mediterranean, and also Inspector General of Overseas Forces.[33] The job had originally been offered to Kitchener, who had turned it down because he hoped to be made Viceroy of India. This did not happen, and Kitchener resented Hamilton for accepting the appointment in Malta, probably because Kitchener hoped that the Malta command would be kept open for him after the Viceroyalty had fallen through.[34] Malta was a magnificent appointment, although for Hamilton a slightly more modest one than Kitchener had been offered. The number of troops in the Command was 37,000, one-third of the British soldiers on overseas garrison duty, while the remaining two-thirds were in India, considered a separate Army. The Mediterranean was to Hamilton a larger-scale version of Southern Command, and in a better climate. His time was spent on inspecting the widely-spread garrisons, and in lavish entertaining at his headquarters on the island of Malta.

It was a four-year appointment and he returned home in 1914, at the age of sixty-one, and was given the honour of becoming ADC to the King. In normal circumstances, no further job would have been available to him, and he would have been retired on grounds of age. However, the declaration of war changed the situation immediately. One of the Prime Minister's first decisions was to appoint Lord Kitchener, who was on leave from Egypt and was in London, to become Secretary of State for War, the political head of the Army. Some people believed that Kitchener had hopes that he would be appointed, and he did not accept it reluctantly.

Hamilton had been Kitchener's Chief of Staff at the end of the Second Boer War, and Kitchener thought highly of him. Hamilton was now certain to be caught up in the new, greater conflict. One of Kitchener's first decisions was therefore to appoint Hamilton to the Central Command in Britain. This was a skeleton formation comprising three armies that were eventually recruited and trained, and its nominal role was to guard against invasion. But Kitchener was determined to find something more active for Hamilton when an opportunity arrived.

Since a war on such a scale was going to change Hamilton's life, it is appropriate to pause briefly to assess his professional strengths and weaknesses. He had spent forty-two years as an officer in the British Army. During this period he had witnessed many changes, and become one of the Army's most seasoned generals. He had garnered an excellent reputation, and his books had some influence on this.

Hamilton had spent six years commanding troops on active service: more than four years as a brave and enterprising junior officer in three short campaigns (including many months recovering from wounds), and almost two years in successful commands during the Second Boer War. He had no experience higher than commanding a division composed of mobile columns. The emphasis of what he had learned was therefore more tactical than strategic.

From the age of twenty-nine, staff appointments occupied him for almost nineteen years. These were mainly concerned with administration: as an ADC, Military Secretary, Attaché to the Japanese Army, and taking a number of steps up the ladder in the A and Q branches of the General Staff. They included senior jobs during two active campaigns on the North-West Frontier of India, although he was deprived by bad luck of

169

commanding troops in the field. During his staff service he had spent virtually no time in the G branch: less than six months as Chief of Staff to Kitchener at the end of the Second Boer War. Military strategy had therefore not played much part in his work on the staff, although he had of course acquired great knowledge of manning and logistics. The rest of his years of service had been as a junior regimental officer in Ireland and India; and in peacetime jobs of growing importance: more than a year at the School of Musketry, four years at Southern Command, and four years in Malta. He had never held any senior regimental appointments, nor had he attended the Staff College.

In summary, Hamilton's career had been distinguished and varied, but unbalanced. For an officer to have spent forty-five per cent of his service as an administrative staff officer was most unusual. Admittedly, Lord Roberts himself had spent a similar period on the staff, but his subsequent experience in senior fighting commands had been more significant than Hamilton's.

This synopsis of Hamilton's career brings me to re-visit the eleven qualities, briefly described in Chapter 1, that in my opinion define whether a soldier has the battery of talents needed to join the ranks of the great captains. Virtually no commanders have possessed all these qualities, but all generals must have some of them, otherwise they would not have been appointed in the first place. I start by looking at Hamilton's strengths, and there were five obvious ones.

• He had moral courage to match his valour on the battlefield. He had always shown himself willing to support publicly arguments that were not always popular: pro-musketry, anti-cavalry, pro-long service, anti-conscription.
• He had a close understanding of and empathy for the men he commanded, without detracting from his belief in military discipline. This was connected with his strong support of long service. He had learned important lessons during the fifty-five per cent of his career he had spent with troops, and these were reinforced during his years with Lord Roberts, who had an extraordinary rapport with the men in the ranks.
• He had considerable raw brain power. He published widely, and his writing was much better than that of any of his military

contemporaries. He was respected by men of first-class talent, e.g. Roberts, Kitchener and Haldane.

• He was a clear thinker: something that was evident from his writings and his conversation and speeches. This was at least partly a legacy of his long experience as a staff officer.

• He was a skilled tactician. He was a strong proponent of musketry (which demanded continuous training to maintain and improve standards); the effective use of ground in attack and defence; fire and movement; the avoidance of infantry 'bunching' to prevent them from being enfiladed; close artillery/infantry cooperation; and a new role for cavalry as mounted infantry.

But he also had two serious weaknesses.

• His strategic understanding was much more limited than his 'feel' for tactics. His vision was limited, possibly another legacy of his long period as a staff officer. In the controversy over compulsory service, he and Haldane demonstrated a far narrower vision of the future than Roberts and Amery. He reported accurately on the Russo-Japanese War, but he had written about tactics to the virtual exclusion of strategy. Although he drew brief but important lessons from that war, e.g. the value of military intelligence, meticulous planning at all stages, and the need for a substantial superiority of numbers in the attack, these points did not seem to have fully penetrated his psyche. Worst of all, he was responsible for publishing a misjudgement that in retrospect was suicidal. This concerned how fully he understood the importance of modern firepower. He appreciated its value in the attack, although this was not proven until the German Army developed its 'storm troop' infiltration tactics in 1918. However, the greater importance of fire power in defence had not made a comparable impact on him. In 1899 a book was published, not by a soldier but by a Polish financier called Ivan Stanislavovich Bloch, who foresaw with uncanny accuracy the future course of the First World War. Developments such as rapid-fire small arms, barbed wire, and entrenchments would make any future war 'protracted and indecisive', and future conflicts would bring nothing but deadlock

171

and attrition. Most soldiers resisted this view instinctively but silently. Hamilton was bold enough to express his scorn in writing:

All that exaggerated reliance placed upon *chassepots* and *mitrailleuses* by France before 1870; all that trash written by Monsieur Bloch before 1904 about zones of fire across which no living being could pass, heralded nothing but disaster. War is essentially the triumph, not of a *chassepot* over a needle-gun, not a line of men entrenched behind wire entanglements and fire-swept zones over men exposing themselves in the open, but of one will over another weaker will.[35]

Hamilton's views were believed even more strongly in France. These convictions were to bleed France white during the First World War, and were to lead to the mutinies of 1917. Ultimately they led to the Maginot Line and the collapse of the French Army in 1940.

- There were doubts about Hamilton's ability to stand back in detachment to draw up his plans. His life had been characterized by impetuosity, which is a desirable quality in a junior officer, but in a senior it can be a serious problem. As mentioned, Hamilton clearly noted the ability of the Japanese Army to plan ahead, but the importance of this had not been fully registered in his mind.

Some qualities of great leadership only become apparent when a general reaches high command, and this did not happen to Hamilton until Gallipoli. I must therefore jump ahead in order to review albeit briefly these other qualities:

- The ability to pick good subordinates. For the Gallipoli expedition, the senior generals were all chosen by Kitchener. Hamilton's eye for talent was therefore not proven.
- Ruthless intolerance of incompetence. At Gallipoli he did not react instantly by sacking incompetent generals after the mishandled landing at Suvla Bay in August 1915.
- Obsessive determination. Hamilton demonstrated this at Gallipoli.
- Understanding the psychology of the enemy. Hamilton was barely conscious of the leaders of the Turkish Army. Liman von Sanders

rates four brief mentions in Hamilton's *Gallipoli Diary*. (In contrast, Montgomery displayed photographs of the leading German generals in the caravan where he lived during his campaigning.) Despite what he had learned in the Russo-Japanese War about the fighting ability of 'native' peasant soldiers trained by German officers, Hamilton had a poor view of the Turkish rank and file before the assault on the Dardanelles.

Enough has been revealed to arrive at one conclusion of great importance. At the time of his appointment to command the Gallipoli expedition, *Hamilton was far more a tactician than a strategist.* Gallipoli was an enterprise full of heroism in the formations and units in Hamilton's command. There were also mistakes, and frequent ill-luck. Also obvious is the hardiness and grit of the Turkish soldiers and the considerable military skills of the Turkish Army's top commanders, a number of whom were German officers. I believe that within this complex mixture of factors that eventually led to the British failure, Hamilton's own bias towards tactics rather than strategy was an important part of the mix, and it therefore made an unfortunate contribution to the British defeat.

Notes

1 Frederick Maurice, 'Douglas Haig,' *Military Lives. Intimate Biographies of the Famous by the Famous* (Hew Strachan, ed.) (Oxford: Oxford University Press, 2002), p.181.
2 Ibid., pp.179–81.
3 Douglas Haig, *Diaries and Letters* (Douglas Scott, ed.) (Barnsley, South Yorkshire, UK: Pen & Sword Military, 2006), p.213.
4 C. F. Aspinall-Oglander, 'Ian Standish Monteith Hamilton,' *Military Lives. Biographies of the Famous by the Famous*, p.197.
5 Field Marshal Lord Carver, *Britain's Army in the Twentieth Century* (London: Macmillan, in association with the Imperial War Museum, 1998), p.15.
6 Aspinall-Oglander, 'Ian Standish Monteith Hamilton,' pp.197–8.
7 Richard Burdon Haldane, *An Autobiography* (London: Hodder & Stoughton, 1929), p.197.
8 General Sir Ian Hamilton, *Compulsory Service. A Study of the Question in the Light of Experience* (London: John Murray, 1910).
9 Ibid., p.22.
10 Carver, *Britain's Army in the Twentieth Century*, p.16.
11 Hamilton, *Compulsory Service*, pp.145–7.

12 Major General Sir C. E. Callwell, *Field Marshal Sir Henry Wilson. His Life and Diaries* (Volume 1) (London: Cassell, 1927), p.89.
13 Ibid., p.100.
14 Hamilton, *Compulsory Service*, p.12.
15 Ibid., p.45.
16 Ibid, p.44.
17 Ibid., p.68.
18 Ibid., pp.84–7.
19 Robert Graves, *Goodbye To All That* (London: The Folio Society, 1981), p.83. (Originally published in 1929.)
20 Hamilton, *Compulsory Service*, pp.116–33.
21 Ibid., pp.178–81.
22 R.C.K. Ensor, *England, 1870-1914* (Oxford: Oxford University Press, 1936), p.526.
23 Hamilton, *Compulsory Service*, p.148.
24 Ibid., p.147.
25 Field Marshal Earl Roberts, *Fallacies and Facts. An Answer to 'Compulsory Service'* (London: John Murray, 1911).
26 David James, *Lord Roberts* (London: Hollis & Carter, 1954), pp.450–1.
27 Roberts, *Fallacies and Facts*, p.116.
28 Ibid., pp.10, 45, 20.
29 James, *Lord Roberts,* p.449.
30 Ibid., p.551.
31 Roberts, *Fallacies and Facts*, pp.17–18.
32 Sir Ian Hamilton, *The Commander* (Major Anthony Farrar-Hockley, ed.) (London: Hollis and Carter, 1957), pp.94–5.
33 Aspinall-Oglander, 'Ian Standish Monteith Hamilton,' p.198.
34 Hamilton, *The Commander*, pp.122–5.
35 Hamilton, *Compulsory Service*, pp.121–2.

CHAPTER 10

'Corpses Lined Up Like Rows of Broad-Beans'

T he title of this chapter – such a homely but bitterly poignant image – comes from the diary of a Turkish officer who saw through his field glasses the mortal remains of British troops who had stormed V Beach on the Gallipoli Peninsula.[1] Even in a war that had seen and was still to see so much bloodshed, the British and ANZAC assault on Gallipoli was a story of rarely paralleled heroism and sacrifice. It is an epic that has attracted a vast literature, but the purpose of this book is not to repeat the rich and plentiful accounts that have already been published. My purpose is to puzzle out why the soldiers were committed to V Beach in the first place.

The issues I shall be addressing at different times are the following: were the enormous numbers of casualties suffered during the initial assault inevitable? Were other landing places feasible and preferable? Did the assault have to take place at such an early date, when the attackers were so ill-prepared? And, most importantly, was the force deployed large enough for its substantial task? These are all matters of strategy, and strategy can be a slippery subject. To contain ambiguity, I am starting with six definitions that are an analysis of different levels of military planning: definitions formulated during the 1930s by Basil Liddell Hart, the first historian who succeeded in dissecting the First World War to uncover the lessons to be drawn from it, and whose insights came from his unrivalled knowledge of the long and unhappy history of past conflicts all over the world.[2]

• *The rôle of grand strategy is to co-ordinate and direct all the resources of a nation towards the attainment of the political object of the war – the goal defined by national policy.*
• *Pure strategy is the distribution and transmission of military means to fulfil the ends of policy.*
• *Pure strategy, the art of the general, depends for success, first and most, on a calculation and co-ordination of the end and the means.*
• *The purpose of pure strategy is to diminish the possibility of resistance, and it seeks to fulfil this purpose by exploiting the elements of movement and surprise.*
• *As regards the relation of strategy to tactics, while in execution the borderline is often shadowy, and it is difficult to decide exactly where a strategical movement ends and a tactical movement begins, yet in conception the two are distinct.*
• *When the application of the military instrument merges into actual fighting, the dispositions for and control of such direct action are termed tactics. Tactics lies in and fills the province of fighting. Strategy not only stops on the frontier, but has for its purpose the reduction of fighting to the slenderest possible proportions.*

Ian Hamilton, being the local commander, was in no way responsible for the grand strategy of the Gallipoli campaign. But the pure strategy, 'the art of the general', was directly his concern. This included a realistic appraisal of the size of his force, the distribution of this force, and the underlying plan and timing of the attack. Since his plan should in Liddell Hart's judgement have been aimed at reducing 'fighting to the slenderest possible proportions', Hamilton's decisions were to have an important although indirect influence on the tactics of the ensuing combat. These decisions were to lead inexorably to the landing on V Beach. It is a story with complicated antecedents and these must be recounted in some detail, starting with a description of how Turkey, which was not a factor in the European balance of power, came to be involved in the First World War.

Germany's Eyes Turn South-East

The First World War started with 'some damned silly thing in the Balkans', just as Bismarck, the first Chancellor of the German Empire had predicted twenty years before.[3]

Europe in 1914 was made up of independent nation states, some large and some small. They included three continental empires: Germany, Austria-Hungary and Russia, each headed by an autocratic hereditary ruler. Each empire occupied great tracts of territory, and the population of each was heterogeneous. Austria-Hungary was a ragbag of multi-lingual ethnic groups, and the German and Russian Empires had each been formed from groups of separate states. On the periphery in the south-east was the Ottoman Empire of Turkey. She dominated the Middle East and once ruled the Balkans, but had been forced back towards Asia and by 1912 retained only a tiny corner of territory in Europe. She therefore had a grievance over the Balkans and, most importantly, she had a geographical position dangerous to both Britain and Russia. If Turkey were to go to war with Britain, this would endanger Britain's shortest sea route to India and the Far East; and if she fought Russia, this would be certain to block Russia's access to the Mediterranean and her main ally France. However, this threat to the British was brought to an end by Allenby's campaign in the Middle East in 1917 and 1918. In the end, Turkey shared the fate of the three large continental empires and was dismantled by the victors at the end of the First World War. Today's troubled Middle East is composed of separate countries most of which were once part of the Ottoman Empire.

Germany was the strongest of the continental empires from every point of view, but Kaiser Wilhelm, the last of the Hohenzollerns, was headstrong and unstable. Austria-Hungary was torn apart by internal dissensions, and Franz Josef, Emperor of Austria and King of Hungary, who died two years before his Empire fell, was an astonishing relic of the past and was approaching senility. Russia was geographically the largest but was the least powerful of the great empires, although her industry was growing fast. Nicholas, the Russian Tsar, the last of the Romanovs, was weak and bewildered by the difficulties faced by his gigantic Empire. The character and temperament of these three powerful emperors made for an explosive mixture.

The ancien régime of the Turkish Sultanate that had seen the Ottoman Empire expelled from the Balkans was both corrupt and inefficient, and in a coup d'état in 1908, a group of army officers, the 'Young Turks,' took over the Government and emasculated the power of the Sultan. They modelled their rule on the militarism of Germany, to whom they looked for help, which they received in just the form they needed.

Prussia had grown rapidly during the nineteenth century as a result of both her economic strength and her aggressive foreign policy that gave her additional territory following successful wars against Denmark in 1864, Austria-Hungary in 1866, and France in 1870–71 (when the German Empire was formed). The French and Germans were traditional enemies. The main cause of this enmity, and something that became its prime symbol, was France's seizure of the rich provinces of Alsace and Lorraine during the mid-seventeenth century. Alsace (but not Lorraine) is culturally closer to Germany than to France, and part of the price exacted by Germany for her defeat of France in 1871 was the return of these two prosperous provinces.

France's resentment of Germany and Germany's hatred of France were, not surprisingly, worse than ever after 1871. These antagonisms still existed even after the defeat of Germany in 1918 and again in 1945; and only faded with the birth and success of the European Union, formed in 1957, and which was providing serious economic benefits to its members within a few years (although deep-seated problems eventually made themselves felt). In the last analysis, the antagonism between France and Germany, although not the factor that precipitated the First World War, was the deepest underlying cause of that conflict. After 1871, France was a country deeply divided by internal dissensions – political, religious, military and economic – but the general desire for revenge against Germany was shared by all the competing factions.

The rapid growth of the German economy and the equally rapid increase in the ambitions of the Royal House drove Germany's interests overseas. This was resented by Britain, a country that possessed the most powerful Empire in the world. But in contrast to the continental European empires, the British Empire was enormously widespread and was geared to creating wealth by driving demand for Britain's export trade, which meant that much (but not all) of the wealth created in the colonies remained there to buy British products.

Throughout the nineteenth century, Prussia (expanded after 1871 to become the German Empire) possessed the most impressive army in the world, very large though not quite the largest. But it was the best equipped and most rigorously trained, due to its focus on developing the initiative of regimental officers and non-commissioned officers. And because of the importance of the Great General Staff – whose job was to apply brainpower of the highest quality to military planning – Germany had developed the most sophisticated strategic and tactical doctrines. It also produced the most professional generals, one of whom would shortly find himself in Turkey. Of all the other armies in the world, only the British was comparable, or even superior, in quality because it was an all-Regular force. However, in 1914, the peacetime strength of the British Army was only about ten per cent of that of Germany, with its large numbers of trained reserves who could be speedily mobilized. And a high proportion of the British Regulars were to lose their lives during the first year of the war. An enormous advantage the British possessed was that many British officers and men had actually been under fire in colonial wars, and nothing is more instructive than the whistle of bullets. Many Turkish soldiers had also received this practical training in the firing line during the two Balkan Wars of 1912 and 1913, and this prepared them for Gallipoli, where their fighting prowess was to surprise the British.

Britain as a nation was widely regarded as a leading military power, but it was the Royal Navy and not the Army that was pre-eminent. In the 1890s Germany started building a navy to rival Britain's, which seriously strained relations between the two countries, and Britain began to look towards France as a potential ally. This led to the 1904 Entente Cordiale, an important démarche because it settled colonial disputes, but it did not call initially for any firm commitment of military support in the event of European war. (This commitment was to come later.)

France's defensive ally was Russia, with whom she formed the Dual Alliance in 1894, an alliance which offered strategic and economic advantages to both nations. The German Kaiser had allowed the defensive treaty with Russia, which he had inherited, to lapse which led to Russia joining the opposite camp. The resulting treaty between Russia and France was dangerous for Germany, because she might as a result be forced to fight on two fronts. In 1904 France added, with the Entente Cordiale, a friendly relationship with her neighbour across the Channel. The long-term importance of this agreement to Britain was less political than military, because it was eventually to dictate Britain's military strategy during the whole of the First World War. In1907, Britain also signed a convention with Russia to remove the threat against the British in India. This reinforced the Dual Alliance, a coalition that soon became known as the Triple Entente. Since Russia and Turkey were traditional enemies, the Triple Entente alienated Turkey from Britain and France. Russia had a protective role towards the independent Slav states in the Balkans, Serbia in particular. The problem with Serbia was that she was an uncomfortable neighbour of Austria-Hungary, which was suspicious and antagonistic towards the Serbs, and the feelings were reciprocated. It was here that the trouble began.

Germany was facing a situation of potential peril with two antagonists, one on each flank. France was likely to receive support from Britain, and Russia had small allies in the Balkans. Germany's only realistic course to maintain her dominant position was to continue and strengthen her alliance with the ramshackle Austro-Hungarian Empire, whose ruling class also spoke German because both Germany and Austria-Hungary were rump states of the old Holy Roman Empire, the loose amalgamation of separate aristocratic states that spread over central Europe and lasted for many centuries. Bismarck had followed this policy of friendship since 1879, with the explicit intention of restraining Austria-Hungary's ambitions in the Balkans. Kaiser Wilhelm chose to ignore this important caveat, and his departure from the wise caution of Bismarck was to have terrible consequences. Italy had also been brought in, to form the Triple Alliance in 1882, but when the powder keg blew up Italy remained a spectator and was eventually to join France, Russia and Britain.

As the two great European alliances confronted one another with mutual suspicion, Germany strengthened her gaze towards the south-east, and eyed Turkey as a potential ally. During the nineteenth century, the Ottoman Empire had remained friendly with Britain despite some causes of tension, and the two countries had been allies during the Crimean War against Russia, whose ambitions were always a menace to Turkey. But with the signing of the convention between Britain and Russia in 1907 everything changed, and the Young Turks who came to power in 1908 turned immediately towards Germany. Germany had long-standing plans to extend her empire to the Middle East and had made steady overtures to Constantinople, where the Germans had appointed exceptionally able ambassadors since1897. Germany now provided the type of help that the Young Turks valued most. She began to train the Turkish Army in German methods, as she had done with the Japanese. Germany also gave Turkey the services of a number of highly professional officers. The result of all this was that the Turkish Army, which was large and recruited from hardy peasants accustomed to long hours and short commons, was transformed into a formidable fighting force. Its high quality was soon to be appreciated by the soldiers of Britain, Australia, New Zealand and France at Gallipoli.

On 28 June 1914, the heir to the throne of the Austro-Hungarian Empire, the Archduke Franz Ferdinand and his wife Sophie, were paying an official visit to Sarajevo, capital of the recently-annexed province of Bosnia and Herzegovina. This province was populated by a number of ethnic groups and rather less than half the population was Slav. Serbia, with whom she shared a frontier, was even more dominated by its Slav population. The visitors were not warmly welcomed, because the population looked for the friendship of Serbia, a nation that in turn had her eyes on Russia, the leading Slav power. Gavrilo Princip, a sickly Serbian student who was a cat's paw for a secret society of violent nationalists, assassinated the Archduke and his wife with pistol shots as they were driving past in an open car.

On 28 July the Emperor and the Government of Vienna despatched a furious ultimatum to Serbia demanding recompense. (The delay was mainly due to the time taken for the Empire to mobilize its armies.) But before the ultimatum was delivered the German Kaiser had been consulted and he, in an astonishingly casual fashion, gave what was later described in a famous metaphor as a blank cheque of unqualified support. The Kaiser, who did not even see the details of the ultimatum, seemed quite oblivious to the possible consequences of his action. Serbia capitulated substantially – although not totally – but Vienna was too furious to be assuaged by Serbia's willingness to give way.

Since Germany had promised her support, the Emperor and his Government did not hesitate to declare war on Serbia on 28 July, and the guns of the Empire began to thunder. As should have been foreseen, Russia prepared to give military support to the small and overwhelmingly threatened Serb state, and began mobilizing her armies on 31 July. This was immediately regarded by Germany as a casus belli, and since the Russians did not halt the order, Germany declared war on Russia on 1 August. Again with total predictability, this made it inevitable that France would support Russia and declare war on Germany. On 2 August, Russian troops moved against Germany and German troops moved against France. The fuse was lit and the explosion was about to take place.

The entry of France into the war did not of itself cause Britain to come in. The specific German aggression that made Britain act was the invasion of Belgium. A Treaty signed in 1839 – the famous 'Scrap of Paper' – committed Britain to guarantee the independence of Belgium, which became a Kingdom after her separation from the Netherlands. There was self-interest in Britain's desire for a free and independent Belgium, because Britain could not countenance an enemy country controlling the mouth of the great River Scheldt that enters the English Channel beyond Antwerp. An enemy on the Scheldt was considered in 1914 – as it had been during the Napoleonic War – to be disastrous to Britain's control of the English Channel.

On 4 August 1914 Britain went to war. The declaration of war sparked an immediate and quite astonishing burst of rejoicing in Britain, France and Germany. These warring nations seemed to have released their long pent-up tensions, and cheering crowds thronged the streets. The populations of these countries felt that the war would be brief, intense and full of dramatic events; and of course every nation was confident that she would be victorious. There was not much thought about the blood that was likely to be shed.

When war broke out Turkey was well on the way to becoming an ally of Germany. In December 1913 military co-operation between Turkey and Germany had been given a great boost by the arrival in Constantinople of a military mission of seventy officers, under General Otto Liman von Sanders (who would be Hamilton's opponent at Gallipoli). This German general became the Inspector General of the

Turkish Army – de facto Commander-in-Chief – and immediately took a 'grip' on his new command, which he considered quite unfit for war. This had nothing to do with the quality of the men in the ranks, but was due to the hopeless lack of equipment; some men did not even have boots. During the years before the war, as had also happened in Japan, the Turkish Navy was being instructed by Britain's Royal Navy. The German Admiralty now decided to take steps to weaken Britain's position. It therefore sent out the *Goeben*, a glittering example of German naval power, on an extended visit to Constantinople. She was a new battle cruiser, the largest ship that had ever entered the Dardanelles, the strait connecting the Mediterranean and the Black Seas, and this could not fail to make an immediate impact on Turkish opinion. The *Goeben* did more than anything else 'to secure Turkey as Germany's ally'.[4]

During 1914, the German Ambassador in Constantinople began a diplomatic offensive, making extravagant promises to induce Turkey to become Germany's formal ally. Although Enver Pasha, the thirty-one-year-old leader of the Young Turks, pressed hard for such an alliance – and despite a secret agreement concluded at the end of July – the rest of the Turkish Government was undecided. Their uncertainty was reinforced by Britain's entry into the war on 4 August, when the threat of the Royal Navy attacking the Dardanelles became an increasingly frightening possibility. By then the Turkish Army had begun its slow mobilization, a process that was hindered by a crippling shortage of ammunition. An even more important action was taken by the Turkish Navy: it began to lay three lines of mines across the Dardanelles, something that was to have devastating consequences on the eventual British assault up the narrow channel.

The factors that eventually stiffened the sinews of the Turkish Government were two naval events of first importance. The first was that two new battleships under construction in British shipyards – ships that had been partly paid for by public subscription in Turkey – were summarily taken over by the British. These ships would have been the pride of the Turkish fleet, but the Royal Navy could not allow such mighty vessels to be in the hands of a potential enemy. The British move outraged the Turks. The second event was the skilful moves of the *Goeben* and her accompanying light cruiser *Breslau*. When Britain declared war, these ships were in Sicilian waters preparing to attack French convoys, and they immediately became the quarry of the Royal Navy. There was an exciting long-distance chase, but the two German ships eventually got to Constantinople, and their escape was considered an impressive demonstration of German naval prowess. In Constantinople they were formally purchased. They became part of the Turkish Navy and some of the crew members were given Turkish uniforms. The *Goeben* and *Breslau* became the foundation of a force that would guard against any incursion by the Russian Black Sea fleet.

Supplies of desperately needed ammunition now began to arrive by train from Germany through the Balkans. The British Embassy in Constantinople, in the light of Britain's lack of preparation for war in the Middle East, took all possible diplomatic steps to keep the peace. The British ignored the flagrantly belligerent moves of the Turkish Government, but they nevertheless could not permit any Turkish ships to sail into the Mediterranean, and a squadron of the Royal Navy was posted to the mouth of the Dardanelles as a block. On 27 September the Turks closed the Dardanelles and additional mines were laid, which meant that there could be no further traffic from the Mediterranean to the Black Sea, thus stopping communications between Russia and the West. By now the Germans were pressing the Turkish Government to abandon neutrality. This had the result that before dawn on 29 October the Turkish fleet, commanded by the German Admiral Souchon, crossed the Black Sea and bombarded Odessa and Sebastopol. Russia removed her diplomats from Constantinople, and Britain and France soon followed suit. The Young Turks and the Germans had their War at last.[5]

'The Attack on Turkey holds the Field'[6]

The Gallipoli expedition was solely aimed at gaining control of the strait between the Mediterranean and the Black Sea (shown on **Map 5**), a stretch of over 220 miles, with Europe on the north side and Asia on the south. For the first forty-one miles from its entrance on the Mediterranean, the passage known as the Dardanelles is three miles wide at its mouth and, at the most constricted part, the Narrows, is only a mile across. The Gallipoli Peninsula is forbiddingly high ground on the north shore of the Dardanelles, and when the British Army became involved, Hamilton's objective was to control that north shore, to ease the passage of the British ships towards Constantinople. At the eastern end of the Dardanelles, the strait enters the glassy Sea of Marmara – the Marble Sea – a lovely lake that measures 120 miles from west to east. At the eastern end of the Sea of Marmara there is a narrow gut, the Bosporus, leading to the Black Sea. Constantinople (now Istanbul) is spectacularly situated where the Sea of Marmara joins the Bosporus, and straddles both the European and the Asiatic shores.

The military importance of the strait had been known for millennia. During the time of ancient Greece, it was the passage used by the invading Persian armies. Afterwards, in war after war it was an important artery, and Napoleon fully appreciated its importance. There was nothing new about the idea of forcing the passage. It was such an obvious strategy that the Turks were certain to take early precautions against it: hence the mining of the Dardanelles before war was even declared. Therefore when hostilities started there was no secrecy about the possibility of the Royal Navy sailing aggressively through the strait. If this were done successfully, it would hasten the victory of the Entente powers, by supplying Russia. There were also political advantages, since the Cabinets of the Entente were to learn that:

> the Dardanelles was the enemy's heel of Achilles; that a success at this point might rally the wavering Balkans to the banner of the Entente; that the forcing of the Straits might prove the beginning of the end. But by the time this knowledge had been assimilated the opportunity for successful action had gone.[7]

Before the end of 1914 it was clear that the Western Front had reached a deadlock that would be very difficult to break. It is therefore no surprise that the most important naval, military and political figures in Whitehall began to consider an alternative strategy, specifically a naval assault on the Dardanelles, and this became a preoccupation of the War Council, the inner Cabinet of eight members who exercised overall control of Britain's conduct of the war.[8] The two senior service ministers, Lord Kitchener, Secretary of State for War, and Winston Churchill, First Lord of the Admiralty, both supported a direct attack on the Dardanelles, although Kitchener's support was based initially on the plan for an exclusively naval operation. Sir Maurice Hankey, a former officer in the Royal Marines, who was the exceptionally able and influential Secretary of the Council, saw the great value of taking the Dardanelles, but recommended carrying out the task by using a British army to co-operate with 'the Balkan States, which had defeated Turkey shortly before the war, in an attack on their old enemy'.[9]

Kitchener, whose prestige and experience gave him a virtually dominant voice in all matters of strategy, was pulled by three conflicting demands as he considered the Dardanelles venture: first, he was strongly inclined to make the attack to provide practical help to Russia, and also give some recompense to the Russians, whose ill-prepared armies had attacked Germany in 1914 to relieve pressure on the French and British. The Russians were in any event desperately short of all types of ammunition. But on the negative side, the second point was that an expedition to the Dardanelles was already meeting the vociferous opposition of Sir John French, Commander-in-Chief of the BEF in France, who saw it as a dangerous dispersion of effort. And third – a pressing practical problem for Kitchener – he was totally unable to find the 150,000 men he believed would be needed to mount a successful naval and military operation. Kitchener's estimate of numbers was probably sound. He had an extraordinarily acute strategic judgement. The failure to find these numbers was the ultimate cause of the catastrophe at Gallipoli.

While Kitchener remained indecisive, Churchill took the initiative and instructed his staff officers to start making plans for a naval assault. In this he was enthusiastically supported by Lord Fisher, the powerful naval reformer whom Churchill had brought out of retirement to become First Sea Lord, the professional head of the Royal Navy. At the age of seventy-four, Fisher was as energetic and imaginative as ever, although he began to reveal considerable instability later in 1915. The heading of this section of the chapter is taken from a memorandum that Fisher wrote on 3 January 1915.

The planning was now under way. The opening of the Dardanelles would be a job for the Royal Navy, but if the Army was going to make any contribution, there was no question about the availability of as many as 150,000 men. The plan therefore began to turn into a gamble, not least because the Turks never stopped believing that the British would mount an assault. As if to give the Turks a positive warning of what was to come, the Royal Navy now showed its hand. The Commander of the British naval squadron at the Dardanelles was Vice Admiral Carden, an able and aggressive officer. As early as 12 January, Fisher had drawn up a plan for a substantial force of ships to carry out an assault on the Straits, and these were in due course despatched.[10]

On 19 February British ships in blustery weather began to bombard fortifications on the Gallipoli shore, doing a great deal of damage. The British ships also swept the first six miles of the strait for mines, although they did not by any means find them all. Shelling continued intermittently for three weeks in the face of increasing Turkish retaliation. During this period, a number of parties of marines were landed to blow up Turkish defensive works. They faced little opposition at first:

> On this very spot, where a demolition party of thirty men had moved about with impunity on 26 February, the 29th Division exactly two months later lost 3,000 men before nightfall.[11]

But again Turkish opposition soon stiffened.

Churchill had by now taken the bit between his teeth, and he pressed Kitchener, in the presence of the Prime Minister, to prepare a military force to support the naval attack. Kitchener developed a plan, and on 10 March announced to the War Council the approximate strength of the force he had put together.[12] At this stage, the force was intended for only a supporting role, but things quickly changed. By now there was considerable Turkish resistance at the mouth of the strait and the naval bombardment was losing its effectiveness. Then a sudden and unexpected problem arose. While Churchill was continuing to press for action, Carden's health failed, and he was forced to pass the command to his deputy, Vice Admiral de Robeck, an officer who did not have the same tenacity as his predecessor, something that was to have an unfortunate effect on the naval participation in the assault. De Robeck's Chief of Staff was Roger Keyes, a Royal Navy commodore (a one-star flag rank in modern terminology). He was brave, imaginative and aggressive and was to end his career as a five-star admiral of the fleet. But at this stage he could not overcome de Robeck's caution. Later in the year Keyes proposed a 'death-or-glory' assault that he proposed to lead, but this was all too late and was turned down, much to his disappointment.

However, de Robeck started well. Little realizing that the minesweeping had not been thorough enough to clear the multiple mine barriers across the strait, he decided to mount a huge demonstration of naval force. He assembled and deployed sixteen large but old battleships, and, on 18 March, six British battleships in line abreast 'advanced majestically to the execution of a momentous plan'.[13] They were followed by a second line of four French, and a third line of six further British vessels. There was now a repeat in the Dardanelles of what had happened in the Yellow Sea ten years before. While the mighty armada was sailing forward, all the time engaging Turkish fixed fortifications and mobile artillery that was always able to slip away, mines started exploding. Five battleships were knocked out, three being sunk and two heavily damaged, and some smaller ships were also put out of action. With more than a quarter of the naval squadron now lost, this was a very serious setback to the whole enterprise, and it had an unfortunate effect on de Robeck's nerve. Ian Hamilton had already arrived and witnessed the naval battle. He quickly recognized that he would have to accept the baton that de Robeck was anxious to pass to him, and de Robeck made this clear at a meeting on 22 March. It was inconceivable at this time that there should be a supreme commander responsible for both sea and land. (This had to wait until the dominance of the Americans in the Second World War.) In 1915, the Navy and Army co-operated closely, but they fought their own separate battles, and one did not take orders from the other.

'You Are to Have Command'[14]

The order that Kitchener gave Hamilton to proceed to the Dardanelles was typically cursory and extremely direct. On 12 March, Hamilton was summoned to see Kitchener at the War Office, and the Secretary of State devoted only a few sentences to tell Hamilton what was to happen, and included the five words quoted above. Hamilton, at sixty-two, was certainly old by today's standards. Besides the officers already employed in the BEF, at least two men were slightly younger and had much more experience than Hamilton in senior commands in the field: Sir Archibald Hunter, aged fifty-nine, and Sir Herbert Plumer, aged fifty-eight. But there is no evidence that Kitchener considered anyone other than Hamilton, and he was obviously influenced by their close association in South Africa.

As must have been realized, Hamilton knew little about the terrain of the Gallipoli Peninsula, and nothing about the size and dispositions of the Turkish Army. Because of these uncertainties, Hamilton remained with Kitchener and started asking questions. The General Staff in London had not studied the Ottoman Empire in detail before the war, and all they could produce for Hamilton's instruction were 'the text book on the Turkish Army and two small guide books'. Kitchener and Hamilton discussed the topography of the Gallipoli Peninsula, relying on 'Lord K's small and featureless map'. The Admiralty almost certainly had more detailed maps of the Dardanelles, but it was enough for Kitchener to rely on Hamilton and his staff to equip themselves with tactical maps of the Dardanelles and the Gallipoli Peninsula once operational planning was under way. However, with the use of his own schoolboy map, Kitchener talked exclusively about an attack in the south of the peninsula, and guessed that the Turkish Army on Gallipoli numbered about 40,000 men. (His estimate was close, as became apparent when the peninsula was invaded.)[15]

The composition of Hamilton's command was going to be as follows; these are real figures since Kitchener had only given approximations:

29th Division	18,000 men	56 guns
Royal Naval Division	11,000 men	6 guns
ANZAC	34,100 men	76 guns
Total:	63,100 men	138 guns[16]

At the last minute, Kitchener found another 4,000 men to add to Hamilton's force. This was an Indian Army brigade of four 'native' battalions, with highly mobile mountain guns, and this splendid formation brought his force up to a rounded figure of 67,000. In addition, Hamilton commanded a French division of 18,000 men in colourful pre-war uniforms, with forty guns. The French were intended for the Asiatic shore; although they later worked on occasions alongside the British troops on the Gallipoli Peninsula, they generally operated independently. (Hamilton was instructed not to employ British troops anywhere south of the

Dardanelles.) But on the negative side, the only formation with a full complement of artillery was the 29th Division; and a large Russian corps was also mentioned, but it never appeared. There was another point: Hamilton's force included only a minority of Regular troops: one division, plus the Indian brigade. The 29th Division, later to be known as the 'Incomparables', was composed of first-class Regular units assembled ad hoc, but they had never trained and worked together as a formation. The Royal Naval Division had infantry but virtually no artillery. It was newly organized and substantially untrained, although the men were of high quality. The Australian and New Zealand Army Corps (ANZAC) was a superb formation of volunteers, but they were barely prepared for modern warfare although they were to learn quickly. An overall problem was the general shortage of artillery and shells throughout the campaign.

With an estimated Turkish force of 40,000 men on the Gallipoli Peninsula, Hamilton's superiority – based on his own force of 67,000 – was illusory. The trained and fully-equipped attacking forced comprised only the 29th Division and the Indian brigade, which meant that the realistic balance of numbers was 22,000 attackers against 40,000 defenders. After Hamilton's experience in the Russo-Japanese War, he should have been alarmed by this disparity. And these figures were all quite different from the force of 150,000 men that Kitchener had originally thought necessary for success.

There was also a surprising complication about the chain of command. The way in which Kitchener handled Hamilton's job broke the rules and disrupted normal military channels of communication. Kitchener held a political appointment, and orders to Hamilton should have come from the military staff in the War Office, to whom he should also have reported. In fact Sir James Murray, the Chief of the Imperial General Staff, and his subordinates did not know of Hamilton's appointment until after he had himself been told. Kitchener never understood that he was not the Commander-in-Chief of the British Army, and the difficulties in his co-operation with politicians were obviously influenced by how he interpreted his own job description. Hamilton and the other generals were in awe of Kitchener, and nobody attempted to tell him that his job was a civilian one, which meant that he could no longer operate like an autocrat.

Kitchener was bullish overall about the proposed attack. The main weight was going to be carried by the Royal Navy, and when it approached Constantinople, the Turks would almost certainly collapse. The Army might be called upon to support the Navy, but Kitchener did not think that the Army would have to bear the burden of the attack. This was, however, before the unsuccessful naval incursion on 18 March, which changed the situation totally. Kitchener later sent Hamilton a memorandum of instructions covering eleven points, which summarized what the two of them had actually discussed. Kitchener emphasized that the Turkish positions 'had been fortified and armed for determined resistance'.[17]

For Hamilton, everything from now on was improvisation on a heroic scale. He departed the next day, 13 March, travelled through France by rail, and sailed from Marseilles in a Royal Navy ship, arriving at Tenedos, a large island twenty miles south-west of the Gallipoli Peninsula, on the afternoon of 17 March. He was accompanied by Major General Braithwaite, his Chief of Staff whom Kitchener had appointed; other senior staff officers, all nominated by the War Office, would be delayed although they were badly needed. The day of his arrival at Tenedos was the day before de Robeck's impressive but unsuccessful incursion into the Dardanelles, the incursion that totally changed the job that Hamilton had to do. And there was another date that was to become important. Hamilton's Army eventually assaulted the Peninsula on 25 April. From the date of his arrival at Tenedos, there would be thirty-nine days before the attack, which made it a very tight margin into which Hamilton would have to pack all the necessary organizational work and strategic planning. For comparison, the planning for the invasion of France in June 1944 took *seventeen months*. (Although the 1944 invasion was much larger and vastly more complicated than Gallipoli, the difference in the length of the planning processes for each was still startlingly great.)

Hamilton immediately set about two tasks. First, he had to see something of the forbidding landscape of the Gallipoli Peninsula. He therefore embarked on a naval vessel early on 18 March and travelled around the coast. He sailed from Tenedos, which was an unsuitable base of operations for the invasion, to Lemnos, which he chose as his headquarters. Lemnos is an island inconveniently situated forty miles west of Gallipoli, but it has a long, narrow harbour at Mudros. The voyage from Lemnos round the west and north of the peninsula and back – a distance of 100-odd miles – took seven and a half hours. Hamilton could not take in the peninsula in much detail, although he was struck by the obvious strength of the Turkish lines. But this cursory reconnaissance had perforce to provide enough information for the decision about the place or places where his army was going to assault. It was at the end of this voyage that Hamilton saw at some distance the unsuccessful naval attack on the Dardanelles, which made it imperative that the army would have to take the initiative, although Churchill continued to urge de Robeck not to stop bombarding the Turkish fortifications.

Hamilton's second task was to pull his command together and set up a sensible organization, and he had to do this without the help of his senior A and Q staff officers, who had not yet arrived. Hamilton himself had spent many years on the staff in these two branches, so he had the necessary expertise. But this work swallowed his attention when he should have devoted himself to questions of strategy.[18] Stores had already been landed and – typical of the chaotic arrangements – the loading had been carried out with a startling absence of thought:

> water-carts in one ship; water-cart horses in another; guns in one ship; limbers in another; entrenching tools anyhow. . . transports have been loaded up as in peace time and they must be completely discharged and every ship reloaded in war fashion . . . it takes three times as long to repack a ship loaded at haphazard as it would have taken to have loaded her on a system in the first instance.[19]

There was no alternative to sending the cargo ships back to Egypt to be properly loaded. Hamilton also decided very quickly that the army could not concentrate on Lemnos, and that it must be properly reorganized in the wider spaces of Egypt. On 24 March he was on his way to Alexandria, accompanied by the Royal Naval Division. The 29th Division was not due to arrive from Malta until early April, so that it could be routed directly to Egypt.

Hamilton arrived in Egypt on 26 March. He immediately started the wheels turning, meeting the political and military leaders, inspecting British, ANZAC, Indian and French troops, and involving himself in such administrative matters as supplies of ammunition and water and loading transport ships correctly. From now on the administrative arrangements, especially for the transport of troops, were running fairly smoothly. And important details were provided for, e.g. the supply of 500 copies of maps of the Gallipoli Peninsula, arranged on 10/13 April.[20] Hamilton also conducted a lively correspondence with Kitchener, in fine disregard of military protocol: 'K is my soldier chief ' (although officially he was not).[21] What is striking about all the correspondence between Hamilton and the War Office before the assault on the peninsula is that it is so much devoted to logistical matters, with only the most intermittent reference to the strategy of the campaign.

Hamilton was also confronted with stories in the Egyptian press revealing the forthcoming attack on Gallipoli, although they did not presumably tell the Turks much they did not know already. (Such indiscretion was not unique: in later wars, radio broadcasts on the public airwaves revealed information that should have been kept under wraps.) Hamilton's A and Q staff officers arrived (perhaps appropriately) on 1 April. Since he was now partly relieved from his routine planning, Hamilton could at last turn to matters of strategy. In this, he was stimulated by a telegram he received on 4 April from Kitchener, whose views coincided with Hamilton's to land at the southern tip of the peninsula.[22] He continued to be impressed by all the troops he inspected – something that boosted his customary positive attitude – and he made a telling remark that was later to rebound: 'If we don't win, I won't be able to put it on the men.'[23] Hamilton left Egypt on 8 April and arrived at Lemnos early on 10 April. By that time, with his usual optimism and impetuosity, he had made up his mind how to mount his attack. There were fifteen days to go. On the ship, Hamilton had – for the first time – immersed himself in the Appreciations of the Situation made by his three subordinates, Major General Aylmer Hunter-Weston of the 29th Division, Lieutenant General Sir William Birdwood of ANZAC, and Major General Archibald Paris of the Royal Naval Division. He was confronted with three very different opinions. The ideas of Birdwood and Paris were wide-ranging and diffuse, although Paris gave some support for the attack on Cape Helles in the south (as had Birdwood when he had earlier been in contact with Kitchener).

A military appreciation must cover the topography of the battleground, a realistic appraisal of the forces on both sides, and a clear statement of the objective. Hunter-Weston's appreciation was the only one that bore any relation to reality. It is no coincidence that Hunter-Weston was the only one of the four top commanders, Hamilton, Hunter-Weston, Birdwood and Paris, who had already seen any serious fighting since the outbreak of the war. He had commanded a brigade in the BEF in 1914, and had done well. For a start, Hunter-Weston understood the key objective of helping the Fleet, but he was cruelly realistic about the difficulties of the landing:

> The Turkish Army having been warned by our early bombardments and by the landings carried out some time ago, has concentrated a large force in and near the Gallipoli Peninsula. It has converted the Peninsula into an entrenched camp, has, under German direction, made several lines of entrenchments covering the landing places, with concealed machine gun emplacements and land mines on the beach; and has put in concealed positions guns and howitzers capable of covering the landing places and approaches with their fire.[24]

Hunter-Weston thought that Cape Helles and Suvla were viable landing places, but he favoured Helles because of its proximity to the strait. But he was by no means optimistic about the chances of success:

> No loss would be too heavy and no risks too great if thereby success would be attained . . . But I would repeat; no action should be taken unless it has been carefully thought out in all its possibilities and details and unless there is a reasonable *probability* of success.[25]

At a meeting on 10 April with de Robeck and his naval colleagues, Hamilton sketched his plan in broad outline, and the sailors nodded their agreement, although their contribution would be confined to the important roles of transporting the troops to the beaches and providing fire support to the landings.

> 1. The first objective was to upset the equilibrium of Liman von Sanders, by making a full-strength attack in the main landing places, and (in Hamilton's own words) throwing 'every man we

can carry in our small craft in one simultaneous rush against selected points'.

2. Because of the small size of the beaches, the 29th Division would land at a number of different places, and it was eventually decided to land the troops on five beaches on either side of Cape Helles. A particular problem was going to be the fortified village of Seddulbahir. The objective for the 29th Division on the first day was to reach a line five miles inland, and in the longer term it was the Kilitbahir plateau, on the shore of the Narrows, thirteen miles from Cape Helles. Kilitbahir had been discussed with Kitchener at the meeting in London on 12 March.

3. The ANZAC force would land on a beach half way up the western coast with the aim of seizing 'the high backbone of the Peninsula'. Their purpose was to impede the flow of Turkish troops to – or (it was hoped) away from – Cape Helles.[26] In modern military language, their role would be called interdiction, and their objective for the first day was a position three miles inland.[27] With more optimism, Hamilton called the ANZAC landing 'a strong feint, which may, and we hope will, develop into the real thing'.

4. There would a diversion to the eastern end of the northern coast, at Bulair. This would be a job for the Royal Naval Division.

5. Hamilton estimated that fewer than ten per cent of the defending force, i.e. 4,000 Turkish troops and ten guns, would be anywhere near Cape Helles within two days. (He had not yet discovered how quickly the Turkish Army could respond and regroup with mobile reserves.)

Many days before this meeting, Hamilton had made up his mind to make the main attack on Cape Helles. He had talked to Kitchener in these terms during their meeting in London, and Kitchener had reiterated his advice in his telegram of 4 April. Hamilton's rapid voyage around the Gallipoli coast had persuaded him that no other landing place was suitable; and he admitted to himself, as early as 22 March, that he was going to concentrate on Cape Helles in order to be close to the Fleet.[28] Birdwood, the British officer who was the ANZAC Commander, had suggested Cape Helles to Kitchener even before Hamilton was appointed, and Birdwood had put into Kitchener's head his own estimate of 40,000 Turkish soldiers on the Gallipoli Peninsula.[29] Finally, Hunter-Weston's extremely circumspect endorsement in his appreciation, supported by Paris's, confirmed the choice of Cape Helles. However, Hamilton himself agreed with Hunter-Weston about the strength of the Turkish defences:

> The Peninsula itself is being fortified and many Turks work every night on trenches, redoubts and entanglements . . . German thoroughness and forethought have gripped the old go-as-you-please Turk.[30]

The decision was made for good or ill; unfortunately it was mostly for ill.

Hamilton's Choice of the Least Bad Alternative

The topography of the Gallipoli peninsula and the strength and dispositions of the defending troops were going to make for a very difficult invasion. There was no landing place that could have been considered good. Hamilton's dilemma was how to choose the least bad from a number of unattractive alternatives. With hindsight, what can now be said about these alternatives?

As can be seen in **Map 6**, the Gallipoli peninsula is like an irregular triangle. At the eastern end is a neck three miles across, the Bulair Isthmus, where the peninsula is connected to the European mainland. Constantinople lies more than 100 miles east of Bulair. The arm of the triangle running west from Bulair is thirty miles long and ends at Suvla Bay. From there, the second arm runs south to Cape Helles in a concave loop, eighteen miles as the crow flies. From Cape Helles, the third arm of the triangle runs for the forty-two miles of the Dardanelles back to Bulair. The peninsula is everywhere beautiful, especially in the spring. It is very hilly, and the tilt of the land progresses gradually upwards from Cape Helles to the north shore, a short distance to the west of Bulair. Here is a brief description of the alternative landing places that would have been possible for Hamilton to assault.

BULAIR: Bulair is a relatively flat region and it would have been easy to land there, although Hamilton was afraid that the Turks had strongly fortified the Isthmus. These fears were not justified since some of the entrenchments were relics of the Crimean War. The attraction of Bulair was that it was the most suitable place for an advance on Constantinople by a large army. Being so narrow, the Isthmus could have been seized and fortified, and the main force could then have marched east. However, Hamilton was not instructed by London to attempt a coup de main against Constantinople: a matter of grand strategy for which Hamilton did not have nearly enough troops. He had not in any event been invited to discuss and contribute to the politico-strategic plan for his army. His actual job was different. He commanded a relatively small force and his task was to support the Fleet, so that unless the ships had already passed through the Dardanelles, Bulair was not a realistic option. There was the possibility that Hamilton could have taken and occupied Bulair, then advanced along the north shore of the Dardanelles. But the size of his force was also totally inadequate for such a task, since there would have been nothing to stop Turkish troops from crossing the strait from the Asiatic shore to reinforce the peninsula.

SUVLA: Along the coast line, forbiddingly steep hills reduced the number of possible landing places for troops. The coast from Bulair to Suvla is precipitous, except for Ejelmar Bay, six miles east of Suvla itself. Suvla provided an excellent landing place for large numbers of troops, as the British were to discover in August 1915, although the failure to move forward at that time was the result of the astounding lethargy of the force that landed there. In between the many hills and ravines of the peninsula there are some broad stretches of low ground. The most important of these are the ten miles from Ejelmar Bay to the Dardanelles strait, and the similar distance (although interrupted by a few hills) from Suvla also to the strait. A landing in the north-west, at Suvla Bay, maybe with a subsidiary landing on the smaller beach at Ejelmar, was a viable alternative. Both Birdwood and Hunter-Weston gave it limited support; and Hamilton himself, during his brief voyage around the coast, thought it suitable. However, he rejected it for a compelling reason: 'Merely to hold our Line of Communication we should need a couple of Divisions.'[31] Suvla was only possible if Kitchener could be persuaded to boost the size of the Gallipoli Force by fifty per cent. Hamilton did not consider this possible.

CAPE HELLES AND ANZAC: On the side of the triangle from Suvla to Cape Helles, there are a reasonable number of beaches, but most of them within a short distance meet steep, scrub-covered hills and ravines. One of the beaches here became famous as Anzac Cove, named for the attacking ANZAC soldiers. South of Anzac Cove is a plateau that stretches west to east from the coast to the Narrows, which is, prima facie, an attractive place to land, but was ignored by Hamilton. At Cape Helles, selected as the main point of attack, the 29th Division would be landed on five beaches. These were, from east to west, S, V, W, X, and Y. The landings on S and Y would be to protect the flanks; the main thrust would be from V, W, and X, clustered on either side of the Cape. Inland from Cape Helles, the terrain rises only gradually, but the low ground was nevertheless dominated by fire from the gentle slopes. (See **Map 7**.)

Hamilton selected the most obvious place, which was unfortunately exactly where the Turks expected him. An assault on unfamiliar beaches at Cape Helles meant that it had to be done in daylight, in the face of well-prepared Turkish fortifications covered by heavy artillery and small-arms fire. But this choice raised two additional questions. The first concerned the ANZAC operation, which was to employ Hamilton's largest formation. It was natural that Hamilton would use the 29th, his sole Regular division, for the most important task. But since the two ANZAC divisions could not crowd into the small X, W, and V Beaches, what role could they play that would make full use of their considerable strength? As mentioned, Hamilton visualized that the ANZAC troops would be used for interdiction, an essentially secondary job. Hamilton also had at the back of his mind that the 29th Division at Helles and the ANZAC troops would quickly link up. However, this never came close to realization. The second question concerned the Turks. Where exactly were the Turkish defensive positions? And how many Turkish troops were in the southern part of the peninsula, including reserves that could be quickly moved on interior lines to reinforce the units at the 'sharp end'? Virtually nothing was known about the size and disposition of the Turkish defenders.

The Turkish force in the European sector (including Gallipoli) was made up of ten Regular divisions, three provisional divisions and three cavalry brigades, almost half the strength of the whole Turkish Army. Each division had about 9,000 front-line infantry, a smaller number than a British division.[32] Since the arrival of the German Military Mission at the end of 1913, Liman von Sanders had transformed the Turkish peasant soldiers into a formidable fighting force, commanded by many officers – mostly Turkish but some German – who would later make names for themselves. The quality of the Turks as fighting men was to be a surprise to the British. Colonel Kannengiesser, the shrewd German staff officer attached to the 9th Division, covering Cape Helles, found the Turkish peasant:

> well trained and well led, an ideal soldier. His demands for housing and feeding are remarkably small, if one can even use the word demand. He is accustomed from his youth up to sleep on a hard floor. The Turks don't know beds. The most they know are carpets and mattresses which are pulled out of a cupboard for the night and laid anywhere on the floor. Rice and flesh is a feast for him. Their iron rations, as and when available, consisted of a piece of bread and some olives, the latter generally wrapped in the corner of a more than doubtful-looking handkerchief.[33]

Liman von Sanders was the best type of highly professional Prussian officer, well-educated, experienced and independent:

> a tall, stern, military-looking man, very self-contained, quick in decision, clear in his orders, scanty of praise, sharp in reprimand and in following up a decision once taken . . . not concerned with politics.[34]

As part of his energetic training programme for the Turkish Army, he paid particular attention to improving roads on the peninsula, to speed the transfer of reserves to meet threats, a key element in Turkish (and German) defensive strategy. Liman von Sanders now formed a new Fifth Army, under his personal command, and spent the four weeks before the arrival of the British in a furious programme of training. Out of the total Turkish Army of thirteen divisions in the European sector, he deployed four divisions: the 5th, 7th, 9th, and 19th on the Peninsula; plus two additional divisions, the 5th and 11th on the Asiatic shore. Birdwood's estimate of 40,000 Turkish soldiers on Gallipoli – the estimate that went to Kitchener and was then passed to Hamilton – indicated a correct order of magnitude. Liman von Sanders drew his troops back from the dispersed positions they had formerly occupied and put them into three mobile formations which could move on interior lines. In contrast, Hamilton's forces were split up during and after the landing, which meant that the Turks would always have greater numbers when the two sides met in battle. The commander of the Turkish 19th Division was a lieutenant colonel, aged thirty-four, who had a name to conjure with, Mustafa Kemal.[35] Kemal, then totally unknown, made an immediate impression on Kannengiesser:

> a clear-thinking, active, quiet man who knew what he wanted. He weighed and decided everything for himself, without looking elsewhere for support or agreement to his opinion. He spoke accordingly but little, and was always reserved and retiring without being unfriendly. He did not appear to be very strong bodily, although extremely wiry. His stubborn energy gave him apparently complete control, both of his troops and of himself.[36]

Liman von Sanders's own appreciation of the situation before the British landing estimated that three sectors were vulnerable. In order of importance, these were Cape Helles, the north-west coast, and Bulair.[37] He therefore paid most attention to Cape Helles. His Turkish subordinates resented his criticisms of their earlier policy of dispersion; they were already correcting it themselves before the new German commander ordered mobile battle groups to be formed. Just before the British attack, the 9th and 19th Divisions were positioned to cover the British landings in the south of the peninsula. The 7th, 9th and 19th Divisions formed III Corps, commanded by Brigadier Esat Pasha, who had graduated from the Prussian War Academy – a rare distinction – and who had exceptional experience in war and peace. Many of the men in the 9th Division were reservists who had fought in the Balkan Wars of 1912–13 and had earned a strong fighting reputation.[38] Kannengiesser was with them.

At Cape Helles, which was covered by the Turkish 9th Division, the British were faced with well-planned defensive positions with strongpoints 'held by well-led, well-trained and confident troops'.[39] These defences were occupied by a tightly-controlled Turkish regiment (equivalent to a British brigade) which held back plentiful reserves, and whose troops 'had been working on improving the defences for more than eight months'; the positions were thick with barbed wire. The artillery fire plan, using 150mm guns and 105mm howitzers, field gun batteries and 37mm pom-pom quick-firing guns, had been carefully planned and rehearsed. The artillery commander was the officer whose description of the dead British soldiers in rows like broad-beans is quoted in the title of this chapter. The ANZAC landing was covered by the 19th Division, whose forward infantry – three companies protecting the coast and one in immediate reserve – 'were well dug in, occupied positions that dated back to 1912 and had spent months improving both their positions and their communications'.[40]

In summary, the Turkish troops defending Cape Helles and the ANZAC landing relied on carefully-planned and continuously improved permanent fortifications, and plentiful artillery. Mobile reserves of infantry could be rushed forward to reinforce the modest numbers of defenders in the front line, who had at least enough men and firepower to cause the attackers to halt temporarily. Above all, commanders at all levels in the Turkish Army were fast on their feet and were to demonstrate time after time how quickly they could respond to British moves.

Five Beaches and Fifteen Victoria Crosses

Hamilton's first and most important job, although not his only one, was completed when his men were launched into combat, at the stage when strategy became tactics. Responsibility for success now depended on two large bodies of men: those in the British army's chain of command, down to the stoic and bloody-minded soldiers in the ranks, and the Turkish defenders of their homeland. As explained, this book is more concerned with Hamilton's decisions than with the progress of the fighting, but the story would be seriously incomplete without a sketch of the actual landings on the peninsula and the fierce but inconclusive battles during the days and weeks that followed.

Cape Helles is on a headland, and the five British landings were intended to converge, thus concentrating the British force. In the event, this took some time to happen, because of the intensity of the fighting on the beaches. The landings at Cape Helles were made possible by typically British improvisation. In the Second World War, landings from the sea were relatively easy with the use of custom-designed landing craft of different sizes, fitted with ramps at the front to enable troops and vehicles to get onto the shore. In early 1915, the Army did not have the benefit of such specialist vessels, but the Navy came up with a solution. They provided a number of small steam-powered pinnaces that pulled behind them trains of open rowing boats, each containing half an infantry platoon. Every soldier carried an extra-heavy load of eighty pounds – 250 rounds of ammunition and rations for three days – which caused some balance problems in the boats, although there were no disasters, at least on the short journey to the shore. For the landing on V Beach a naval officer, Commander Edward Unwin, produced out of his imagination the idea of a Trojan Horse, with men in its belly. This was an old collier, the *River Clyde*, which would be driven by her own steam as far onto the beach as she could go. Unwin became its very gallant commander. The soldiers were to emerge from sally ports – open panels in the side of the hull – and charge across a bridge of smaller boats that had been pulled along by the *River Clyde*. A substantial number of men were delivered, but they were unfortunately in full view of the enemy. The assault from the sea began in the early morning of 25 April.

Fifteen Victoria Crosses won on 25 and 26 April provide evidence enough of the ferocity of the fighting on those five small beaches (plotted on **Map 7**). On S Beach, the site of the flanking assault furthest east, the smallest of the five landing parties reached the beach. The Turks – unusually – were surprised, and the infantry, marines and sailors, together less than a battalion in strength, landed without too much trouble despite suffering sixty-three casualties. But V Beach was a different story.

V Beach has a shallow gradient that faces rising ground where the sand meets the shore. There are headlands on both sides of the beach, including the fortified village of Seddulbahir. The Turks, realizing the vulnerability of their position, had reinforced their defences with four machine guns, and four 35mm pom-poms. Three British battalions were to land in stages, because the *River Clyde* could only carry a single battalion, and the naval tows for the other two could not land the rest of the men all at once. The bridge of boats from the *River Clyde* had partly broken loose during the landing, but two sailors, Commander Unwin, the originator of the plan to use the *River Clyde* and who was her captain, accompanied by Able Seaman Williams, jumped into the water under heavy fire and improvised a crossing place for the soldiers, and winning

Victoria Crosses for themselves. But the soldiers who had emerged from the *River Clyde* were visible to the enemy. The big ships of the Royal Navy were too far offshore to provide close covering fire, because the sailors were reluctant to land shells close to the disembarking troops. The result was slaughter on the beach, and the water around the *River Clyde* was red with blood. The survivors spent an unpleasant night, but managed the next day to drive the Turkish defenders away from the beach and from Seddulbahir. During one of these attacks, Corporal William Cosgrove, of the 1st Battalion Royal Munster Fusiliers, won one of the nine Victoria Crosses awarded for valour on V Beach.

The largest landing of all was made on W Beach, a 200-yard stretch of sand, barely ten yards deep. At the end of the sand, there were hills which provided good firing positions for the defenders. The 1st Battalion Lancashire Fusiliers, loaded in thirty-two boats, were the first battalion to reach the beach. They were faced with barbed wire and heavy small-arms and machine-gun fire, and a little later they met a number of Turkish counter-attacks. But the Fusiliers eventually won the day, by displaying the grit and fighting skill based on long training and regimental discipline that characterized the pre-1914 British Regular Army. They won six Victoria Crosses in the process, and were soon afterwards reinforced by four new battalions. The newspaper story about 'six Victoria Crosses before breakfast' won by the Lancashire Fusiliers became one of the epics of the First World War. This was a vivid piece of journalism, and the story is not spoilt by the fact that the members of the battalion had actually eaten their breakfast before the landing!

Farther to the west, the landing on X Beach by the 2nd Battalion Royal Fusiliers was successful. Later in the day two follow-up battalions were strongly counter-attacked, although these Turkish forays were contained by naval gunfire. The troops on the last beach, Y, six miles up the coast, which had been intended to provide flank protection to the main landings on V, W, and X, were to experience a day of mixed fortunes. Two thousand men landed, but they did not immediately dig in to consolidate. Some men even advanced tentatively into, and then withdrew from, the small town of Krithia (which was to witness a pitched battle a few weeks later). At the end of the afternoon, Y Beach was heavily shelled and counter-attacked. There was much confusion, and many wounded and unwounded men were taken away by sea. Hamilton, on the battleship *Queen Elizabeth*, observed briefly what was happening, but he did not issue any direct orders to the troops to hold on.[41] And Hunter-Weston did not exercise a firm 'grip', since he was distracted by the other beaches. Nevertheless, on 26 April, the British held a tenuous position beyond the beach, although this was so far from the main landings that there could be no question of the men on Y Beach linking up with those near the tip of the Cape Helles headland.

On 25 April, independent of the British landings, the French had successfully captured KumKale, a village on the north-west tip of the Asiatic shore. They held off numerous Turkish counter-attacks, despite confusion that led to many French and Turkish troops being mixed up in the village itself. However, after the loss of 250 men and the capture of 500 Turkish prisoners, the French line stabilized on the 26 April, and the French troops were securely on the Asiatic shore of the Dardanelles.

On the European shore, the soldiers on X and W Beaches had linked up and held a crooked three-mile line running north and south. As yet this excluded V and S Beaches. Six miles farther to the north, the defenders of Y held their isolated perimeter. To have made relatively successful landings, although they had to rely on improvised methods of getting onto the beaches, and to have faced such well-defended Turkish positions when they got there, was a formidable achievement. It was, alas, a pyrrhic victory. The losses represented much more than a decimation, and worse was to come.

Enemy Trenches Twenty Yards Away

Unlike the landings at Cape Helles, which had a defined strategic aim – the capture of the Kilitbahir Plateau and the Narrows – the ANZAC landing on the western coast of the Gallipoli Peninsula (Z Beach) lacked a clear strategic objective. There was a barely articulated plan for interdicting Turkish reinforcements to the Cape Helles sector, and perhaps moving south-east to link with the 29th Division, which it was thought would soon be advancing. Of these two objectives, the first was partially fulfilled; but the second, not at all.

What made the ANZAC assault so difficult was that the landing place was a constricted beach faced with steep hills: hills that became barriers hard to climb, to defend and to traverse. The three words *climb*, *defend*, and *traverse* define the course of the heroic and unrelenting fighting that took place for more than eight months, much of this period in baking summer weather in which disease was to become an even greater enemy than the Turks.

The ANZAC commander was Lieutenant General Sir William Birdwood, a highly experienced Indian Army officer whom Hamilton knew well. Like most officers in the Indian Army, Birdwood had been under fire on many occasions. The operational plan was to land the ANZAC troops at dawn in open boats on a wide expanse of sand, codenamed Brighton Beach, north of the Gaba Tepe promontory. However, the navigation went wrong in the dark, and the troops were mixed up and landed in a small, rather beautiful bay a mile further north, a bay that became known as Anzac Cove. A visitor today is immediately struck by its tiny size for the task, which was to land two full-strength infantry divisions, with their animals, transport wagons, and artillery. The shortage of artillery and a good deal of confusion in organizing the batteries and the gun positions were serious problems on the first two days. The Turks had six guns ready for action at Gaba Tepe, plus a number of others in reserve, waiting for ammunition. Formidable hills dominate the cove, and are even more forbidding than those at Brighton Beach. This mountainous country was where the fighting was to take place, in the steep hills and gullies that stretch for five miles north-east, approximately parallel to the coastline. Small features of the terrain were later immortalized by names given them by the soldiers, often the surnames of officers commanding battalions and companies. In places, the two opposing lines were indeed only twenty yards apart.

The Turkish defensive positions were not on the beaches, like most of those on Cape Helles. The Turks dominated the beaches from the hills, and even when the ANZAC troops were in the boats, they began to suffer casualties from deadly aimed sniper and machine-gun fire. They started taking even heavier losses as they began to swarm up the hills. The result was confusion in the scrub and steep valleys, heavy defensive fire, Turkish counter-attacks, and an inevitable mixing of ANZAC men from different units. In some cases there were fifty per cent casualties, and about 1,600 men were evacuated by the end of the day. Morale began to falter as a few battalion commanders began to lose control of their units. But most battalions were solid and the troops managed to stick it out.

One problem was enemy fire from the south in the Gaba Tepe area, and the focus of the ANZAC activity began to move right, to the south. The troops were supported in that sector by effective fire from two ships that sailed close inshore. This was exceptional: most of the naval gunfire that day was less effective because it was poorly directed. Also the move to the right weakened the centre and left, and when the Turks made a heavy counter-attack, something approaching a crisis occurred.

During the afternoon of 25 April, reinforcements were landing only slowly and by the end of the day only half the total body of men had arrived on the beach. Some officers in the hills were sending requests to start to withdraw, and some groups of men were already straggling down towards the water. By the evening, the force had suffered 3,000 casualties. Birdwood left his ship and came ashore. The Turkish 27th Regiment, which was part of the 9th Division responsible for the southern sector, had been given the job of keeping watch on part of the western shore of the peninsula. By 0545 hours on 25 April, its commanding officer was fully aware of what was going on and shortly afterwards the word reached Lieutenant Colonel Mustafa Kemal, who commanded the 19th Division, responsible for the north-west. Kemal responded with furious energy to reinforce the 27th Regiment in attacking the troops in Anzac Cove and the hills facing it. Liman von Sanders had ordered Kemal to send forward a single battalion. But Kemal, sensing the danger from the serious size of the ANZAC assault, led forward a regiment of three battalions. He took a company forward to see for himself and put in a fierce counter-attack.[42] This was one of the main causes of the ANZAC troubles, despite the fact that the Turks lost many men to the naval gunfire. It marked the beginning of Mustafa Kemal's rapid rise to prominence.

There was now a meeting of the senior ANZAC officers. Birdwood, as a result of his extensive fighting experience, was in favour of hanging on. But he felt obliged to send an urgent message to Hamilton, who was on the *Queen Elizabeth*, to say that the two divisional commanders recommended evacuation. Hamilton was roused from his bed and, being an experienced tactician, which made him appreciate the great difficulties of any re-embarkation, refused to countenance any withdrawal, and was firmer than he had been at Y Beach:

> Your news is indeed serious. But there is nothing for it but to dig yourselves right in and stick it out . . . You have got through the difficult business, now you have only to dig, dig, dig, until you are safe.[43]

Within days the situation reached a degree of stability, although the ANZAC front was characterized from now on by perpetual attacks and counter-attacks, with a constant drain of casualties. As summer arrived, there was stifling heat, the smell of unburied corpses, and infestations of flies. On the Turkish side:

> The plague of flies was, under these conditions, insupportable. The walls of the tent inside were black. When eating, in spite of every precaution, there were always two or three flies on every mouthful. We bore the plague more willingly as we learnt from English papers that our enemy were suffering still more from it. The health of the troops suffered severely in the continuous tropical heat. In three battalions scurvy broke out as a result of the unchanging rations and the lack of vitamins.[44]

Water was a perpetual problem. Many Turkish soldiers on the high ground found fresh spring water, but the attackers had to transport their water in cans to the front line. This was usually only possible by loading mules, which had a particularly hard job climbing the gullies of the ANZAC sector. With a piece of splendid improvisation, the British managed to construct a pressure station and pipeline, connecting the ships to a section of the firing line.

Before and during the landings at Cape Helles and Anzac Cove, Hamilton had mounted a demonstration by the Royal Naval Division at Bulair. This was intended to distract the attention of the Turks and persuade them that there would be a landing on the Isthmus. The initial part of the demonstration was Freyberg's solitary swim on the night of 24 April to light flares on the beach. The next day, various naval manoeuvres took place and were noticed by Liman von Sanders. But he was not easily fooled:

About twenty large hostile ships, some war vessels, some transports, could be counted in front of us. Some individual vessels were lying close in under the steep slopes of the coast. Others were farther out in the Gulf or were still underway. From the broadsides of the war vessels came an uninterrupted stream of fire and smoke and the entire coast including our ridge was covered with shells and shrapnel. It was an unforgettable picture. Nowhere, however, could we see any debarking of troops from the transports.[45]

The initial clash of arms had now taken place. For the remaining months of the campaign, the fighting at both Cape Helles and Anzac resembled the attritional warfare that had already set in on the Western Front before the end of 1914. The Helles front was narrow, stretching three miles across the neck of the Helles promontory. At Anzac, the hills and gullies forced the troops on both sides into sometimes ferocious close-quarter combat. In many places the Turks occupied trenches that had been strongly constructed before the war. By now Hamilton had received twelve heavy (60-pounder) guns, but not enough ammunition for them. Both in Gallipoli and on the Western Front there was constant aggressive activity. But this was self-cancelling and left a more-or-less stable front line. Gallipoli was hotter than the Western Front, and there was more disease.

Before 14 May the total number of British casualties had reached 14,000, or more than a fifth of the strength of Hamilton's initial army on the peninsula, and an even higher proportion of his infantry, his front-line bayonets.[46] Kitchener combed the British army in Egypt to find troops to reinforce Hamilton. In addition to the Indian Army brigade that he had found before the original attack, Kitchener now sent two untrained Territorial divisions. The Royal Naval Division (now reduced to two brigades) and the French Division were also thrown into the Cape Helles sector. During a series of five bitter battles at Cape Helles between early June and mid-July, the British and French losses mounted by another 16,800, for the most meagre gains of ground.[47] The original strength of the 29th Division had by now been eaten up, and it consisted largely of reinforcements. Finding more men now became a matter of pressing urgency, and Kitchener was forced to do something about the situation. New, untrained and poorly-led formations were going to make possible the next – and final – phase of the Gallipoli campaign. By this time, Hamilton's force at Cape Helles had almost gained its ultimate line. This was a good deal short of the objective that the 29th Division should have reached *by the end of the first day of the assault.*

The Last Roll of the Dice

The two major assaults that had taken place during the campaign had followed the same pattern. The first phase was a fierce opposed landing from the sea to establish a foothold on land. The second was an immediate Turkish counter-attack that was barely contained by the British troops. (Such a counter-attack strategy was the embodiment of traditional German methods, which dictated that positions should be defended with the use of mobile reserves. This strategy was still being followed by the German Army in France in 1944.) The third phase was the consolidation of the British positions, a process that led rapidly to deadlock, as the battlefield became dominated by defensive fire power. In contrast, the landing at Suvla Bay in August was uncontested, but not exploited. When the British eventually advanced, there was the customary sharp Turkish response, which inevitably led not long afterwards to the usual deadlock.

By early August 1915 Hamilton had received a large new formation, most of whose troops had not yet done any fighting. This was IX Corps, commanded by Lieutenant General Sir Frederick Stopford, who was younger than Hamilton but appeared much older. Stopford was well known for his charm, his total lack of experience of commanding troops in war, and his astonishing physical fragility.[48] IX Corps comprised three New Army Divisions, two Territorial Divisions, a Mounted Division of Yeomanry; and Hamilton added the depleted two brigades of the Royal Naval Division. The new force had more men than Hamilton's original army.

The idea of assaulting Suvla Bay had first been mooted before the end of June, and it was discussed so extensively that the precise objective of the assault was lost, or perhaps it was never articulated. There were two possibilities: first, to establish a port that could be used for future operations on the peninsula; or second, to support a planned advance from the left of the ANZAC position, which was down the coast from Suvla. A third objective was not discussed, and not even considered: to hurl the troops ashore and immediately drive them on a ten-mile advance south-east through the terrain – which was much less forbidding than the rest of the peninsula – to reach the Dardanelles. By the time the Suvla assault was being planned, Hamilton and his staff had probably become pessimistic about any chances of breaching the Turkish positions. As a result of these divided counsels, Stopford had no clear idea of what he was supposed to do. Hamilton had to be faulted for this, although Stopford was painfully slow and was even more to blame.

The northern coast of the peninsula stretches from Bulair in the east to Suvla Point in the west. Suvla Point is a promontory with a hilly spine. Immediately south of the Point lies Suvla Bay, shaped like an open-mouthed circle, the neck of which – from Suvla Point to Nibrunesi Point – is two miles across. From Nibrunesi, the coast falls back south-east to Anzac Cove, only five miles away. Inland from Suvla Bay is a large salt lake which has an outlet to the sea called the Cut. The Suvla plain stretches three miles inland before reaching a range of prominent hills, the other side of which is the plateau that runs parallel with the north coast of the peninsula.

On 6 August the ANZAC troops, and the sole Indian Army brigade which was now attached to them, began their long-prepared assault on a major feature the Sari Bair Ridge, to the left (or north) of their positions. With the ANZAC troops attacking to the north, Stopford, who was about to land his IX Corps at Suvla, sent one of his New Army divisions south in support of his ANZAC comrades. Beginning at 0930 hours on 6 August and lasting over two days, Stopford landed his two remaining New Army divisions to the north of Suvla, on A Beach in the Bay, and C and B to the south of it; 27,000 men were disembarked, and they were observed from the hills by 3,000 Turks.[49] The remaining British troops landed during the following days. After the near-disastrous landings on V and W Beaches on 25 April, the British hastened the production of armoured, engine-powered craft called 'Beetles' to carry the troops to the shore, 500 men at a time. The irony of this was that the landings at Suvla were unopposed. There was not much urgency about the British landings, and the reason was Stopford's belief that he was there to establish a port in addition to adding weight to the ANZAC assault, for which he had already detached a division. Because Stopford thought that there was no urgency, twenty-four hours were lost, which meant that the Turks were able with their customary rapid response to contain any further British advance. The commander of the Turkish defences was now Mustafa Kemal, newly promoted Colonel: this elevation had not tamed his naturally aggressive instincts. He was still the commander of the 19th Division, which met the ANZAC attack on Sari Bair.

On 7 August, Kemal was given command of a group of seven under-strength divisions, all commanded by experienced officers including an outstanding German, Major Willmer. There was confusion at first because Kemal did not have time to take a 'grip' on his new command, but this period of uncertainty did not last long. Liman von Sanders rushed two of Kemal's divisions from the rear to the front line, and Kemal began a series of co-ordinated counter-attacks on 9 August. He led the most important of these himself on 10 August:

> Mustafa Kemal crept forward with his scouting screen in order
> personally to give the order to attack at the critical moment when
> a brief artillery bombardment ended. Kemal hugged the ground
> while the Ottoman artillery and machine-gun fire raked the enemy
> positions over his head and then, at the exact moment when the
> firing ceased, he raised himself up and pointed to the enemy line
> with his riding crop (his own pre-arranged signal to attack).[50]

Hamilton nowhere mentioned Kemal in his *Gallipoli Diary*, which suggests that he was unaware of his most dangerous Turkish opponent. Kemal's powerful style of leadership from the front was also Hamilton's style. However Hamilton, because of the demands of overall command, was forced to spend his time fretting on the island of Lemnos, forty miles from the firing line. Hamilton (like Rommel and many other generals) preferred to be where the bullets were flying.

In this way all forward movements by the British and ANZAC troops were blocked. The capture of Sari Bair might have been decisively important because of its commanding position above the other hills. The Indian Army brigade seized it with dramatic heroism, but the troops were unsupported and were driven off by shell fire. However, despite this setback, there was now a continuous British line running north to south for eight miles, from the sea east of Suvla Point down to Anzac Cove. It cut across the low-lying Suvla Plain and ended in the hills and gullies of the ANZAC positions. This line was to remain stable until the end of the campaign. But stability did not mean inactivity. There was unceasing fire from artillery and small arms, and a constant trickle of casualties. Aggression on either side was countered by the other, just as had happened on the Western Front. At Anzac on 16 August:

> We shoot from here pretty often at the Turkish guns. Last night the Dardanelles droned on for hours. This morning the machine guns on both sides were going like dentists' drills.[51]

As late as 30 November, at Lone Pine, the scene of brutal fighting and enormous ANZAC and Turkish losses, the local Turkish Company Commander reported, as these events were happening:

> Can spot and follow shells in the air. They shine like suns and come straight down. Their burst is extremely violent. Some fail to explode. Enemy periscopes pop up from behind four embrasures protected by steel plates. That anyone should try to observe under such a bombardment is quite astonishing. Emerge from my observation post to fire one rifle-clip at enemy periscopes.[52]

In these battles Hamilton's troops suffered 18,000 battle casualties and 40,000 losses from sickness. The butcher's bill was beginning to resemble the Western Front. Before the campaign came to an end, large numbers of reinforcements had arrived on both sides, and at least 503,000 warriors had become casualties either from battle – killed, wounded and missing – or from deaths and evacuation as a result of illness. Of this huge total, 205,000 were British and ANZAC, 47,000 French, and 251,000 (and probably more) Turkish.

On 15 August, after the obvious failure at Suvla and Sari Bair, Hamilton sacked Stopford, two divisional commanders and a brigadier. This was more than a week after the landing and it was too late; it calls into question Hamilton's capacity to take urgent steps to get rid of incompetence. Liman von Sanders had no such qualms, and always responded instantly:

When a reserve Turkish division at Helles was withdrawn on the morning of 7 August, the German Chief of Staff with the Turkish Southern Group was seized with panic and suggested that all the Turkish troops should be transferred to the Asiatic shore. The Marshal instantly removed him from his post, and instructed his successor that not one yard of ground was to be surrendered voluntarily. Again, when the commander of the two Turkish reinforcing divisions from Bulair postponed his attack on reaching Suvla on 8 August, the Marshal at once replaced him by Mustafa Kemal.[53]

In the Second World War, Montgomery was even more unrelenting.[54] Because Hamilton allowed compassion to undermine his resolve to sack weak commanders, valuable time was lost. By now Hamilton's own position was in peril. There were criticisms of him in military and political circles in London, and a good deal of press speculation about his competence. Many of the attacks came from a trenchant and unpopular Australian journalist called Keith Murdoch, whose son Rupert was to make this Murdoch family famous.

The Gallipoli expedition itself was also being sniped at. The criticisms from the BEF that it was a dangerous diversion of resources had spread during the months of the expedition, and many authoritative figures in London were impressed by such arguments, notably the CIGS Lieutenant General Robertson, who was anyway a 'Westerner'. Churchill was by now out of office, and Kitchener's own position was being unobtrusively scrutinized by members of the Cabinet. Two Regular divisions that could have been sent to Gallipoli were moved in September to the new front that was being opened at Salonika. The French politicians had a plan to concentrate attention on Salonika, 'putting Johnnie Hamilton under Sarrail' (the French general commanding in Salonika). [55] These were the words of Henry Wilson, a senior and wonderfully devious staff officer in London who had served under Hamilton during the Second Boer War. Salonika was to be another disappointment.

Hamilton was recalled on 14 October and returned to London, being replaced by Lieutenant General Sir Charles Monro, an army commander in the BEF. After Gallipoli, Hamilton was offered no further employment. Monro was an able but orthodox soldier, much more conventional than Hamilton. And coming from the Western Front, he was instinctively out of sympathy with the Gallipoli 'sideshow'. After surveying the various Gallipoli battlefronts, on 31 October Monro recommended evacuation;

as Churchill put it: 'He came, he saw, he capitulated.' Kitchener, who was unconvinced, sailed to Gallipoli to see for himself. He reluctantly agreed with Monro. But Suvla might not after all have been Britain's last throw of the dice. On 17 October, the aggressive – and frustrated – Commodore Roger Keyes pressed de Robeck to allow a squadron of ships, which Keyes himself would command, to steam up the Dardanelles and brave all the destruction that the Turkish mines and shore batteries could inflict. De Robeck refused to accept the idea, but he permitted Keyes to go to London to try and sell it to the Admiralty. With Churchill now off the scene, Keyes's journey and his brave proposal came to nothing. It was too late, since the decision to evacuate the Gallipoli Peninsula was now very close.

The evacuation was planned to take place in December 1915 and January 1916. Many people forecast disastrous losses in the process. The evacuation was much more carefully and imaginatively planned than any of the offensives that had taken place, and Kitchener – with another flash of strategic insight – said that the naysayers were wrong and that the evacuation would be made with no loss of life. He was right, and the British got away scot-free. But Gallipoli, with its promise and disasters, remained a legend, as did Hamilton's own part in the enterprise.

Three Questions Revisited
Chapter 1 posed three questions. I have now given enough detail of the Gallipoli operation to attempt some responses.

First, given the state of military technology in 1915, was the assault on the Gallipoli Peninsula a viable operation of war?

Second, if time and resources had been available, would greater force and more effective army-navy co-operation have been successful, given no change in the basic strategic plan?

Third – and most importantly – could the Gallipoli assault have succeeded with a different strategic plan?

It is clear after the event that the Gallipoli expedition, as it was carried out, was not a viable operation. Hamilton did not have the necessary superiority in numbers of men. And he chose Cape Helles, the most obvious place for the assault by the 29th Division, the very place where the Turks were expecting the landing to take place. It is the site that Kitchener favoured, and Hamilton was obviously influenced by his old chief. It also received qualified support from his subordinate commanders (as mentioned earlier). But Hamilton did not have the force necessary for a successful assault on Cape Helles. Without more troops, plus a more sophisticated deception plan, plus effective fire control to provide continuous naval gunfire support, the choice of Helles was not defensible. Hamilton also chose to land the ANZAC troops at a place where there could be no close co-operation between them and the 29th Division. There were two separate attacks with no common objective. Hamilton was well aware of the possibilities offered by a landing at Suvla, but he correctly appreciated that he would have needed six and not four divisions to achieve success there. For these fundamental reasons, I believe that there is no merit in the often-expressed view that a few lucky breaks would have enabled Hamilton to snatch victory from the jaws of defeat.

With many more men (the War Office's responsibility) and a better and more imaginative strategy from Hamilton, the operation might have been viable, although it is never possible to guarantee success in war. I believe that the following five specific requirements might have made all the difference, and the Dardanelles would have been opened, which would have made a major contribution to winning the First World War:

- *150,000 men, or eight infantry divisions.* This was Kitchener's original estimate, and one of his remarkable qualities was his occasionally astonishing strategic insight. The larger strength would of course also have called for considerable logistical support.
- *More time to work out a plan.* The tactics should have been based on a much more detailed examination of the terrain, and better intelligence about the Turkish Army.
- *A larger number of boats*, with well-trained crews, to ferry the troops to the beaches: perhaps three infantry divisions for the initial assault, carried in a minimal number of 'lifts', with only short intervals between them; and then followed up by the transport of five follow-up divisions. There was no question of designing special landing craft like those used in the Second World War, but

the 'Beetles' used at Suvla might have been made available earlier. (They were being built in Britain.)

• *A meticulously-prepared fire plan for using the big guns of the Fleet* to support the landing and the subsequent phases of the fighting. Although the battleships had to remain in deep water, the reach of their heaviest guns was over ten miles, which would have been enough to support the troops all the way to the Dardanelles, provided that an effective method of fire control could be worked out and practised beforehand. This called for experiments to find out how the high trajectory of the naval guns could be used to search the contours of the terrain of the peninsula.

• *A landing place large enough for three divisions.* Suvla Bay, with a possible satellite at Ejelmar, would probably have been large enough, and would also have provided a more open route to the strait, via the large plateau stretching across the peninsula.

The remaining unknown is Hamilton's own capacity for the job. Did he have sufficient drive and ruthlessness? Did he have enough experience of high-level operational command? His weakness was that his magnetism and tactical skill did not compensate for his lack of a strategic 'feel'. The lessons of the Russo-Japanese War – the importance of meticulous planning based on knowledge of the terrain and intelligence about the enemy, and the need for superior numbers in the attack – seem to have passed him by. Nor did he grasp Liddell Hart's fundamental point that *the purpose of pure strategy is to diminish the possibility of resistance. Strategy has for its purpose the reduction of fighting to the slenderest possible proportions.* Finally, Hamilton's dismissal of Bloch's forecast that defensive fire power would come to dominate the battlefield, surely came back to haunt him.

At the end of Chapter 5, I raised the danger that long years of staff service in the administrative branches might (barely perceptibly) blunt an officer's mental capacity for war. The danger is two-fold: it could erode the instinct to scrutinize the directives of his superiors in a questioning but not destructive frame of mind; and it could slow the speed of the officer's reactions. I believe that Hamilton's failure at Gallipoli can be partly attributed to these lingering legacies of his long years on the staff in India.

Hamilton did not seriously question the strength of the force he was to command to assault Gallipoli. The estimated size of the Turkish army on the peninsula was such that the British would not have the superiority in numbers of trained and fully-equipped troops necessary for a decisive assault. Hamilton deferred to Kitchener. His attitude was quite different from Montgomery's in the Second World War. Montgomery refused to give way to political pressure to attack at El Alamein until he felt that his army was ready. And before the invasion of Normandy in June 1944, he refused to proceed until he was given more infantry divisions for the assault. If Hamilton had insisted on a bigger army for the Gallipoli expedition, he would probably have lost his job. He had the moral courage to accept this, but he did not take this step because the lesson from the Russo-Japanese War that superior numbers really matter had obviously not sunk in.

Hamilton's speed of response to enemy moves could not be compared to Mustafa Kemal's. But Kemal was in tactical command, which Hamilton was not. Hamilton was reluctant to issue direct orders when they were needed at Y Beach, although his instruction to Birdwood at Anzac only a few hours later was decisively important. As an overall commander, Hamilton was slow to sack incompetent generals at Suvla, although he had no hand in selecting them in the first place. He should however have evaluated their capacity more carefully before they were sent into battle.

If one takes a broad view, Churchill did more than anyone else to get the Gallipoli enterprise off the ground. But the individual most responsible for the débâcle must be seen to be Kitchener, because he dictated the inadequate size of Hamilton's force, although Hamilton himself deserves a major share of the blame. But it is very hard not to sympathize with Kitchener, who was a big man in every sense of the word, and who was compelled to carry the main responsibility for the successes and failures of the British Army in a mighty conflict in which Britain was totally unequipped to confront on land a first-class enemy. Kitchener was distracted and overworked, mainly because he was a poor delegator, and he found the corridors of power in London a totally uncongenial environment.

With his fine-tuned strategic instinct, Kitchener was the sole voice in London who predicted at the beginning that it would be a long war. He therefore single-handedly embarked on a mission that no one had ever carried out before: he built from scratch a New Army large enough to fight a war on a continental scale. He abandoned the Territorial Force structure – a highly questionable decision – and this increased the burden on him personally. In addition he made significant contributions to the fighting in France. In 1914, he rushed – in uniform – to the headquarters of the BEF to knock some sense into the head of Sir John French to make him stick to his job and not give up the fight. And, in 1915, Kitchener was forced to respond to pressure from the BEF for artillery ammunition, the lack of which was a desperate problem (as it also was in Gallipoli). This shortage was a legacy of Britain's lack of preparation before the war.

The Gallipoli enterprise came on top of all this. The grand strategy for the campaign was immensely alluring, because opening the strait would have transformed the position of Russia. But this could only have been done by driving the Royal Navy through the Dardanelles, and this needed an army on the Gallipoli Peninsula. However, because of the constant pressures on him – pressures that would have destroyed a smaller man – Gallipoli never received Kitchener's undivided attention and he, autocrat and proconsul that he was, was forced to do something he had never done before. He was compelled to compromise. He was recruiting, supplying and training his enormous New Army; Churchill was urging action on Gallipoli; the Western Front was demanding reinforcements and munitions; and politicians who were amateur strategists with no knowledge of war were staking claims for opening new fighting fronts. In view of all this, Kitchener would have been well advised to exercise his well-known power to say 'no' to all the arguments in favour of Gallipoli. But Kitchener had never in his life taken advice. And Hamilton – who was in awe of him – would not have been listened to, even if he had worked out a highly persuasive master plan for how to invade Gallipoli with a much better chance of success. Hamilton made this point himself in something he had written in 1905. He heard of a general who, like Oliver Twist, had asked for more, and Kitchener replied: 'Your reasons for not doing what you were told to do are the best I ever heard; now go and do it!'[56]

The tragedy of Gallipoli was not a matter of lost opportunities or discredited reputations. It was the sacrifice of so many brave soldiers from Britain, Australia, New Zealand, India, France, and Turkey.

Notes

1 Lieutenant Mehmed Fasih, *Gallipoli 1915. Bloody Ridge (Lone Pine)* (Istanbul, Turkey: Denizler Kitabevi, 1997) p.9. The officer quoted was Major Mahmut Bey, who commanded the formidable Turkish artillery defences at Cape Helles.

2 Liddell Hart, *The British Way In Warfare* (London: Faber & Faber, 1932), pp.98–100.

3 Bismarck made this observation to a German named Ballen, who recounted it to Winston Churchill two weeks before the British entered the war. Churchill included the remark in a speech in the House of Commons. This was reported in the *Hansard Parliamentary Proceedings,* Volume 413, Column 84.

4 Brigadier General C. F. Aspinall-Oglander, *History of the Great War. Military Operations: Gallipoli* (Volume 1) (London: Imperial War Museum, 1992) (First published in 1929), p.6.

5 Ibid., pp. 6–20.

6 *Admiral of the Fleet Lord Fisher, Memorandum to the First Sea Lord dated 3 January 1915.* Winston S. Churchill, *The World Crisis* (Volume 2) (Norwalk, CT: The Easton Press, 1991) (First published in 1923), p.95.

7 Aspinall-Oglander, *History of the Great War. Military Operations: Gallipoli* (Volume 1), p. 9.

8 Philip Magnus, *Kitchener, Portrait of an Imperialist* (London: John Murray, 1958), pp. 309–16.

9 Lord Hankey, *The Supreme Command, 1914–1918* (Volume 1) (London: George Allen and Unwin, 1961), p.251.

10 Churchill, *The World Crisis* (Volume 2), p.109.

11 Aspinall-Oglander, *History of the Great War. Military Operations: Gallipoli* (Volume 1), p.79.

12 *The Dardanelles Commission* (Part 1, 1914-1915) (London: The Stationery Office, 2000) (First published in 1917), pp.202–3.

13 Churchill, *The World Crisis* (Volume 2), p.225.

14 General Sir Ian Hamilton, *Gallipoli Diary* (Volume 1) (New York: George H. Doran, 1920), p.2.

15 The meetings at the War Office, and Hamilton's journey are described in Hamilton, *Gallipoli Diary* (Volume 1) pp.2–25.

16 Ibid., p.3; also *The Dardanelles Commission* (Part 1, 1914-1915), p.203.

17 Sir George Arthur, *Life of Lord Kitchener* (Volume 3) (London: Macmillan, 1920), pp.122–4.

18 Hamilton, *Gallipoli Diary* (Volume 1), pp.26–53.

19 Ibid., pp. 27, 44, 61.

20 *British Army Papers* (Kew, London: Public Record Office), WO158/574: C413227, 1915.

21 Hamilton, *Gallipoli Diary* (Volume 1), p.54.

22 Ibid., p.76.

23 Ibid., p.83.

24 Ibid., pp.89–90.

25 Ibid., pp.92–3.

26 Ibid., p.97.
27 Aspinall-Oglander, *History of The Great War. Military Operations: Gallipoli* (Volume 1), pp.130–52.
28 Hamilton, *Gallipoli Diary* (Volume 1), p.48.
29 Field Marshal Lord Birdwood, *Khaki and Gown. An Autobiography* (London: Ward Lock, 1941), p.254; also *British Army Papers*, WO158/574: C413227, 27 February and 3 March 1915.
30 Hamilton, *Gallipoli Diary* (Volume 1), pp.22–3.
31 Ibid., pp. 90, 30; also Birdwood, *Khaki and Gown. An Autobiography*, p.254.
32 Aspinall-Oglander, *History of The Great War. Military Operations: Gallipoli* (Volume 1), pp.19–20.
33 Hans Kannengiesser Pasha, *The Campaign in Gallipoli* (London: Hutchinson, 1927), p.148.
34 Ibid., pp.21, 63.
35 Edward J. Erickson, *Gallipoli. The Ottoman Campaign* (Barnsley, Yorkshire, U.K.: Pen & Sword, 2010), pp.207–8.
36 Kannengiesser, *The Campaign in Gallipoli,* p.126.
37 Otto Liman von Sanders, *Five Years in Turkey* (Annapolis, MD: United States Naval Institute, 1927), pp.57–60. (His surname was Liman von Sanders.)
38 Erickson, *Gallipoli. The Ottoman Campaign*, pp.35–7, 207.
39 Ibid., p.65.
40 Ibid, pp.49, 66.
41 John North, *Gallipoli, the Fading Vision* (London: Faber & Faber, 1936), pp.275–6.
42 Ibid., pp.272–3.
43 Hamilton, *Gallipoli Diary* (Volume 1), p.144.
44 Kannengiesser, *The Campaign in Gallipoli,* p.192.
45 Liman von Sanders, *Five Years in Turkey*, pp.63–4.
46 Aspinall-Oglander, *History of the Great War. Military Operations: Gallipoli* (Volume 1), p.362.
47 Alan Moorehead, *Gallipoli* (Norwalk, CT: The Easton Press, 1988), p.219.
48 North, *Gallipoli, the Fading Vision,* p.267.
49 Erickson, *Gallipoli. The Ottoman Campaign,* pp.148–59.
50 Ibid., p.164.
51 Aubrey Herbert, *Mons, Anzac and Kut* (London: Hutchinson, 1919), p.188.
52 Fasih, *Gallipoli 1915. Bloody Ridge (Lone Pine)*, p.152.
53 North, *Gallipoli, the Fading Vision,* pp.271–2.
54 A story (unusual for being unpublished) says a great deal about Montgomery's justifiable ruthlessness in sacking incompetent officers. Before the battle of El Alamein, Montgomery visited many individual units of the Eighth Army. He called on a prestigious regular regiment of the Royal Horse Artillery, and asked the commanding officer: 'Where are your guns?' A large tactical map was brought for inspection, and the gun positions were shown to be 13,000 yards behind the British Forward Defended Localities (FDLs), about the maximum reach of a 25-pounder. The guns were obviously sited for defence (i.e. to support troops being driven back) rather than attack (i.e. to support advancing troops). Montgomery responded immediately:

'Colonel, who is your Second-in-Command?' This officer was summoned, to be greeted by Montgomery with the order: 'Major, you are now commanding this Regiment.' The colonel was instantly sacked. Although the unfortunate commanding officer had presumably been given his specific task by his direct superior, the Commander Royal Artillery (CRA) of the division, Montgomery was making the point with great brutality that he expected all his commanders to be aggressive and proactive. (A friend, now dead, told me about this incident. He was Major James Baxter MC and Bar, who had been a subaltern in the regiment at the time and had been present during these dramatic interviews.)

55 Major General C. E. Callwell, *Field Marshal Sir Henry Wilson. His Life and Diaries* (Volume 1) (London: Cassell, 1927), p.250.

56 Lieutenant General Sir Ian Hamilton, *A Staff Officer's Scrap Book* (Volume 1) (London: Edward Arnold, 1903), pp.119–20.

CHAPTER 11

Military Philosopher

Ian Hamilton had a long retirement which he used productively. He died in 1947, at the age of ninety-four. During this period, at least until the beginning of the Second World War and then the death of his wife in 1941, he travelled widely with her and they led an active social life, since they had no money worries. Hamilton also spent a good deal of time on two activities directly connected with his army service.

First, he played a leading role in the affairs of the British Legion (now the Royal British Legion), the large organization of military veterans that had been set up, through amalgamation of different bodies, shortly after the end of the First World War. It still flourishes today, and has local branches in all parts of the United Kingdom and also overseas. Its purpose is partly charitable and partly social, by encouraging members to meet regularly to preserve their old comradeship. It gives all types of support – financial, emotional and social – to men and women who have been in the services and their dependants, and is the 'national custodian of Remembrance'. The funds come from a small subscription from every member and a number of fundraising activities, the most important of which is the annual Poppy Appeal during the days leading up to Remembrance Day, the second Sunday in November. (Non-British readers may not know that the poppies, which are artificial flowers for sale made by disabled ex-service personnel in factories owned by the Legion, are worn during the Remembrance period by almost every member of the British public and by people in many overseas countries.)

Hamilton's second activity was as Colonel of the Gordon Highlanders, which meant that he was the figurehead of the regiment. He appeared, splendidly-uniformed, on ceremonial parades and made popular appearances at reunions and, importantly, worked in the background to protect the interests of the regiment among the military chiefs at the War Office. As Colonel, an official appointment recorded in the Army List, he also played a part in vetting potential officers and approving officers' appointments.

This chapter is devoted to something different. Hamilton continued to write for publication. He produced a handful of significant works about soldiering, and these are what I shall discuss here. He brought three special qualities to the writing, which represents his mature best. First, what he said was based on *thought*: thought that was always influenced by his extensive knowledge of the history of peoples, politics, and – importantly – armies and conflicts. His second quality was that his writing was rooted in his long and varied personal experience of soldiering. The third was natural wit with an occasional and refreshing note of scepticism, a refusal to accept received wisdom at its face value. He had never shied away from unpopular causes since his days as a young regimental officer, when he had espoused the cause of musketry in the face of opposition from martinets focused on the barrack square. I shall quote extensively from Hamilton's own words. I am doing this to demonstrate that I am not misrepresenting his views, and also to give a flavour of his limpid and sometimes sparkling prose.

At the beginning of his important book, *The Soul and Body of an Army*, published as early as 1921, he makes the following crushing comment on the British Army Field Service Regulations (FSR), the bible containing the Army's strategic and tactical doctrines:

> Our FSR, Part 1, printed reverentially, as might be a super-axiom of the views of the twelve Apostles, in large deeply-leaded type: **'Decisive success in battle can be obtained only by a vigorous offensive.'** Here the War Office in one sentence lays down its *sine qua non* for success, and shows at the same time that it does not understand the special fighting character of the British soldier. As it turns out, there would have been as much sense, neither more nor less, in saying. **'Decisive defeat in battle can only be gained by a vigorous offensive.'** . . . So long as it stands enthroned there in its leaded type it is a dogmatic denial of everything that happened in a war where all the worst defeats were sustained by a

223

vigorous offensive: i.e. Loos, Passchendaele, Verdun, and that final overthrow which began on 21 March 1918; not to mention that the whole war was a German offensive, and that Germany was defeated whilst actually in France.[1]

Hamilton's point is the difference between a *necessary* and a *sufficient* condition for success. A vigorous offensive is necessary, but it is dangerous folly to conduct it unless many other requirements are fulfilled – highly-trained troops, a sound strategic plan, superior numbers, knowledge of the ground, intelligence about the enemy – elements that together made the Battle of El Alamein, for instance, a strategic and tactical success. It is the lack of all these ingredients that have made so many other battles failures; all they offered was a vigorous offensive.

In his writing, Hamilton concentrated on the underlying principles of military organization, discipline and training, and was less concerned with specific operational recommendations, the things that senior officers should do to improve their commands. As background, and also to demonstrate that Hamilton knew what he was talking about, I shall discuss a number of his predictions that dated from 1921. In everything he wrote, his mind was focused on the future and not the past: a future that he visualized with sometimes startling accuracy.

The Crystal Ball
Hamilton's main predictions fall into five groups, each of which can be discussed separately. (1) The end of siege warfare of the 1914-1918 type. (2) The extinction of cavalry in its traditional 'shock' role. (3) The rapid growth in the importance of mechanical arms on the battlefield. (4) The reconstruction of the traditional division into a smaller and harder-hitting formation of all arms. (5) The vision of joint-service planning, with co-ordinated command of sea, land and air. Within twenty years, most of these predictions had come to pass, and they had all become reality well before the end of the twentieth century.

(1) *The end of siege warfare.* Hamilton was unambiguous about the end of static trench lines, where 'men can still be held together under the eye, tongue and auto-pistol of the captain'. Trenches were a merely temporary means of extinguishing:

the individuality, which had been three-quarters of the battle in the wide extensions of a war of movement. . . machines will no longer be denied, and wide encircling movements, followed by distant battles fought between comparatively small forces, will be the order of the world to come.[2]

Even in the Russo-Japanese War, where trench warfare with all its trappings played an important role, 'extensions of attacking infantry were tending to increase in their width'.[3] He did not mention Ludendorff's offensives in 1918 that came close to success in France and Flanders. These demonstrated that trenches could be overcome through the use of imaginatively planned infantry tactics based on infiltration: surprise, violence, speed, and penetration of any small cracks in the enemy front. Hamilton met Ludendorff himself in 1922, which suggests that what the German Army had achieved in 1918 had registered with him.

With hindsight, the prediction of the demise of the trench is obvious. Yet nine years after the publication of Hamilton's words, the French military and political leaders ordered the construction of a magnificent piece of modern engineering, demonstrating their continued belief in the importance of siege warfare. This was the Maginot Line, a chain of forts, many inter-connected, that immensely strengthened France's eastern frontier, and which was in short order scornfully bypassed by Germany's Panzer divisions in 1940.

(2) *The extinction of cavalry in its traditional 'shock' role.* Hamilton had witnessed at first hand in the Second Boer War that any success by cavalry was the result of its deployment as mounted infantry. His view was hardened by the Russo-Japanese War where, using an image that was later to become famous, he described how:

> the brave and thrusting Japanese riders were as clean out of the picture as elephant mahouts. They were so clean out of it that Kuroki, who hated not to 'use up' whatever he had, set them to cook rice for his hard-pressed infantry.[4]

Again, with hindsight, there was nothing surprising about this conclusion. Yet the British Army after the First World War was still influenced by cavalry generals, and money for expensive mechanization was always short. At last, by the end of the 1920s, the first regular cavalry regiments began to be mechanized, but the process was not completed before the imminent outbreak of war in 1939. Some yeomanry regiments took their horses with them when they were despatched overseas and some traditional cavalry actions were fought in 1941.

(3) *The rapid growth in the importance of mechanical arms.* Hamilton drew an elegant parallel between his image of future warfare and the 1916 Battle of Jutland. This was the last and biggest of the conventional naval engagements between ships of all sizes, from battleships to torpedo boats, and in it the German and British fleets manoeuvred to blast each other out of the water. Hamilton's parallel is precise, and so is the way in which he amplified his argument:

> replace Jellicoe's ships by heavy armoured tanks and Beatty's by light armoured racers: let whippets stand for the destroyers: plaster the sky with airships and aeroplanes: paint them there as thick as stars; do this and you will gain a truer impression of the crash tactics and high velocity strategies of the future than from poring over false battle pictures by Verestchagin or Meissonier.[5]

> the first step is to bring aeroplanes and tanks into the regimental framework . . . When we sprinkle Lewis guns and Maxims through the battalion and 'reinforce' infantry with automatic rifles that will loose off thousands of rounds in a few minutes; have the speakers ever weighed those cartridges? How are our hungry fire-arms to be fed? There is only one answer. They must be fed by armoured caterpillar transport; i.e. by tanks.[6]

> Aeroplanes are themselves artillery of a sort, and when they are not actually working on reconnaissance or as long-range artillery, their most essential duty is to spot for the divisional artillery, a duty which will be carried out twice as well when the observer and flyer know their gunners and the gunners know them and their manners and air customs.[7]

Hamilton's arguments eventually made a small dent in British military conservatism, but it took the later advocacy of two imaginative but much younger military analysts, J. F. C. Fuller and Basil Liddell Hart, to put flesh on the bones of Hamilton's ideas which, as mentioned earlier, were published only three years after the end of the First World War. The chiefs of the British Army invariably used the argument that money was short in order to frustrate the imagination and force of the arguments of the proponents of mechanized warfare. But the German Army listened more attentively than the British Army, and the thinking of Fuller and Liddell Hart influenced the development of the German Panzer division and the tactics of Blitzkrieg.

One thing that Hamilton strangely failed to mention was the highly successful 'all arms' offensive of Rawlinson's Fourth Army in August 1918. In this huge assault, infantry, artillery, armour and air all operated under a unified and carefully phased plan. Despite the eloquently expressed views of Hamilton and then those of Fuller and Liddell Hart, the 'all arms' offensive was a wheel that had to be reinvented by the British Army in 1942 when, in the middle of a massive war, it started to build properly-balanced armoured divisions, one in the UK and one in Egypt.

(4) *The reconstruction of the traditional division.* During the First World War, Hamilton's antennae were sensitive enough to detect a gradual change in the sensibility of the British soldiers in the fighting ranks. This took the form of a widening of what they saw as their military family: from the battalion to the brigade, and finally to the division. This happened because battalions and brigades no longer fought alone. As warfare had increased in scope, it was the division – composed for long periods of the same battalions – that was the piece that the generals moved on the chessboard of war. It became 'the pivot of the battle; sharp in its outline, vibrant to the word of its commander, crowned with ever-green traditions'.[8] Many divisions developed a powerful loyalty, a process that continued during the Second World War. From that widespread conflict, it is easy to think of many divisions that became the military families of their officers and men: Guards Armoured, 7th Armoured (the 'Desert Rats'), 51st (Highland), 56th (London), 1st Airborne, 6th Airborne, 2nd New Zealand, 9th Australian and 4th Indian.

To Hamilton, the division was the equivalent of the Roman Legion of 6,200 men; the history of the Roman army is essentially the history of its legions. However, modern warfare now demanded that divisions had to be radically reconfigured. The traditional size of the British division was 20,000 men (although its actual strength was usually fewer, because of casualties). This was made up of twelve battalions (reduced in 1918 to nine), plus all the supporting arms necessary to make a division a complete orchestra of war, at least for how war was fought between 1914 and 1918. Shortly after 1918, Hamilton began to visualize a radically smaller division, one that had much greater mobility (because of mechanical transport and a shorter 'tail'), and more 'punch' (because of greater firepower). 'Divisions will have to be *portable*; say 6,000 all told; engineers, artillery and all other tools and engines of war.'[9]

Balance was all-important. Because infantry was the only arm that could meet all four key demands – to move, fire, charge, and hold – the infantry remained queen of the battlefield. But the division had to be composed of 'all arms', to reinforce the fighting capability of the infantry (but not to take its place). Despite Hamilton's rather archaic language, his meaning is quite clear: 'Organise the infantry of each division to include land machines, and to organise the divisional artillery to include air machines.'[10]

It took a long time for the American and British Armies to move wholeheartedly in the direction pointed by Hamilton, although the system of Air Observation Posts (AOPs) became important for artillery spotting during the latter part of the Second World War. However, in both the United States and Britain, much more radical changes began to take place during the 1960s. It is unlikely that the planners at that time had ever heard of Hamilton. Yet the major battlefield formations in both the American and British armies today bear a strong resemblance to Hamilton's 'small' division (e.g. the 'square' brigade, with two battalions, two armoured regiments and strong artillery). An interesting and not unimportant example of military nomenclature comes from the First Gulf War. British armour had fought in the North African desert during the Second World War, and in Iraq in 1991. In both campaigns, the 'Desert Rats' were prominently at the 'sharp end' of battle. But this evocative name was the property of formations of different sizes: the 7th Armoured Division in North Africa, and 7 Armoured Brigade in Iraq (which had been part of 7th Armoured Division fifty years before'.

(5) *The vision of joint-service planning.* It is evident from Hamilton's words that have been liberally quoted in this chapter that his thinking moved strongly towards joint planning by all the fighting services, and it was not too radical a step for such co-ordination to become *control.* This is apparent from the following steps in his argument, leading to an inexorable conclusion:

> The staffs of the Army and Navy will always be brought up in a different way until they are brought up in the same way. But the sooner they are brought up in the same way, the better for all of us. They should have a common doctrine and similar methods and, speaking as one who has worked in closest touch with the Navy both in peace and war, I assert positively that there is no more reason the Army and Navy should be 'unconscious' of one another's problems than that infantry and artillery should be 'unconscious' of one another's problems.[11]

> Take the Defence Minister. He would bring Admirals and Generals out of their opposite corners where, since the days of the Stuarts, they have growled at one another, and make them work hand in hand under his own eye. The eccentricities with which four centuries of ploughing lonely furrows have endowed the Admiralty and the War Office would then be shown up. Instead of going into a third corner or joining part the Navy and part the Army, the new Air Marshals would fall in.[12]

> Directly the new Defence Minister was appointed, he would set about forming a united general staff; not for the three branches of one service, as at present, but for all three services. And he would stress urgency as it must take five years before the strange elements shake down together and another five years at least before they become a band of brothers putting doctrine above the interests or traditions of any one service.[13]

The most obvious comment that can be made on these ideas is that, in both the United States and Britain, they have actually been accepted and are successfully in operation. The first British Minister of Defence was Churchill, who in 1940 combined this appointment with the premiership. After 1945, the system re-emerged in the early 1950s and grew in importance until 1964, when the modern Ministry of Defence was set up with a Chief of the Defence Staff. There is even at the moment talk in Britain of something even more radical: a total fusion of all three branches of the services.[14] However, this idea will almost certainly founder on the rocks of conservatism and service loyalty, although it has already been implemented with the Israeli Defence Force (although unsuccessfully in Canada).

Hamilton was also sufficiently ahead of his time to visualize a unified leadership and co-operative planning at an *international* level between allies, in particular the American and British Armies.[15] By 1942 – five years before Hamilton's death – the Combined Chiefs-of-Staff Committee was directing the strategy for all Anglo-American military efforts. And in General Eisenhower's headquarters, during the successful campaigns in North Africa, Sicily, Italy and North-West Europe, there was a *single* staff composed of equal numbers of American and British officers. One of the secrets of the success of this arrangement was that Eisenhower was determined to make it work. He was quite happy for his staff officers to vent their spleen against one another. The American officers were allowed to call the British officers 'SOBs', but they were strictly forbidden to call them 'British SOBs'. The same directive applied to the British, merely replacing 'SOBs' with the even choicer epithets that enrich the vocabulary of British soldiers of all ranks.

Organization, Discipline, Training

An army is easy to define: a lethal weapon forged by a government for the commander to whom it is entrusted. But the effectiveness of this lethal weapon depends on three factors: organization, discipline and training. Hamilton was clear about the priorities. Organization comes first.

***Organization*:**

> the art, or science, of building up a symmetrical whole by a number of parts, just as the human frame is built up by heart, liver, brain, legs, etc. It is not until you have a forefinger that you clearly grasp the advantage of a thumb.[16]

However, military organizations tend to be either blindly conservative or systematically disorganized. Hamilton's generally favourable view of the

230

United States National Guard was qualified by his conclusion that 'the units just grew', because different states had different priorities: some wanted certain types of unit, others wanted different ones.[17] The ultimate purpose of the total force was not defined, and this had to wait until war arrived in 1917 and again in 1941, when the National Guard had to be shaken into the shape of regular divisions. This worked well; and in Iraq and Afghanistan today, the National Guard is integrated into the Regular Army.

The acronym SNAFU describes military chaos, but this was not an exclusively twentieth-century phenomenon. British military history is full of deplorable stories of disorganization. 'In all her long history England had never sent forth a more splendid body of troops' as those who sailed for the Crimea in 1854. However:

> although the distance from the beaches to the front was only five miles – 8,800 yards – say 10,000 paces, yet neither flour nor blankets could fly over even that short distance. No genius imagined a metalled road; no superman had the happy thought of a railway. So the flower of the Army sank into their graves and the proud hearts of those left were broken.[18]

The Crimean War sent up warning signals. The Cardwell reforms, in particular the system of linked battalions, rationalized the structure of the Army. Yet too many military chiefs held the obscurantist view: 'organize the British Army and you ruin it.' Hence, the shocking problems that characterized the first months of the Second Boer War. It took leadership on the ground by the powerful figures of Roberts and Kitchener to put some order into the flaccidity and confusion.

Major reforms had to wait for Haldane, the Secretary of State for War from 1905 to 1912, who did so much to prepare the British Army for a continental conflict that came in 1914. There were three. First, he focused on the specific purpose of the British Army. The numbers of six Regular divisions sent to France and the fourteen Territorial divisions for home defence may appear to have been made by guesswork. But they were not. The traditional Regular Army could not be expected to expand, so that the flood of new recruits would serve for 'hostilities-only'. The well-established Territorial organization at home was geared for this expansion:

the County Associations, who knew all about making, clothing, feeding and keeping troops, would have stamped out duplicates, triplicates and quadruplicates of their original quotas of Territorial troops, without too much friction or effort.[19]

It was not Haldane's fault that Kitchener chose to ignore this carefully prepared mechanism, since he preferred to improvise. This raises another important point. Any military organization must be in place during peacetime. Expansion of an existing army when war is declared may not be as simple as flicking a switch. But it is immeasurably better than starting from scratch, which is the principle on which Kitchener set up his New Army.

Haldane's second contribution was that he virtually invented the shape of the modern British division:

Off his own bat he did it; lopping off excrescences, adding guns, sappers, signallers, field hospitals, and all Army Service Corps administrative services.[20]

This was important to Hamilton because (as has been described) his own vision of the army of the future was based on the division, albeit one that was reconfigured to include more mobility and firepower.

Haldane's third reform was the foundation he laid for the General Staff at the War Office. Chapter 9 mentions that the early Chiefs of the Imperial General Staff did not have the weight of personality to do the job effectively. Another serious and unexpected difficulty was that, after Haldane's time, the General Staff was badly shaken by the Curragh crisis, which came close to a mutiny by British officers serving in Ireland. As a result of this, the Secretary of State for War and the CIGS left office in 1914, accompanied by the Deputy CIGS and the Adjutant General. However, during the First World War the mechanism worked effectively, despite underlying conflict between the staff and 'the frocks' (the slightly derogatory name given by the soldiers to their political masters).

The army staff is the most important building block of military organization, and Hamilton's comments on it are valuable for what they reveal, and also for what they imply about his own approach to warfare. The concept of the General Staff comes from the Prussian, later the German, Army, with its *Grosser Generalstab* (*GGS*), or 'High General

Staff'. It originated in a very tentative form during the mid-seventeenth century, and was given weightier responsibilities in the 1860s by General Albrecht von Roon, the War Minister (roughly equivalent to Adjutant General). Von Roon's reinvigorated system was based on the one that Wellington had used with great success during the Peninsular War.

During that war, Wellington commanded an army whose size varied from time to time, but was always made up of a number of divisions: a larger force than the British had ever before put into the field. Wellington had a very small Staff Corps composed of engineers who had a technical function. To this he added another small and select group to control his army, a tightly-structured staff of about twenty officers and a number of non-commissioned clerks who all marched with him. The Chief of Staff was named Quartermaster General, although the staff, like its commander, was most concerned with strategic planning.[21] When he was not actually fighting battles, Wellington spent each morning with his senior staff officers, listening to their reports and issuing instructions. In addition, he employed about a dozen ADCs, aristocratic young 'gallopers' mounted on thoroughbred chargers, who carried orders to subordinate formations and units. In addition, they acted as their commander's eyes and ears within the divisions in the field, the same job as that carried out by Montgomery's young liaison officers mounted in Jeeps during the campaign in north-west Europe in 1944–45.[22] Wellington's admirable staff system was abandoned with relentless predictability when peace arrived in 1815, and British generals and regimental officers hastened to return to 'real' soldiering.

The von Roon reforms boosted the prestige of the *GGS* and divided its responsibilities in two, carried out by separate categories of staff officers: (1) the administrative, or A and Q sub-branches, responsible respectively for recruitment and man-management and for logistics; and (2) the 'intellectual' branch, devoted to:

> the more abstract consideration in the evolution of armies – the dangers to be apprehended, the best way to meet them, the scale of preparations – the adoption or rejection of innovations in training, weapons, etc., etc.[23]

This second branch was a broader version of what became the British G branch, which is confined to operations and intelligence, and senior to the A and Q branches.

However, in the British Army, the only officers in the G branch who are involved in high politico-military strategy are the top men, the Chief of the General Staff, CGS (formerly the Chief of the Imperial General Staff, CIGS), and the Chief of the Defence Staff. Although all these men had, and have, the ability to reach the peak of their profession, the most powerful of them all was unquestionably Sir Alan Brooke, who was CIGS for four-and-a-half years from the end of 1941. In tandem with Churchill, who was a big thinker although an erratic one, Brooke made a greater impact on Anglo-American strategy than any other man of either nation until the autumn of 1944, when the number of American troops in north-west Europe began to exceed significantly the number of British. On the other side of the hill, the dominance and blind inflexibility of Adolf Hitler prevented the many German generals with high strategic talent from having anything like the influence wielded by Brooke (not to speak of Ludendorff, who operated as unrestricted Commander-in-Chief of the German Army during the First World War).

The German *GGS* was recruited and trained to think with total objectivity and (until the ascendancy of Hitler) independence:

> Prince Karl of Prussia once pregnantly summed up this Prussian conception of obedience to an over-servile staff officer. The King, he said, had put him on the Staff, because he had expected him to know when to disobey.[24]

The *GGS* was always small, and was the natural route to high-level command appointments. In the Second World War, it never numbered more than 800 officers, one man in 5,000 of all the German soldiers under arms. Of these 800 officers, an unknown number, but at least 200, lost their lives for complicity in the 20 July 1944 bomb plot against Hitler, something that demonstrated their clear sense of where the war was heading. In these circumstances they believed that their country was more important than its leader. These men had always followed Hitler without enthusiasm. They looked down on him for his plebeian origins, inadequate military education, and increasing reluctance to accept facts; even his flashes of intuition lacked staying power.

It will be remembered that Hamilton's own long experience as a staff officer had been almost exclusively in the A and Q branches. I have made the point on a number of occasions that Hamilton was a tactician and not a strategist. At Gallipoli, with his intense focus on the troops on the ground, not to speak of his constant worries about manpower and ammunition shortages, he regarded the conflict in a different way from his main opponent, Liman von Sanders. Liman von Sanders had a broader outlook, and was fixated on protecting Constantinople. He operated mainly by shifting his reserves on interior lines to prepared positions, and then letting them get on with countering enemy threats. Like all German generals, he had been promoted to command positions from the *GGS*. Before joining that tiny and carefully-selected group of officers, he had been taught to think in strategic terms at the War Academy at Potsdam, universally accepted as the best such institution in the world. The British Staff College at Camberley was modelled on it. (As described in Chapter 4, Hamilton sacrificed the chance of going to Camberley when he accepted the job of ADC to Sir Fred Roberts.)

Discipline:

> The moment organization grips an individual it tends to produce a certain habit; the habit a part acquires of harmonizing itself with the whole. As in a machine, the parts were held together by rivets – that is to say, by discipline. [25]

The traditional form of discipline was a 'mechanical, subconscious obedience to the percussive shout of the commander'.[26] The soldier had to obey or face the consequences, which could be ferocious. But this system was constructed for an era when soldiers came from the most disadvantaged and uneducated levels of society, and fought shoulder-to-shoulder within sight of their officers and NCOs. As times changed, and in particular as soldiers had to become more independent and self-reliant in the field, the form of discipline had to be modified. Armies found ways (to use a metaphor) of injecting into their soldiers' bloodstreams a serum to make them continue to do their duty unhesitatingly in all circumstances; and – an extension of this point – to accept responsibility and take command if their superiors were killed or disabled. In this way, discipline eventually becomes *self-discipline*.

Hamilton analyzed this serum into four constituents: sense of duty, force of example, military cohesion, and a soldier's fear that he might himself show fear. These four ingredients all have some influence, but Hamilton emphasized most strongly the third of them: military cohesion, or esprit de corps. This is derived from the regiment in which the soldier spends most of his service: the regiment that relishes its independence and its differences from all the others. This is a constant reminder that the giver and receiver of orders are both members of the same closely-knit family, and they play sports together.

The central importance of the regiment is felt more strongly in Britain than in other countries, although there are exceptions. (In the United States armed forces, strong esprit de corps is a characteristic of the United States Marine Corps, and also of a few army formations, e.g. the 101st Airborne Division.) In both world wars, many British battalions suffered horrendous casualties. Reinforcements arrived, and in some mysterious way the regimental esprit de corps normally impregnated the newcomers.[27] As a result, discipline could be reasserted and the reconstituted battalions would fight as effectively as before.

There is widespread anecdotal evidence to corroborate Hamilton's emphasis on the importance of regimental esprit de corps. Here are examples relating to two old-established British regiments. The first comes from Oliver Lyttelton, later Viscount Chandos, who was a highly-decorated officer in the Grenadier Guards (first raised in 1656). He served throughout the First World War, and went on to become a leading British industrialist, and a politician and member of Churchill's War Cabinet:

> I have seen many institutions in my life, universities, colleges, government offices, joint-stock companies, colonial administrations, Cabinets, but the best human organisation, the most efficient and the most closely-knit of which I know is the Brigade of Guards. The system is built upon a discipline as strict in its way as the Prussian; but the guardsman is taught that there is no one like him, and is instructed in the history of his regiment from the day he becomes a recruit. Pride and discipline, discipline and pride are the keys.[28]

The second regiment is the Royal Welch Fusiliers, raised in 1689. Here are the words of a Special Reserve officer who served throughout the First

World War. He was Robert Graves, the poet and man of letters. He described as follows his first encounter with the soldiers of the 2nd Battalion:

> We were going down the village street. The men sitting about on the doorsteps jumped up smartly to attention as we passed and saluted with a fixed, stony glare. They were magnificent looking fellows. Their uniforms were spotless, their equipment khaki-blancoed, and their buttons and cap-badges twinkled. An officer shortly afterwards added: 'in trenches I'd rather be with this battalion than with any other I have met. The senior officers do know their job, whatever else one may say about them, and the NCOs are absolutely to be trusted, too.'[29]

Frank Richards was a highly-decorated regular private soldier in the same battalion as Robert Graves, and he recounts a bloody incident that took place in 1915:

> With the exception of eight men the whole of B Company had been blown up by the mine . . . the part of the trench near the mine-crater was now only between three and four feet deep because of the showers of earth that had fallen into it, and there I found the survivors of B with 'Hammer' Lane, an old soldier, in command. There wasn't a Lance-Corporal left.[30]

Among the changes in the British Army since the end of the Second World War, one of the most problematical is the weakening of the regimental system through disbandment and amalgamation. This has been done to save money and to meet changing demands on the Army to take part in conflicts in different parts of the world, mostly small but some long-lasting. It is not certain that the politicians or even some senior soldiers are fully conscious of the dangers of what has happened and will continue to happen. Regimental esprit de corps is not an especially delicate plant, but there are limits to how much it can be neglected, although in compensation soldiers today have a loyalty to their comrades, their mates, something that is perhaps growing as strong as their loyalty to their regiments.

Training:

> The course of instruction and exercises whereby self-confidence is imparted to the individual soldier by letting him feel that his mind and body have been well-prepared to play their part with credit in God's grand competitive examination of the nations; in the art of using space and time, ground and weapons like a professional as opposed to an amateur.[31]

Hamilton believed that, without organization and discipline, training is of very little value:

> Organization in the guise of internal economy gave the men a cup of hot coffee before they entered upon the thirty hours' struggle on the heights – a cup of coffee without which their skill at arms would certainly have failed them. Discipline enabled them to control their fire even in the tumult and confusion of the night attack – discipline which saved the situation when the men had begun to use their 'training' to shoot one another.[32]

He was nevertheless devoted to the value of training, confident that the soldiers whom he trained were well enough organized and disciplined. (Foot- and arms-drill on the barrack square play a role in instilling this.) But Hamilton was essentially concerned with musketry – individual aimed firing – and fieldcraft. This covered a range of activities: digging trenches, map-reading, choosing good fire positions, covering fire, using dead ground, concealment and camouflage, movement without bunching, leapfrogging. All these activities are taught by practice, and battalions followed a training cycle, a sequence from individual to section, to platoon, to company, and to battalion.

Hamilton's views on training were published in 1921, and he admitted that most such training had become irrelevant when soldiers fought a static war in trenches. 'Movement died away and with it went the best half of the value of training.'[33] His concern was now with training for a new type of warfare. In his view, this was simply not happening. But there was a good reason.

Revolutionary new military hardware, in particular effective tanks which were anyway in short supply, meant that it was unrealistic to develop training programmes until the Army had actually worked out how to use the equipment. During the 1920s and 1930s the British Army, within the confines of tight budgets, made a number of attempts to work out the best tactical employment of armoured formations, and a complete armoured division – still largely experimental – was created in Egypt in 1939. The best lessons come from battles. Those in the Western Desert taught the British Army many practical lessons, one of which was that its armour could not fight on equal terms against the German tanks, and particularly the deadly 88mm anti-tank guns. It also became clear that an armoured division had to contain strong infantry – at least a brigade – plus a number of artillery regiments, and close support from the air. This was the system created in North Africa and employed on a broader scale during the invasion of north-west Europe in 1944, with the addition of the powerful Tactical Air Force which was able to bring fire to bear, especially from rocket-armed fighter planes, controlled by RAF officers accompanying troops on the ground.

It took the defeat in France in 1940, rather than what Hamilton had written, to get the British Army to gear itself for all-arms training, a decade after the German Army had led the way. With lessons provided by the fighting in the Western Desert, all-arms training now became realistic. Coincidentally, it was accompanied by a parallel revival of infantry field training for open warfare. The British Army pioneered the Battle School, which was an up-to-date development of what Hamilton had been doing as a regimental officer and junior staff officer in India. It was only during the 1960s that the British Army introduced a rifle with the rounds fed automatically to increase the rate of fire. And at about the same time, the Vickers medium machine gun was finally retired from service, having done wonderful work since the reign of Queen Victoria (when the original Maxim gun was introduced). The British Army went to war in 1914 with two Vickers guns per battalion; the German Army had four equivalent weapons, and the guns from two or three different battalions were usually massed together. Hamilton, who had attended German Army manoeuvres in 1908, told the War Office about this, but the response was (characteristically) that more machine guns would be impossibly expensive.[34]

In addition to all its advantages in numbers of men and quantities of equipment, the British army that invaded Normandy in 1944 was trained for a contemporary war and not for the last conflict. And although its performance is open to criticism – not least because its hardware, in particular its tanks, had grave deficiencies – the eventual victory was decisive. By the autumn of 1944 the American Army had begun to field much larger numbers of troops than the British, but throughout the campaign, the British army demonstrated its ability (to use a modern metaphor), to 'punch above its weight'. Montgomery was a ferocious proponent of training for battle, and realistic training had a great deal to do with the triumph of British arms.

Command
I must explain why command – the single factor that more than anything else determines the success or failure of an army – is discussed last. There is a chronological reason. Ian Hamilton thought about command over the whole course of his life, and the papers he wrote about it were only collected and edited into a book, *The Commander*, published ten years after his death.[35]

After the end of the First World War, the notion of military genius – the divine spark that strikes and radiates from the small number of generals who are long remembered – lost all its cachet. Generalship became generally regarded as 'hard, slogging, methodical, matter-of-fact work'.[36] This is not at all surprising, considering how the fighting on the Western Front had been conducted for more than four years. But Hamilton thought differently. Chapter 8 describes his disappointment with General Kuroki's decision to limit, for reasons of safety, the extent of his right-flanking sweep at the Battle of the Yalu. Marlborough, Napoleon and Lee would have taken more risk and reaped a far greater reward. But Kuroki, good though he was, was a general of a different calibre. Hamilton *did* believe in military genius which, as he saw it, is made up of four parts: imagination, energy, enthusiasm and courage.[37] He believed (writing as early as 1921) that Churchill approached genius in his politico-military vision in seeing the opportunity offered by the Dardanelles, and in his tactical prescience in pushing so hard to develop the tank. (It is fortunate that in the Second World War, the CIGS, Brooke, had enough moral courage and strategic judgement to restrain some of the rampaging of Churchill's imagination. His most fruitful ideas were very carefully scrutinized before they were put into action.)

Hamilton shared the normal belief that an army's effectiveness depends most on the quality of its generals. Where do these men come from? Chapter 1 lists eighteen figures who, in my opinion, emerged from the Second World War as members of this special cadre. The two Russians came from peasant families, but the other sixteen all came from the customary officers' background: the educated bourgeoisie or, occasionally, a more aristocratic family. They all possessed a sound education with a military orientation, and exhibited the personal qualities of independence and initiative that are needed by a young man before he is granted a commission. It is no surprise that Hamilton believed that great captains should have these same origins. In Britain in 1921 officers had normally been educated at a public (i.e. private) school, and then Sandhurst or Woolwich (at both of which fees were charged). But in this and many other ways Hamilton was not dogmatic.

'Wully' Robertson, who had spent ten years as a private soldier and NCO before being commissioned, eventually climbed to the pinnacle of field marshal. And Hector Macdonald, a colour sergeant in Hamilton's battalion of the Gordon Highlanders, rose to become a major general before his tragic end (described in Chapter 3). Hamilton certainly believed that, within limits, officers might come up from the ranks. When he was Adjutant General, he sent a confidential memorandum to all battalion commanders ordering them to prepare a secret list of three NCOs who could be commissioned immediately on the outbreak of war. But he added an important qualification: the choice had to be 'based on character and manners, not on an examination in which all the orderly-room clerks would come out on top and all the fighting leaders be at the bottom.'[38]

During the First World War the social composition of the British officer corps changed. Since Kitchener's New Army, unlike the old Regular Army, was a cross-section of the country as a whole, the vast numbers of Kitchener Army officers who were promoted from the ranks were more educated men than the pre-war rank and file. But they did not all have the same origins as Hamilton thought appropriate for the best officers, a change that Hamilton accepted although not with much enthusiasm. The traditional method of recruiting officers was restored at the end of the First World War. But, from 1939 onwards, the demands of a vastly expanded Army meant that some officers had to be men with different types of education and civilian jobs. This process did not stop in 1945, and has subsequently been driven by the way in which British society as a whole has become more egalitarian. The officer corps today has a relatively broad recruitment base, as had been true of Kitchener's New Army, although a small number of 'fashionable' regiments still cling to their traditional potential officer 'pool'. Officers today include fewer public school men; the majority are university graduates; and in recent years women have served in nearly all branches of the service. New officers sign up for a finite period of service and not for a full career although this opportunity is often offered later. In the twenty-first century the 'thin red line' is thinly-stretched and constantly engaged in action and peace-keeping throughout the world, but the officers are as professional as ever, if not more so.

Assuming that an officer, with the advantages of seniority, ability, patronage and luck, beats the odds and becomes a general, what are the factors that will determine whether or not he will be a great one? Hamilton had a clear view. He saw six qualities as important: (1) self-confidence and initiative; (2) perception; (3) the ability to organize; (4) the ability to inspire men; (5) physical and moral courage; and (6) selflessness. Two things stand out of this not totally complete menu. First, these are all qualities that Hamilton himself possessed to a high degree, and they go a long way to explaining his success as a commander. Second, the qualities are more innate than acquired. The ethos of public schools aims to nurture them, but it can be argued that they had to be there in the first place. With the right people, public schools are however able to develop these qualities to a pronounced degree.

As an afterthought that appears more than 100 pages later in *The Commander*, Hamilton added a very important additional quality to his list: (7) 'he must understand clearly the difference between strategy and tactics, and be a master of both.'[39] Such an understanding can be developed, and much of an officer's training should be devoted to acquiring it.

Hamilton's most penetrating insights into generalship came from his favourable – and unfavourable – descriptions of six men he had known well, plus two top figures he had met for long enough to understand something about them. They were Earle, Buller, French, Haig, Roberts,

Kitchener, and then Foch and Ludendorff. His paladin was Earle, the victor of the 1885 Battle of Kirbekan:

> He believed that a General should lead his force, like a Lieutenant, from the front and gallop here and there into, and up to the head of, engagement and skirmish. Towards the end of the day of our battle at the head of the Nile, he was the first to reach a hut lying between the two principal hills, in which a small party of Dervishes had taken shelter to continue the fighting. A shot through the window killed the first soldier to reach it; and the soldier was our Commander.[40]

Earle was brave, self-confident, an inspirer of men; above all a *tactician*.

A lack of self-confidence, perception, and tactical expertise was the cause of Buller's failure and delays during the 1899 advance on Ladysmith. When he eventually reached the town, he refused 'to pursue the flying Dutchman', and he and 50,000 men sat on their hands for a period of two months. [41] His solicitude for his men was legendary, and his soldiers were devoted to him. But it exacted a harsh penalty. If he had driven them forward unrelentingly, with little sleep and short rations, he would have brought the conflict to a swifter solution and saved his men in the long run. Roberts did this, and so did Hamilton himself.

French and Hamilton had soldiered together during the Second Boer War as divisional commanders, French with the cavalry and Hamilton with the infantry and later mounted infantry. French had a splendid fighting record. He was tireless, self-confident, able to inspire his men, and was a good tactician. He had the full confidence of Roberts and Kitchener. But when he commanded the BEF in 1914, he began to become unstuck, and the situation got worse in 1915. French was lost in the throes of a gigantic siege war, which became inevitably a war of organization and planning. He was always uncomfortable with commanding from a desk rather than 'from the saddle'. The staff headquarters put in place for the BEF was anyway too large, although as the army grew the staff was in place to handle it.[42] However, the staff, large and competent though it was, could not provide leadership. French was not a strategist, and he became lost in the difficulties of his job because he lacked the brainpower to handle them.

Haig was French's highly efficient chief of staff for most of the Second Boer War. In 1914 he became one of French's immediate subordinates, in command of a corps and, from the beginning of 1915, an army. Hamilton agreed that Haig was the ablest and most experienced general staff officer of his time. When he succeeded French as Commander-in-Chief of the BEF at the end of 1915, he was totally at home in the by now rather bloated BEF headquarters. But he was short in imagination and force of personality, and was never able to cut through to essentials. The First World War was:

> a General Staff war. So framed was it; so calculated; so elaborately worked out; every risk so heavily insured, that, in practice, it reacted against them, became without form as these calculators – dark engineers – ground out the lives of their splendid armies with the plans conceived in their gigantic, remote headquarters.[43]

The tragedy of French was that in 1914 he was promoted above his ceiling. The tragedy of Haig was that his temperament made him only too comfortable with military bureaucracy. He possessed energy, self-confidence, organizing ability, selflessness; but he was not close enough to the troops to inspire them, although his state funeral was attended by huge crowds, including vast numbers of old soldiers who recognized his role in the foundation of the British Legion. Haig's problem was that he failed to see that the main job of a commander is to provide aggressive and visible leadership. This demands a real grasp of tactics and strategy. He focused on strategy, but in executing his plans he totally lacked tactical judgement, in particular an appreciation of the destructive capacity of modern defensive firepower. And Haig's writing provides little evidence of vision or any other intellectual gifts, despite the time he had spent at Oxford. (Very few Army officers at the time had received a university education.)

Hamilton was devoted to Roberts and recognized that Roberts had made all the difference to his own career. As discussed in Chapters 3, 5 and 7, Roberts possessed an impressive range of qualities, which made him the supreme exponent in the British Army of command 'from the saddle'. But when Hamilton was discussing Roberts as part of a broad evaluation of the qualities needed by a great commander, he concentrated on Roberts's wonderful rapport with troops and his talents as an administrator.[44] What

Hamilton does not emphasize is that, in small wars, Roberts had shown a mastery of both tactics and strategy: first, with his brilliant plan that won the Battle of Peiwar Kotal in 1878. Second, in 1900–01, when the British Army was engaged in a larger conflict than any in which it had fought up to that time, Roberts within months had won the major pre-guerrilla phase of the operations. He had a clear plan and the force to execute it. In contrast to Buller, who was slothful and had weak judgement, Roberts demonstrated both tactical 'grip' and broad strategic vision.

Hamilton wrote more about Kitchener than any of the other generals whose command styles he analyzed. Kitchener was a bigger man than any of them, but he had the most extraordinary deficiencies:

> Herbert Kitchener, a man without any personal feel for his troops; a man who centralized most of the responsibility in his own hands – and got away with it! . . .The NCOs and men were immensely interested in the Kitchener enigma; they were proud of Kitchener; they were glad to have him scowl at them.[45]

> Here was the Master of Expedients at work indeed; never the organiser. . . Since K demanded that he should see *everything* of importance first, should make *every* decision of importance, should work out the execution of *every* plan himself, I was but a high-ranking confidential secretary.[46]

> With matter at his command well worthy of the Commentaries of a Caesar, he produced epistles which, for total lack of any touch of human interest, are – if that was his aim – miracles. At last I suggested writing out rough drafts and he closed with my offer. We adopted the same procedure for his speeches, but in this case it was not so easy to remove the burden from him, for the speeches had to be learnt![47]

> K ran everything that mattered himself, from the highest to the lowest level, leaving only the final, tactical application of the troops on the ground to the local commander. This, too, was natural enough: since K had no interest in that side of soldiering, he had made no effort to acquire any knowledge of it.[48]

> His methods then, as later, were the outcome of a never-ending struggle between his common sense and a mania for secrecy in which the mania almost always had the upper hand.[49]

K struggling to raise a national army – in which he succeeded so well – and, above all, struggling to keep his head above water as a member of the War Cabinet and Head of the War Office.[50]

What an astonishing litany! It is a description of a man who had no close sympathy with the soldiers in the ranks; who refused to delegate; who smashed organizations and relied on expedients; who, although he was able to rap out large numbers of clear, brief orders, was an uncomfortable writer of any connected narrative and an awkward public speaker; who was uninterested in military tactics; who was secretive; and who had to struggle to work with equals when, no longer a commander, he became Secretary of State for War. But Hamilton's picture of Kitchener is tinged with respect, almost awe, and he saw Kitchener's weaknesses as nothing more than rather surprising and certainly not mortal deficiencies. Some of the things he was no good at simply showed a lack of interest on his part.

The gaps in Kitchener's military expertise were indeed outweighed by the strength and substance of his character, something described (in a metaphor from ocean-going ships) as his 'bottom'. His personality made an enormous impact. He was listened to – and feared – although some of his subordinates, including Hamilton, were able to release some of his rather surprising sense of humour. Most important of all, he gave repeated evidence of military and strategic vision. Thirteen years after the débâcle of Wolseley's 1884–85 expedition to rescue Gordon, Kitchener reconquered the Sudan. When he began his planning, he immediately took a strong 'grip' on the enterprise. He built a large enough body of men with the necessary logistical support – a process that took two years – and his army moved relentlessly upstream to meet and vanquish the Dervish hordes on the open plain of Omdurman. During the guerrilla phase of the Second Boer War, he alone saw that the war had to be won by a lengthy process of building engineering works, the lines of blockhouses. When he was Commander-in-Chief in India, Kitchener confronted eye-to-eye his immediate superior, the Viceroy. And the Commander-in-Chief, through the weight of his personality, seized financial control of the Indian Army after a very public conflict that saw the resignation of the Viceroy, Lord Curzon. Curzon was able, shrewd, conscientious, rich, aristocratic, and strong, but not as strong as Kitchener.

In the First World War, Kitchener sensed earlier than any other British leader that the German Army in August 1914 was engaged in a broad right-hand sweep through Belgium and northern France.[51] He was virtually the only man who in 1914 foresaw a long war and started making furious preparations by building his New Army. Also, it is not well known that he was conscious of the growing importance of air power, and took active steps to increase significantly the size of the Royal Flying Corps.[52] At about the same time, he was one of the small handful of men who saw the enormous strategic opportunity that would have been opened by forcing the Dardanelles, and was right in seeing the need for 150,000 men (a number he was unfortunately unable to deliver). Finally, he also forecast that the Gallipoli landing places would be evacuated with no loss of life. This was probably his most startlingly correct prediction.

Hamilton provided brief but penetrating insights into Foch and Ludendorff. Foch was cold, ironic, and clever: 'thoughts gushed out of his brain so fast that each sentence was a test sufficient for the listener to make himself a long sermon.'[53] After his painful experiences in 1914, 1915 and 1916, when the French conviction about the power of the all-out offensive bled the French Army white, Foch was sidelined for a year and spent the time *thinking*. This detached but rigorous contemplation enabled him to develop the system he would put into effect when in the spring of 1918 he became Generalissimo, overall co-ordinator of the national armies of France, Britain, America and Belgium. His job carried much authority although Foch was never formally Commander-in-Chief. When the Allies were ready to take the offensive the Generalissimo, operating from a headquarters of minimal size, drove to and from the various national army headquarters and issued personal directives (but not detailed orders). In this way he orchestrated attacks on different fronts, not at the same time but one after the other. This was the strategy that unbalanced the German Supreme Command, and brought the Allies close to victory, although not quite there.

In the autumn of 1918 the Allies on the Western Front, having halted the expensive German offensives in 1918 and starved the German homeland through blockade, were moving in for the kill. But it was the collapse of Bulgaria, on the distant Eastern Front, that was the final and decisive cause of the German defeat. Ludendorff, whom Hamilton met

247

in 1922, made a rather unexpected point. Ludendorff thought that the distinction between the Eastern and Western fronts was false. In his view the only two fronts were Germany and her enemies:

> In a way of fortifications, the breach – rather than the locality of the breach – was the fact that really mattered: a hole big enough to allow armies to march into our vitals with safe lines of communication behind them was clearly the end of things.[54]

This quotation reveals that Ludendorff had a strategic vision of unusual breadth, a vision matched by Kitchener and Churchill when they saw how forcing the Dardanelles in 1915 would have altered the course of the war. It would have been shortened, so that success at the Dardanelles would have saved enormous numbers of lives.

Much of Hamilton's discussion with Ludendorff concerned Russia. Ludendorff, being a conservative and a realist, saw that Germany was still a force to be reckoned with, and would inevitably become the bulwark against Bolshevism.[55] He had learned something about the fighting efficiency of the Red Army before the Russian surrender in 1917. He also saw that Communism knew no frontiers. Ludendorff's crystal ball was as clear as Hamilton's own. Shortly after the end of the First World War, during his travels throughout Europe, Hamilton saw repeated evidence of the resentment caused by the re-drawing of European frontiers in conformity with the principle of national self-determination (but occasionally denying it, as in Czechoslovakia and Yugoslavia). He detected internal tensions in Austria, Czechoslovakia, and Poland that were strong and would lead to conflict in 1939, just as Ludendorff had foreseen the Russian peril that Germany would confront in 1941.[56] Hamilton's views of the future were not confined to Europe. The Anglo-Japanese Treaty of 1902 had brought stability to the countries of the Pacific Rim, a stability imposed by the Pax Britannica. Japan fought alongside Britain during the First World War, despite the traditionally close relationship between the Japanese and German Armies. But with the lapse of this Treaty in 1921, Hamilton foresaw that there would no longer be any restraint on Japan's oriental-irredentist ambitions, and he feared that the Pacific would be transformed into an enormous field for Japanese aggression.[57] More prophetic words.

The Legacy

Hamilton's writings about armies and commanders have been forgotten, perhaps a legacy of his unfortunate command at Gallipoli. This is regrettable since, unlike that of most other soldiers, his writing reveals clarity, wit, and style. It is even more unfortunate that his writings have disappeared because of his forecasts made in 1921 – that trench warfare would disappear, that horsed cavalry would almost immediately lose its importance, that mechanization on the ground and in the air would transform armies, that the traditional division would be reconfigured, and that command and operations would become all-arms affairs, even on an international basis – all these fanciful visions would come true, most within two decades.

Equally remarkable is that Hamilton's broad picture of the future of war did not include a realistic character study of the great captains of the future. Until the end of his life, Hamilton remained a total believer in the general's role as a tactician, and this was of course an expression of his love of soldiering at the 'sharp end'. But Hamilton always lacked a feel for the even greater importance of strategy. Of the eight leading generals whom he named for their high profiles, four of them – Roberts, Kitchener, Foch and Ludendorff – were strategists who conceived big plans. But when Hamilton wrote about the two he knew best, Roberts and Kitchener, he downplayed their strategic abilities in favour of their other qualities. Hamilton probably continued to associate strategic planning with the crushing incubus of military bureaucracy: the bureaucracy that Haig assembled around him. However, as Foch (and Wellington) had already demonstrated and Montgomery was later to do, a bloated staff was not a requirement for success so long as the general himself was imaginative enough to cut a swathe through the staff officers with the identifiable red tabs on their lapels, and make a direct impact on his troops.

Hamilton's concept of generalship – exemplified by Earle, Mustafa Kemal, Lawrence, Rommel and Wingate when they charged around the battlefields where the bullets were flying – demonstrated a dash and valour that had an immediate effect on the morale of the troops. At Gallipoli, Hamilton disliked having to be forty miles away at Lemnos. Mustafa Kemal, in the firing line, was directing his soldiers forward with his riding crop. But meanwhile, the cool Prussian Liman von Sanders was at his headquarters, taking the pulse of the action on the battlefield, moving his reserves forward to prepared defensive positions, and ultimately defeating Hamilton's heroic and exhausted army: an army that had relentlessly battered itself against the strength of the Turkish defences.

Notes

1 Sir Ian Hamilton, *The Soul and Body of an Army* (London: Edward Arnold, 1921), pp.21–2.
2 Ibid., pp. 117–18.
3 Ibid., p.119.
4 Ibid., p.273.
5 Ibid., p.280. Rommel's mobility in the Western Desert in 1941–42 has been compared with naval warfare. See Desmond Young, *Rommel* (London: Collins, 1950), p.135.
6 Hamilton, *The Soul and Body of an Army*, pp.282–3.
7 Ibid., p.288.
8 Ibid., p.260.
9 Ibid., p.266.
10 Ibid., p.269.
11 Ibid., p.58.
12 Ibid., p.246.
13 Ibid., p.251.
14 Con Coughlin, 'Armed forces merger would give us a lean, mean fighting machine' *Telegraph* (London), 6 July 2011, p.19.
15 Sir Ian Hamilton, *The Friends of England* (London: George Allen & Unwin, 1923), pp.85–6.
16 Hamilton, *The Soul and Body of an Army*, pp.78–9.
17 Ibid., pp.24, 54–5.
18 Ibid., pp.86–8. A railway was actually built there by an Irish engineer.
19 Ibid., p.79.
20 Ibid., p.73.
21 Wellington's staff organization is hardly discussed in the vast literature on the Peninsular War. I am indebted to the well-known military historian Gordon Corrigan for explaining this admirable system to me.
22 Arthur Bryant, *The Great Duke* (London: William Collins, 1971), pp.345–7.
23 Hamilton, *The Soul and Body of an Army*, p.35.
24 Walter Görlitz, *The German General Staff. Its History and Structure, 1657–1945* (London: Hollis & Carter, 1953), p.76.
25 Hamilton, *The Soul and Body of an Army*, p.91.
26 Ibid., pp.97, 105.
27 Robert Graves, *Goodbye to All That* (London: The Folio Society, 1981), pp.84, 87. First published in 1929.

28 Oliver Lyttelton, Viscount Chandos, *The Memoirs of Lord Chandos* (London: The Bodley Head, 1962), p.35.
29 Graves, *Goodbye to All That*, pp.114,116.
30 Frank Richards, *Old Soldiers Never Die* (London: Faber & Faber, 1933), p.168.
31 Hamilton, *The Soul and Body of an Army*, p.145.
32 Ibid., p.147.
33 Ibid., p.175.
34 Ibid., p.203.
35 General Sir Ian Hamilton, *The Commander* (Major Anthony Farrar-Hockley, ed.) (London: Hollis & Carter, 1957).
36 Hamilton, *The Soul and Body of an Army*, p.188.
37 Ibid., pp.189–98.
38 Ibid., p.131.
39 Hamilton, *The Commander*, pp.32, 35, 150.
40 Ibid., p.77.
41 Ibid., p.39.
42 Ibid., pp.133–4.
43 Ibid., pp.135,137.
44 Ibid., p.96.
45 Ibid., pp. 67, 69.
46 Ibid., p.103.
47 Ibid., p.114.
48 Ibid., pp.111–12.
49 Ibid., p.104.
50 Ibid., p.129.
51 Major General Sir C. E. Callwell, *Field Marshal Sir Henry Wilson. His Life and Diaries* (Volume 1) (London: Cassell, 1927), p.163.
52 Marshal of the Royal Air Force Lord Douglas of Kirtleside, with Robert Wright, *Combat and Command* (New York: Simon & Schuster, 1966), pp.68–9.
53 Hamilton, *The Commander*, p.144.
54 Ibid., pp.141–2.
55 Hamilton, *The Friends of England*, p.51.
56 Ibid., pp.114, 138.
57 Ibid., pp.243–56.

Index

The soldiers, sailors and airmen listed in this Index are in nearly all cases given their final ranks and titles. During the episodes described in this book, these men normally held more junior positions.

Afghanistan, 27, 31, 33, 36, 41, 80, 231

Afghan War, First , 38

Afghan War, Second, 39–41, 43–6, 96

Africa, 25

Aiho River, 140

Air Observation Posts (AOP), 228

Aisne, Battle of the, 12

Alberts, Paul, 104

Alanbrooke, Field Marshal Lord, 5, 16, 47, 240

Alexander, Field Marshal Lord, 3, 16, 234

Alexander the Great, 1

Alexandria, 192

Allenby, Field Marshal Lord, 5, 113, 151–2

Alsace, 178

Amery, Leo, 166–7, 171

Anderson, Lieutenant General Sir Kenneth, 2

Anglo-Japanese Alliance, 132, 248

Anglo-Russian Convention, 180–1

Antung (Manchuria), 142

Anzio, Battle of, 2, 151

Armies:
  Aircraft, Role in land battle, 226, 228, 239, 249

  Amalgamation of Armed Services, 230

  Anglo-American Joint Command (Mediterranean and North–West Europe), 230

  Armour and mechanization, Growth of, 224, 226, 228, 238–9, 249

  Battle Schools, 239

  Battle, Success in, 224

Brigades, 'Square', 228

Bureaucracy, Military, 240, 244, 247

Cavalry in traditional role, 45, 53, 94–5, 111, 132, 149, 160, 224–6, 249

Command, General principles of, 240–9

Command 'from the saddle', 10, 11, 19, 107, 114, 155, 243–4

Command, Responsibilities of, and necessary qualities for, 3–4, 6, 10, 15, 40, 82–3, 100, 107, 113, 170–3, 212, 242–3

Command, 'Top–down', 53, 57–8

Discipline and its constituents, 203, 230, 235–7

Esprit de Corps, Regimental, 236–7

Infantry, Field deployment and training of, 29–30, 54, 76, 94, 118, 145, 152–3, 225, 238

Joint Army/Navy/Air Command, 188, 224, 228–30, 249

Logistics, 10, 86

Officer selection, 241–2

Organisation of army formations, 11, 15, 224, 227–8, 230, 232–5, 249

Training, 230, 238–40

Trench/Siege Warfare, Demise of, 224–5, 249

Army Council, British, 133, 157

Arnhem, Battle of, 151

Arthur, Sir George, 219

Asia, 184

Aspinall-Oglander, Brigadier General CF, 84, 173–4, 219–20

Asquith, Herbert, Lord Oxford, 187

Atrocities/farm burning/concentration

Index

camps in South Africa, 114, 121–2, 124–5

Auchinleck, Field Marshal Sir Claude, 2

Australia, 49, 87, 108, 112, 181, 218

Austria, 79, 177, 248

Austria–Hungary, 167, 177–82

Balkans/Balkan Wars, 177, 179–80, 184

Ballard, Brigadier General C, 128

Bangalore, 66

Basutoland, 122

Baxter, Major James, 221

Beatty, Admiral of the Fleet Lord, 226

Belfast, South Africa, 124

Belgium, 152, 182,247

Belisarius, 1

Bennett, Air Vice Marshal Donald, 46–47

Bey, Major Mahmut (Turkish artillery commander at V Beach), 219

Bird, Brevet Major WD, 155–156

Birdwood, Field Marshal Lord, 193–194, 198, 204, 206, 217, 220

Bismarck, Prince Otto von, 105, 177

Black Sea, 184–185

'Black Week' (1899), 107

Blockhouse lines, South Africa, 114, 125–126, 144, 246

Blair, Andy Clay, 16–17

Bloch, Ivan Stanislavovich, 171–172, 216

Bloemfontein, 88, 104, 104–105, 108–109, 111–114, 117

Boers/Boer Republics, 51–54, 61, 86–89, 113, 118
  Artillery, 88, 91–92, 97, 99
  The Great Trek, 52, 87
  Military abilities, 52–53, 90–91, 95–96, 113
  Racial segregation, 51–52, 96
  Religious fervour, 51, 56
Boer War, First, xxiii, 31, 48, 51, 54–62, 86

Casualties (killed, wounded, missing, prisoners), 60–61

Boer War, Second, xxiii, 2, 6, 8–9, 31, 33, 41–43, 51, 62, 69, 82, 86–127, 131, 152, 170, 213, 231, 243, 245
  Casualties (killed, wounded, missing, prisoners), 93, 95, 97, 100, 102–103, 106–107, 111, 114, 121–123

Bonaparte, Napoleon, 2, 49, 140, 182, 240

Bosnia & Herzegovina, 181

Bosporus, 185

Botha, Louis, 101–103, 120, 127

Braithwaite, General Sir Walter, 191

Brandwater Basin, 122–124

The Breslau, 183–184

Brevet ranks, 34

Britain/British Empire, 87, 89, 107, 112, 178, 181, 227, 247

British Army:
  British Army Papers, 219–220
  Budgets before First World War, 158, 165, 167, 239
  Cadet Corps, 159
  Commander-in-Chief, 49, 129–130
  Conservatism, 129, 226, 231
  Components before Haldane Reforms, 158–159
  Experience of active service, 179
  Field Service Regulations, 223
  Formations and Units:
  British Expeditionary Force (WW1), 9–10, 93, 116, 130, 132, 159, 163, 186, 188, 231
  Fourth Army (WW1), 227
  Australian & New Zealand Army Corps (ANZAC)(WW1), xxii, 13, 175, 211, 189–190, 192, 198, 204–208
  IX Corps (WW1), 209–210
  Cavalry Division (2 Boer War), 93–95, 111, 113, 117–119, 160
  Royal Naval Division (WW1), 152, 189, 192, 207–209

Guards Armoured Division (WW2), 227
7th Armoured Division (WW2), 227
Mounted Infantry Division (2 Boer War), 111–121, 131
3rd Division (WW1), 160
29th Division (WW1), 152, 187, 189, 192, 195, 198, 204, 208–209, 215
51st (Highland) Division (WW1 & WW2), 18, 227
56th (London) Division (WW1 & WW2), 227
1st Airborne Division (WW2), 227
6th Airborne Division (WW2), 227
9th Australian Division (WW2), 227
4th Indian Division (WW2), 227
2nd New Zealand Division (WW2), 227
2 Cavalry Brigade (2 Boer War), 112, 118
2 Mounted Infantry Brigade (2 Boer War), 112
Highland Brigade (2 Boer War), 107
19 Brigade (2 Boer War), 112
21 Brigade (2 Boer War), 118
29 Indian Brigade (WW1), 189
City Imperial Volunteers, 112
1st Devonshire Regiment, 94
Gordon Highlanders, 18, 20, 24, 26, 40, 43–46, 48, 63, 80, 96, 222–223, 241
1st Gordon Highlanders, 51, 74–78, 119
2nd Gordon Highlanders, 55, 92
Grenadier Guards, 236
Imperial Light Horse, 94
1st Lancashire Fusiliers, 203
1st Manchester Regiment, 94
5th Punjab Cavalry, 45
2nd Rifle Brigade, 99
Royal Artillery, 91, 101, 104, 118–119, 163, 189–190, 208, 232
Royal Engineers, 125, 163
Royal Horse Artillery, 114, 220–221
2nd Royal Fusiliers, 203

1st Royal Munster Fusiliers, 203
Royal Scots Greys, 25
Royal Welch Fusiliers, 236–237
Scots Guards, 25
Seaforth Highlanders, 25
12th (Suffolk) Regiment, 23–24, 118
75th (Stirlingshire) Regiment, 51
French Army, cooperation with, 163–164, 180
Linked battalions, 50–51
Militia, 158–159, 162
New Armies (Kitchener), 165, 209, 218, 241, 247
Regular Army Reserve, 158, 162–163
Reorganisation before First World War, 130, 162–165
Service – long/short, 26, 43–44, 50, 66, 92, 161–168
Support services, 163, 232
Territorial Force, 162, 165, 167, 209, 231
Volunteers and Yeomanry, 159–160, 162, 209, 226
British Legion, *see* Royal British Legion
British Labour Government (1945), 65
Brooke, *see* Alanbrooke
Brusiloff, General Alexei, 5
Bryant, Sir Arthur, 250
Bulgaria, 247–248
Buller, General Sir Redvers, 2, 75, 97–105, 109, 113, 124, 242–243
Burma, 42, 97, 112, 142
Byng, Field Marshal Lord, 113

Cadorna, General Luigi, 14
Caesar's Camp, Ladysmith, 98, 100
Cairo, 74, 87
Calcutta, 149
Callwell, Major General Sir CE, 173, 221, 251
Cambridge, Duke of, 7, 66, 129
Campbell-Bannerman, Sir Henry, 157
Canada, 49, 87, 108, 230

Index

Cape to Cairo Railway, 87
Cape Province/Cape Town, 87–88, 90,
    103, 105–108, 113, 120
Carden, Vice Admiral Sir Sackville,
    187
Cardwell, Edward, 21, 49–51, 231
Carthaginian Army, 7–8
Carver, Field Marshal Lord, 173
Cavagnari, Sir Louis, 40
Ceylon, 112
Chamberlain, Lieutenant Neville, 65
Chancellorsville, Battle of, 40
Chandler, David, 64
Changuion, Louis, 104
Chaotao, Battle of, 134, 146
Chardeh Valley, Afghanistan, 45
Charlemagne, 1
Cheam School, 19–20, 24
Chief of the Imperial General
    Staff/Chief of the General Staff,
    133, 157, 229, 232, 234
Chiefs of Staff of all three services, 83,
    229
Chitral Expedition, 80
Churchill, Sir Winston, 9, 42, 71, 83,
    103, 108, 114–116, 120–121, 127–
    128, 185, 187, 213–214, 217–219,
    229, 236, 240
Churchill, Lord Randolph, 41–42, 46
Chuikov, Marshal Vassily, 5
Civil War, American, 2, 40, 49
Class, social, in Britain, 18
Colenso, Battle of, 101, 107, 109
Colley, Major General Sir George, 54–
    61
Colley, Lady, 23
Commandos, Boer, 53, 89–90, 101–
    103, 106, 113, 120–121, 124, 126
Commandos, British in Second World
    War, 30
Conan Doyle, Dr Arthur, 112
Constantinople, 9, 181, 184–185, 191,
    196, 235
Coruna, Battle of, 76
Corrigan, Major Gordon, 250

Cosgrove, Corporal William, 203
Coughlin, Con, 250
Cramb, John Adam, 166
Crimean War, 49, 180, 196, 231
Cronje, Piet, 106, 109–111, 114
Cunningham, General Sir Alan, 2
Cunningham, Admiral of the Fleet
    Lord, 5
Curragh Crisis, 232
Curzon, Marquess of, 246
Czechoslovakia, 248

Danchev, Alex, 16
Dardanelles Strait, 6, 183–188, 195,
    197, 204, 210, 240, 247
Dardanelles Commission, 219
Dawley, Major General Ernest, 2
Deception, strategic, 151–152
Defence Minister and Chief of Defence
    Staff, 229–230, 234
Defensive Fire Power, 11–13, 172–173
De Guingand, Major General Sir
    Francis, 82
De la Rey, Koos, 91, 106, 109
De Lisle, Lieutenant General Sir
    Beauvoir, 113
Denmark, 178
Dera Ishmael Khan (cantonment), 27
De Robeck, Admiral of the Fleet Lord,
    187–188, 192, 214
De Wet, Christiaan, 89, 91, 109, 114,
    117, 121–124, 127–128
De Wet, Piet, 122
Diamond Hill, Battle of, 120,122
Diamond mining, 87–88, 109
Dill, Field Marshal Sir John, 2
Disease among troops, 99, 111–112,
    152, 205, 207, 212
Dönitz, Grand Admiral Karl, 5
Doornkop, Battle of, 117–119
Douglas, Marshal of the Royal Air
    Force Lord, 251
Dowding, Air Chief Marshal Lord, 5
Drakensberg Mountains, 55
Dresden, 22

Dual Alliance, 179
Dundee, South Africa, 92–93, 97
Durban, 48, 55

Earle, Major General W, 75–76, 94,
    242–243, 249
East India Company,
East India Company School,
    Addiscombe, 36
Edinburgh University, 157
Edward the First, King, 1
Egypt, 72–77, 169, 192–193, 208,
    227
Egyptian Army, 74, 77
Eisenhower, General Dwight D, 1, 3,
    17, 46, 82, 230
El Alamein, Battle of, 15, 224
Elandsfontein, 121
Elandslaagte, Battle of, 93–98, 118
Ensor, RCK, 174
Entente Cordiale, 179–180
Enver Pasha, 183
Erickson, Edward J, 220
Esat Pasha, Brigadier, 200
Esher Committee, 132–133, 157
Eton College, 36
European Union, 178

Falkenhayn, General Erich von, 14
Farrar-Hockley, Lieutenant General Sir
    Anthony, 17, 64, 128, 174, 251
Far East, 177
Farwell, Byron, 47, 64
Fasih, Lieutenant Mehmed, 219
Fenghuancheng, Korea, 139
Ferguson, Niall, 64
Fisher, Admiral of the Fleet Lord, 184,
    186–187, 219
Flaminius (Roman Consul), 122
Florida, South Africa, 118
'Flowers of the Forest', 119
Foch, Marshal Ferdinand, 3–4, 243,
    247, 249
Foesulae (Roman camp), 7
Forbes, Lieutenant 'Polly', 44

Fouriesburg, South Africa, 122
France, 137, 152, 178–182, 218, 225,
    247
Franco-Prussian War, 148, 178
Franz Ferdinand, Archduke, 181
Franz Josef, Emperor, 177
French Army, 163
French Army in the Dardanelles, 189–
    190
French, David, 31
French, Field Marshal Lord, 2, 9–10,
    93–95, 111, 113, 116–119, 130, 186,
    242–244
Frendendall, Major General Lloyd, 2
Frederick the Great, 1
Freyberg, Lieutenant General Lord,
    152, 155, 207
Fujii, Major General S, 145
Fuller, Major General JFC, 104, 227

Galliéni, General Josef Simon, 5
Gallipoli Expedition, 14–16, 116–117,
    150, 154, 165, 176, 181, 249
  British evacuation, 214
  British landing craft, 201–202, 210,
    215
  British naval action and
    bombardment, 187–188, 192, 206,
    216
  British plan, Strategic weakness of,
    155, 197, 214
  British Staff planning, Slow pace of,
    154, 192–193, 214–215
  British troop strengths and casualties,
    154, 186, 189–90, 195, 197, 204,
    206, 208, 210, 212, 214–215,
    217–218, 247
  French participation, 204, 208
  Turkish artillery, 202–203, 219
  Turkish command, German
    contribution to, 154, 181–182,
    201, 209
  Turkish defences, 11, 13, 191–192,
    198, 203, 205, 211, 249
  Turkish soldiers, 154, 173, 179, 181,

189–190, 196, 199
Turkish troop strengths and
    casualties, 189, 195, 198–200,
    206, 212, 218
Gallipoli Peninsula, xix–xx, 8–11, 13,
    100, 189, 191
A, B, C, Beaches, *see* Suvla
Anzac Cove (Z Beach), 195, 197,
    204–212, 217
Bulair, 152, 196–7, 200, 207, 210, 213
Brighton Beach, 204
Climate/heat, xviii, 207
The Cut, 210
Ejelmar Bay, 197, 216
Gaba Tepe, 206
Helles, Cape, 152, 198–201, 204,
    208–209, 214, 219
Kilitbahir, 195, 204
Krithia, 203
Kumkale, 204
Lone Pine, 212
Nibrunesi, 210
S Beach, 198, 202, 204
Salt Lake, 210
Sari Bair, 210, 212
Seddul Bahir, 195, 202
Suvla (A, B, C Beaches), 194, 197,
    209–212, 214, 216–217
V Beach, 175–176, 198, 201–204,
    210
W Beach, 198, 203–204, 210
Water, Difficulties with supply of,
    207
X Beach, 198, 203–204
Y Beach, 198, 203–204, 217
Z Beach, *see* Anzac Cove
Gandhi, Mohandas, 103
Gatacre, Lieutenant General Sir
    William, 2, 106, 113
'The Gay Gordons', 24
Germany, 22, 87–89, 157, 177–184
German/Prussian Army, 11–12, 22, 49,
    83, 130–131, 137, 151–152, 157–
    158, 163–164, 173, 178, 209, 225,
    227, 232–235, 247

German/Prussian General Staff, 95,
    232–235, 250
German/Prussian War Academy, xxi,
    200, 235
Gettysburg, Battle of, 147
Gibraltar, 104, 116
Gilbert & Sullivan, 129
Gladstone, William Ewart, 49, 72
Gobi Desert, 131
The Goeben, 183–184
Gold mining, 87–88, 118
'A Gordon for Me', 24
Gordon, Major General Charles, 42, 48,
    71–72, 78, 84, 107
Gordon Relief Expedition, 48, 71–78,
    98, 246
    Desert Force, 74, 77
    River Force, 74, 77
Gort, Field Marshal Lord, 2
Gort, Lord (Ian Hamilton's maternal
    grandfather), 7
Görlitz, Walter, 250
Göttingen, University, 157
Gough, General Sir Hubert, 14
Grant, General Ulysses S, 1–2
Graves, Robert, 174, 250–251
Greece, 151, 185
Grierson, General Sir James, 116
Guderian, General Heinz, 5
Gurkha soldiers, 146
Gustavus Adolphus, 1

Haig, Field Marshal Lord, 3, 35–36, 47,
    93, 104, 113, 116, 158–160, 163,
    242, 244, 249
Haldane, Richard Burdon, 157–168,
    171, 173, 231
Hamilton, Major General Sir Bruce, 23,
    118
Hamilton, Colonel Christian Monteith
    (Ian Hamilton's father), 18
Hamilton (née Vereker), Cosa (Ian
    Hamilton's mother), 19
The Hamilton family of Westport, 18
Hamilton, Harry (Jean Hamilton's

adopted son), 79
Hamilton, Jean (née Muir) (Ian
    Hamilton's wife), 8, 79–80, 161,
    222
Hamilton, General Sir Ian, xx–xxii,
    2–3, 6, 35, 40, 43–46
    ADC to Sir Frederick Roberts, 63–71
    168
    Adjutant General in Britain, 161, 168
    Bravery, 45, 59, 62, 95, 106, 170,
    211
    Campaigns: References to Hamilton
    under:
        Afghan War, Second,
        Boer War, First,
        Boer War, Second,
        Chitral Expedition,
        Gallipoli Expedition,
        Gordon Relief Expedition,
        Russo–Japanese War,
        Tirah Expedition
    Central Force in Britain, Command
        of (1914–1918), 9, 169
    Clarity, mental, 171
    Classics, Education in, xx, 7, 24
    'Crammer', Education at, 22, 63
    Decorations, 13, 78, 80, 161, 169
    Defensive fire power, Misjudgment
        of, 12–13, 172, 216
    Determination, 172
    Dismissal at Gallipoli, 14, 213
    Enemy, Limited understanding of,
        172
    Failings at Gallipoli, xxi–xxii, 214–
        217
    Germany, Time spent in, 12, 22
    Impulsiveness, 45, 100,172, 193
    Incompetence of subordinates,
        Toleration of, 172, 217
    Intellect, 170
    Languages, 19, 22, 28–29, 131, 139
    Leave in Britain from India, 70, 74
    Mediterranean, GOC before First
        World War, 168
    Moral courage, 170, 217

Promotions, 78–81, 93, 111, 130, 161
Sandhurst, Royal Military College,
    Education at, 12, 21–23
Schools (Cheam, Wellington),
    Education at, 19–20
Southern Command in Britain,
    Command of (before First World
    War), 130, 160, 168, 170
Staff appointments in India (A and Q
    Branches), 71, 78–80, 125–127,
    130–132, 169, 216–217
Strategic vision, Limitations to his,
    167, 171, 173, 216, 235
Subordinates, Selection of, 172
Tactical skill, 171, 235
Troops, Understanding of, 171
Writing:
Lucidity and readability, xx–xxi, 7–8,
    24, 223
Anti-Commando (with Victor
    Sampson), 8, 69, 84, 104, 128
*The Ballad of Hádji and Other
    Poems*, 69, 84
The Commander (Farrar-Hockley,
    ed), 8, 64, 84, 128, 156, 174, 240,
    251
Compulsory Service, 161–168,
    173–174
Erlkönig (translation), 69
The Fighting of the Future, 68, 70
The Friends of England, 84, 155,
    250–251,
Gallipoli Diary (two volumes), xx,
    xxiii, 16–17, 70, 84, 172, 211,
    219–220
Icarus, 69
A Jaunt in a Junk, 8, 68, 84
Jean, 8, 84
Listening for the Drums, 8, 17, 32,
    46–47, 64, 84, 128
Madras Mail, Journalism in, 69
Now and Then, 69, 84
The Soul and Body of an Army, 84,
    223, 250–251
A Staff Officer's Scrap-Book (two

volumes), 8, 17, 69–70, 84, 153, 155–156, 221
When I was a Boy, 8, 17, 31
Hamilton, Ian (Ian Hamilton's nephew), 17, 84, 155
Hamilton, Colonel Meade 'Tiger', 23–24, 118,
Hamilton, Vereker (Ian Hamilton's brother), 19
Hamley, Major General Edward Bruce, 96, 104
Hankey, Lieutenant Colonel Lord, 186, 219
Hannibal, 1, 7
Harris, Marshal of the Royal Air Force, Sir Arthur, 3, 16
Haswell, Jock, 31
Hay, Major, Gordon Highlanders, 58–59
Heilbron, Battle of, 117, 122
'Heilan' Laddie', 24
Heliograph communication, 100, 102
Herbert, Aubrey, 220
'Highland Clearances', 121–122
'Hill of Doves', *see* Majuba Hill
Himalayas, 27–28, 67
Hindenburg, Field Marshal Paul von, 84–85
Hitler, Adolf, 234
Hoffmann, Major General Max, 85
Hohenzollern family, 177
Holland, 87
Holy Loch, Argyllshire, 19
Holy Roman Empire, 180
Holmes, Sherlock, 112
Honourable East India Company, 36
Hungary, 177
Hunter, General Sir Archibald, 98–99, 104, 113, 122–124, 188
Hunter, Archie, 128
Hunter–Weston, Lieutenant General Sir Aylmer, 193–194, 196–197

Ingogo, Battle of, 55
Impati Hill, 97

India, 19, 26, 70, 77, 80, 177, 218
Indian Army, 8, 26–27, 32, 36–37, 66, 74, 83, 92, 131–132, 149, 160, 189–190, 246
Formations and Units:
Army of Southern India, 65
4th Indian Division (WW2), 227
29th Indian Brigade (WW1), 189
5th Punjab Cavalry, 45
Indian Civil Service, 25
Indian Mutiny, 27, 36–37
India Office, London, 42
India – North-West Frontier, 41–42, 124, 169
Infantry, Mounted, 53, 94, 108, 111–132
Les Invalides, Paris, 2
Iraq, 231
Ireland, 122
Ironside, Field Marshal Lord, 2
Israel Defence Force, 230
Istanbul, 185
Italy, 167, 180

Jackson, Tabitha, 104, 127
Jackson, Lieutenant General Thomas 'Stonewall', 40
Jacobs, Frits, 104
James, David, 47, 127, 155, 174
Jameson Raid, 88
Japan, 127, 248
Japanese Army, 131
  Artillery, 141–143, 145
  Commanders, quality of, 140–145, 150
  Digging ability, 142, 152
  Engineering, 141
  German model, 135–136, 143, 145, 148, 150, 248
  Hygiene, 152
  Logistics, and two streams of recruits (fighting soldiers and coolies), 136
  Marching ability, 146, 152
  Military Intelligence, 138
  Musketry, 153

Numbers, 136, 138, 140, 143–144, 146–148
Officers, Education of, 136
Physical strength, 152
Planning, Care in, 140–141, 151
Rations, 137
Secrecy, 139
Spiritual strength, 153
Troops, Overall quality of, 8–9, 136
Japanese Navy, modelled on British Royal Navy, 133–136
Jellicoe, Admiral of the Fleet Lord, 2, 226
Joffre, Marshal Jean-Jacques, 14
Johannesburg, 87, 94, 118–120
Jones, John Philip, 31
Julius Caesar, 1, 245
Jutland, Battle of, 226

Kabul, 40
'Kaisermen'/'High–korrars' (Japanese slang for German officers), 135
Kandahar, 41
Kannengiesser, Major General Hans, 199, 220
Karl, Prince of Prussia, 234
Keegan, Sir John, 17
Kemal, Mustafa, *Atatürk*, 5, 83, 200, 206, 211, 213, 217, 249
Kesselring, Field Marshal Albert, 5
Keyes, Admiral of the Fleet Lord, 187, 214
Khartoum, 43, 71, 73, 78, 107
Kimberley, 87–88, 90–91, 98, 105–109
Kimmel, Admiral Husband, 2
King, Admiral Ernest, 5
Kinteito Island, Korea, 141–142
Kipling, Rudyard, 36, 64
Kirbekan, Battle of, 75–76, 78, 94, 243
Kitchener, Field Marshal Lord, xxii, 1, 9, 16, 78, 82–83, 99, 107–127, 144, 149, 160, 163, 168, 171, 185–191, 193–194, 208, 213–214, 216–219, 231–232, 241, 243, 245–247, 249

Korea, 133, 135–136, 139, 141–142, 149
Kroonstad, 113–114, 117, 122
Kruger, Paul, 87–89, 114, 118–119
Kruger, Rayne, 127
Kuroki, Marshal Baron, 137, 139–148, 151
Kuropatkin, General Aleksei Nikolaevich, 147–148

Ladysmith, Natal, 43, 82, 89–105, 113,119, 243
Laing's Nek, 55–56
Lane, Private 'Hammer', 237
Lawrence, Colonel TE, 5, 151, 249
Lee-Enfield rifles, 64, 91, 132
Lee, John, 17
Lee-Metford rifles, 64, 91
Lee, General Robert E, 140, 240
Lemnos, 191–193, 211, 249
Lettow–Vorbeck, Colonel Paul von, 5, 151
Lewis guns, 226
Liao Yang, Battle of, 137, 139, 145–149, 154
Liberal landslide (1905), 157
Liddell Hart, Sir Basil, 4–5, 17, 175–176, 216, 227
Liman von Sanders, Marshal Otto, xxii, 5, 12, 172, 182, 194, 199–200, 206–207, 212–213, 220, 235, 249
Lincoln, Abraham, 2
Lindley, South Africa, 122
Lloyd George, David, Lord Dwyfor, 157
London, City of, 112
Loos, Battle of, 224
Lorraine, 182
Lucas, Major General John, 2
Ludendoff, General Erich, 5, 85, 225, 234, 243, 247–249
Lyall, Sir Alfred, 26
Lyttelton, Oliver, Lord Chandos, 236, 251
MacArthur, General Douglas, 5, 82

Macdonald, Major General Sir Hector, 44, 57–58, 241
Machadodorp, 119
Madras, 41, 65–66, 79
Mafeking, 90–91, 98, 105, 109, 113
Magaliesberg mountain range, 123–124
Magersfontein, Battle of, xxiii, 107–109
Maginot Line, 225
Magnus, Sir Philip, 128, 219
The Mahdi, 48, 72
Majuba Hill, 'Hill of Doves', Battle of, 23, 54–62, 74, 111
Malta, 168, 170, 192
Manchester Guardian, 17
Manchu (Qing) dynasty, 133
Manchuria, 132–155
Manstein, Field Marshal Erich von, 5
Marlborough, Duke of, 140 240
Marmara, Sea of, 185
Marseilles, 191
Marshall, General George C, 5, 46
Martin, Christopher, 156
Mason, Philip, 32
Massy, General Redan, 45
Matthijsen, Corporal Adriaan, 123–124
Maurice, Major General Sir Frederick, 173
Mauser rifles, 53, 62, 88–89, 91–92
Maxim machine guns, 226, 239
McCallum, Neil, 31
McNeill, William H, 156
Meissonier (artist), 226
Methuen, Lieutenant General Lord, 98, 105–107, 113
Michelli, Alison, 32
Middle East, 177, 181
Mileham, Patrick, 47, 64
Milner, Alfred, Lord, 87
Modder River, Battle of, 106–107, 109, 112, 115
Moltke, General Helmuth von (the younger), 14
Mongolia, 131
Mons, Retreat from, 116

Monash, Lieutenant General Sir John, 5
Monro, General Sir Charles, 213
Montgomery, John, 47
Montgomery, Field Marshal Lord, 3, 5, 15–16, 35, 47, 82, 144, 148, 156, 172, 213, 220 233, 240, 249
Mooltan, cantonment, 27
Moore, Sir John, 76
Moorhead, Alan, 220
Morgan, Lieutenant General Sir Frederick, 82
Motienling Pass, Battle of, 146
Mountbatten, Admiral of the Fleet Lord, 3, 16
Mukden, Battle of, 137, 139, 148–149
Murdoch, Keith, 213
Murdoch, Rupert, 213
Musketry, 28, 33, 67–68, 70, 79, 143, 160
Musketry, School of (Hythe), 28, 81, 94, 170

National Service League, 161, 166–167
Newcastle, South Africa, 55
New Zealand, 49–50, 108, 112, 181, 218
Nicholson's Nek, Battle of, 97–98
Nile River/Cataracts, 41, 73, 75–78, 107
Nimitz, Admiral Chester, 5
Nivelle, General Robert, 14
Normandy, 239
North, John, xx–xxi, xxiv, 220

Odessa, 184,
Olifant's Nek, Magaliesberg mountain range, 123–124
Omdurman, Battle of, 44, 107, 147, 246
Ootacamund ('Ooty'), 67, 79
Orange Free State/Orange River Colony, xxiii, 52, 55, 88, 92, 104, 106, 113, 121–123, 126
Orange River Station, 106
Ottoman Empire, *see* Turkey
Oxford University, 244

Oyama, Marshal Marquis, 144–145, 148

Paardeberg, Battle of, xxiii, 108–109, 111, 114, 126
Pakenham, Thomas, 104, 127–128
Pakistan, 27, 65, 80
Paris, Major General Sir Archibald, 193–194, 196
Pas de Calais, 152
Passchendaele, Battle of, 224
Patton, General George S, 82
Peiwar Kotal, Battle of, 40, 245
Peninsular War, 76, 250
Penn Symons, Major General Sir W, 92–93, 106
Percival, Lieutenant General Arthur, 2
Perry, Commodore, US Navy, 135
Platrand, Ladysmith, 99–100, 119
Plumer, Field Marshal Lord, 113, 188
Poland, 248
Poplar Grove, Battle of, 111
Poppy Appeal, Royal British Legion, 222
Port Arthur, Manchuria, 134, 137–138, 149
Portsmouth, New Hampshire, 149
Portuguese East Africa, 113, 120, 124
Presbyterian Church, 18
Pretoria, 55, 87, 108, 113–114, 120, 122–124, 127
Pretyman, Major General GT, 65
Princip, Gavrilo, 181
Promotions – the Military Pyramid, 34–36
Prussia, 178
Purchase of commissions, 21

Quartermaster–General, Army staff appointment of, 233
Queen Elizabeth, 204, 206

The Rand, 87–88, 118
Rangoon, 149
Ransford, Oliver, 64

Rawlinson, General Lord, 5, 98–99, 104, 113, 167, 227
Reddersberg, Battle of, 114
Rhodes, Cecil, 87–88
Rhodesia, 87, 113
Richards, Private Frank, 47, 237, 251
Rietfontein, Battle of, 97
Riet River, 106
River Clyde, 152, 155, 202–203
Roberts, Lieutenant General Sir Abraham (Lord Roberts's father), 36
Roberts, Lieutenant Freddie (Lord Roberts's son), 101
Roberts, Field Marshal Lord ('Bobs'/ 'Bobs Bahadur'), 33, 36–47, 49, 54, 61, 65–71, 73, 80, 82, 96, 99, 101–104, 107–125, 129–130, 132, 155, 161–168, 171, 174, 231, 235, 242, 244–245, 249
   Commander–in–Chief, British Army, 129–130, 132, 161
   Commander–in–Chief, India, 78–80
   'Roberts Ring', 61, 73, 78–80, 131
   Special rapport with troops, 66–68, 244
Robertson, Field Marshal Sir William, 113, 157, 213, 241
Rooineks/Red Necks, 56, 61
Roman Army, 7–8, 227–228
Rommel, Field Marshal Erwin, 5, 211, 249–250
Roon, General Count Albrecht von, 233
Roosevelt, President Theodore, 149
Royal British Legion, 222–223, 244
Royal Family, British, 13, 47, 129, 168
Royal Flying Corps/Royal Air Force, 229, 239, 247
Royal Navy, 9, 158, 162–163, 179, 183–184, 186, 191, 207–8
   Royal Naval Division (WW1), 152, 189, 192, 207–209
   Royal Navy detachment, Majuba, 56–59
Russian Army, 134, 140, 143–144,

148, 150, 164
Artillery, 143
Cossacks, 150
Musketry, 143,
Russian Empire, 134, 177, 179–182, 184, 186, 248
Russian Navy, 133, 184
Russian threats against India, 77
Russian Revolutions, 134, 149
Russo–Japanese War, 8, 11, 131–132, 135–155, 190, 216, 225

Salerno, Battle of, 2
Salonika Expedition, 213
Sardinia, 152
Salisbury Plain, 161
Sampson, Victor, 8, 104, 128
Sandhurst, Royal Military College, 12, 21–23, 36, 63, 118
Sand River, Battle of, 117
Sannas Pos/Sanna's Post, 114
Sarajevo, 181
Sarrail, General Maurice, 213
Scarfe, Norman, 156
Scheldt River, 182
Scotland, 18
Scottish clans, 18
'Scotland the Brave', 24
Scott, Douglas, 173
'Scrap of paper', 182
Sebastopol, 184
Sedan, Battle of, 147
Serbia, 180–182
Shikar (shooting for sport), 27
Shorncliffe, 76
Short, Lieutenant General Walter, 2
Slavs, 180–181
Slim, Field Marshal Lord, 5, 82
Smit, Commander (Boer), 58
Smith, Lieutenant General Walter Bedell, 82
Smith-Dorrien, General Sir Horace, 2, 109, 113, 115–116, 118, 128
Sobieski, John, 1
Souchon, Admiral, 184

Spiers, Edward, 64
Spion Kop, Battle of, 102–103
St Petersburg, 149
Staff Colleges, Camberley and Quetta, 35, 63, 78, 96, 116, 170, 235
Staff Officers, Roles of, 82–83
Stewart, Brigadier General Sir Herbert, 75, 77
Steyn, Marthinus, 87–88, 114, 123
Stirling, Lieutenant Colonel David, 151
Stopford, Lieutenant General Sir Frederick, 209–210, 212
Stormberg, Battle of, 106–107, 113
'Storm troop' tactics, 12, 171
Strachan, Hew, 84
Strategy, definition of, 176, 216
Suakim, Port of, 73, 77
Suez Canal, 71, 73–74
'Surrender Hill', Battle of, 123
Switzerland, 119

Tabanyama Hill, South Africa, 102
Tactics, Definition of, 176, 216
Talana, Battle of, 92–93, 96–97
Tannenberg, Battle of, 11, 84
Tel-el-Kebir, Battle of, 71
Tenedos, 190–191
Tidworth, 161
Tiger Hill, Korea, 141
Tirah Expedition, 80
Todman, Daniel, 16
Togo, Admiral Heihachiro, 137–138
Tokyo, 134, 139, 144
'Torch' Operation, Invasion of North–West Africa, 46
Trans-Siberian Railway, 134, 147
Transvaal, 54–55, 87–88, 92, 113, 118, 120–121, 124, 126
Trasimene Lake, Battle of, 7
Triple Alliance, 180
Triple Entente, 180, 185
Tugela River, 101–103
Tunisia, 2
Tsushima, Battle of, 137, 153
Turkey/Ottoman Empire, 176–184, 189

Turkish Army, *see* Gallipoli
Turkish Navy, 183–184
Twenty-Sixth of August, Battle of, 146

Uitlanders, 53, 87–88, 94, 118
United States, 41, 87, 127, 247
United States Marine Corps, 236
United States National Guard, 230–231
United States 101st Airborne Division,
    236
Unwin, Commander Edward, 202–203

Vaal River, 52, 55, 118, 122
Verdun, Battle of, 224
Verestchagin (artist), 226
Viceroy of India, 79, 168, 246
Victoria Cross, 38, 43, 62, 78, 95–96,
    101, 201–203
Victoria, Queen, 61, 63, 129, 239
Vienna, 181
Vladivostok, 134

Wagon Hill, Ladysmith, 98, 100
War Council, British (WW1), 185
War Office, Reorganization of, 129,
    132–133
War Museum of the Boer Republics,
    Bloemfontein, 64
Warren, General Sir Charles, 2, 102
Washington, George, 1
Waters, Colonel WHH, 64
Wauchope, Major General Andrew, 107
Wavell, Field Marshal Lord, 2
Wellington College, 19–20
Wellington, Duke of, 1, 20, 233
    Wellington's Staff Corps (Engineers),
        233
    Wellington's General Staff, 233,
        249–250
Western Front (WW1), 11–12, 185,
    208, 218, 224–225, 248
White, General Sir George, 2, 43, 80–
    81, 91–92, 96–99, 104, 113, 116

Wilhelm II, Kaiser, 177, 179–181
William the Conqueror, King, 1
Williams, Able Seaman William
    Charles, 202–203
Willmer, Major, 211
Wilson, Field Marshal Sir Henry, 113,
    167, 213, 221, 251
Wingate, Major General Orde, 151, 249
Witwatersrand, *see* the Rand
Wolseley, Field Marshal Lord, 36, 41,
    61, 71–78, 84, 125, 246
    'Wolseley Ring', 61, 73–74
Wood, Field Marshal Sir Evelyn, 48–
    49, 54, 57, 61–62, 74
Woolwich, Royal Military Academy, 21
Woolls–Sampson, Major Adrian, 94–95
World War, First, xix, 2–3, 5–6, 8, 11,
    43, 70, 79, 93, 126, 176–177, 180,
    185, 225, 234, 236, 240–241, 246,
    248
World War, Second, xix, 2, 5–6, 25, 79,
    124, 135, 230, 239–240
Wright, Robert, 251

Yalu River, Battle of, 137, 139–144,
    151, 154, 240
Yamamoto, Admiral Isoroku, 5
Yellow Sea, Battle of, 133, 137–138,
    153
Yokohama, 149
Yoshirai, Battle of, 146
Young, Desmond, 250
Young, Brigadier Peter, 30,
'Young Turks', 178, 181, 184
Ypres, 13, 132
Yugoslavia, 248
Yule, Major General JH, 97

Zambia, 87
Zhukov, Marshal Georgi, 5
Zimbabwe, 87
Zulu War, xxiii